THE
HIST⊗RY
WARS

THE HISTRY WARS

STUART MACINTYRE
and ANNA CLARK

MELBOURNE UNIVERSITY PRESS

MELBOURNE UNIVERSITY PRESS
an imprint of Melbourne University Publishing Ltd
PO Box 1167, Carlton, Victoria 3053, Australia
mup-info@unimelb.edu.au
www.mup.com.au

First published 2003
Text © Stuart Macintyre and Anna Clark 2003
Design and typography © Melbourne University Publishing Ltd 2003

Typeset in Malaysia by Syarikat Seng Teik Sdn. Bhd.
Printed in Australia by McPherson's Printing Group
Designed by Phil Campbell

National Library of Australia Cataloguing-in-Publication entry

Macintyre, Stuart, 1947-.
The history wars.

Bibliography.
Includes index.
ISBN 0 522 85091 X.

1. Historiography-Australia. 2. History-Methodology.
3. Historians-Australia. 4. Australia-History-Study
and teaching. I. Clark, Anna, 1978-. II. Title

907.2

CONTENTS

FOREWORD

Stuart Macintyre's account of the 'History Wars' is a fascinating study of the recent endeavours to rewrite or reinterpret the history of European settlement in Australia. These endeavours have generated fierce controversy and allegations of lack of scholarship by media and political commentators as well as historians.

Not all historians are shrinking violets, reluctant to step outside the seclusion of the seminar. As Stuart Macintyre points out, the high-profile historians Manning Clark and Geoffrey Blainey have been controversialists who expressed views which had political overtones. Their competing visions of the Australian heritage and Australian culture became the battleground of the History Wars.

Elements of these competing visions of Australia were appropriated by the Labor Party and the Coalition parties, respectively, as persuasive means of articulating their political and electoral goals. The present federal government and its supporters have decried the so-called 'Black Armband' view of Australian history and have emphasised the successful European settlement, the Anglo-Saxon-Celtic legacy, the monarchy, and the sense of national unity and pride in our achievements. This emphasis, which strongly reflects elements of the Blainey view, is a more reassuring Australian story, whether wholly accurate or not, than that offered by Manning Clark.

I say 'more reassuring' because it appears to offer common assumptions based on what was formerly an orthodox account of Australia's past. But the common assumptions taken from the past are, in various respects, under challenge. We live in a multicultural society which is no longer united, as it once was, by very strong common assumptions.

Although the direct conjunction between Australian history and politics may seem surprising to some, strong linkages between history and politics have occurred often. As monarchs and totalitarian regimes recognised, history can be a badge of legitimacy and an instrument in influencing both the present and the future. Totalitarian regimes insisted on the teaching of their version of history in schools and institutions of higher learning. Other versions were proscribed.

There is no one 'right' view of Australian history. There can be no absolute certainty about the past. All too often the primary facts are eminently contestable. When they can be established with any degree of probability, they may be open to competing interpretations.

At the end of the day there can be no denial of the fundamental proposition that the Indigenous peoples of Australia were dispossessed against their will of much of their traditional lands. The extent of the force and violence that accompanied that dispossession is a matter of historical research and debate, but the fundamental proposition remains unshaken.

The revelation of the past by historians, archaeologists and others is an on-going process. So, as time passes, we may acquire a more detailed knowledge of the European settlement of Indigenous lands in Australia. That knowledge will be sharpened by scholarly debate and discussion which, it is to be hoped, will not be accompanied by the invective and verbal violence that has given prominence to the History Wars.

Sir Anthony Mason

ACKNOWLEDGEMENTS

I have been helped in the preparation of this book by a number of friends and colleagues who gave me material, testimony, information and encouragement. They include Fay Anderson, Tony Birch, Geoffrey Bolton, Frank Bongiorno, Verity Burgmann, Michael Cathcart, Sebastian Clark, Cathie Clement, Ann Curthoys, Joy Damousi, Kate Darian-Smith, Graeme Davison, Ross Fitzgerald, Stephen Foster, Robert French, Tom Griffiths, Patricia Grimshaw, Paula Hamilton, John Hirst, Les Holmes, David Hutchinson, James Jupp, Diane Langmore, Martha Macintyre, Michael McKernan, Nicole McLennan, Rob Pascoe, Michael Piggott, Penny Ramsay, Andrew Reeves, Keir Reeves, Tim Rowse and Peter Steele. John Faulkner, John Hirst and Don Watson read drafts and made helpful suggestions. While many provided ingredients, the broth is my own.

The book would not have been written without the encouragement of Louise Adler, who persuaded me to put my other projects on one side. It could not have been written without Anna Clark. She has previously made a study of the Black Armband debate and is currently engaged on a doctoral research project in school history. In addition to contributing a chapter on that subject, she put her research at my disposal, hunted out additional material and was an exemplary supervisor of my own research.

Stuart Macintyre

A number of friends and family read drafts of my chapter and gave much-needed advice. I am especially indebted to Becky Batagol, Simon Booth, Alison Clark, Tom Clark, Cate Elkner, Maya Haviland and Clare Wright. Thanks also to Stuart for allowing me to contribute a small portion of my own work in what has been a large portion of his. And to my father Axel for his love and support, who didn't live to see this book but who would have had a bit to say.

Anna Clark

CHAPTER 1

HISTORY UNDER FIRE

'One of the more insidious developments in Australian political life over the past decade or so has been the attempt to rewrite Australian history in the service of a partisan political cause.' The speaker was John Howard, and he spoke in the aftermath of his electoral triumph in 1996.

The new prime minister was brooding over his tribulations in opposition when he had lost the 1987 election, then the party leadership, until in 1995 a desperate Liberal Party turned to him once again. He could now settle accounts with those who had written him off as an outmoded traditionalist clinging to a Dreamtime in the 1950s when the family was secure behind the white picket fence, when Robert Menzies guided the nation's destinies with patrician dignity and a young Queen Elizabeth embodied a stable moral order.

Paul Keating had been the chief tormenter. He had taunted Howard in 1992 as yesterday's man who yearned to turn the clock back to an era of the Morphy Richards toaster, the Qualcast mower, the Astor TV console and the AWA radiogram, armchair and slippers. Howard now accused Keating of having sought to 'demean, pillory and tear down many great people of Australia's past who had no opportunity to answer back'.

John Howard was also looking forward to the devices that he would employ as he consolidated his national leadership. The campaign slogan in 1996 was 'For All Of Us', but that had captured a bare majority of voters. Once the Coalition was in office, the 'us' needed clarification. An early designation was 'the mainstream', but this was hardly more expressive.

Howard then hit upon 'the battlers', the ordinary Australians who made no claim for special attention and wanted nothing more than a fair go. His avowed intention was that they should feel 'relaxed and comfortable' as they enjoyed a respite from the hectoring pyrotechnics of his predecessor's 'big picture'. An earnest of intentions was his scrapping of the principal multicultural agencies. In the following year he dashed hopes for reconciliation with Indigenous Australians. Then the government refused to agree to an international agreement on greenhouse emissions. Then the republic was despatched, and later the refugees were turned away.

These and other decisions marked out a strategy of refusal, but threaded together they formed more than a necklace of negatives. Each one of them combined conviction and calculation. Howard spoke from the heart but his script was informed by constant measurement of public opinion and careful political management. His government acted in the national interest but with a shrewd appreciation of wedge politics. It erased the components of Keating's Big Picture, one after another, dismissing each one of them as pandering to the interests of a selfish minority.

Keating had painted his Big Picture in the speeches he delivered while prime minister. An aggressively demotic speaker, at his best and worst in impromptu invective, Keating was a more diffident and awkward presenter of prepared addresses; but he appreciated the importance of such statements and developed a close rapport with his speechwriter, the historian Don Watson. He placed particular emphasis on the commemoration of historic sites—Winton for the centenary of 'Waltzing Matilda' and Corowa for that of its federal conference, as well as the Western Front, the Kokoda Track, Changi and Hellfire Pass—and he put new places on the map of Australian history, such as Redfern Park.

At home and abroad he built up a story of a people who had suffered but overcome. They had triumphed over their tribulations and prejudices to embrace diversity and tolerance with an egalitarian generosity that would enable them to engage with their Asian neighbours and flourish in the open, globalised economy. This was the national story that held together the Big Picture and it came under immediate attack from John Howard. Speaking in the Commonwealth parliament in October 1996, the prime minister declared: 'I do not take the black armband view of Australian history . . . I believe that the balance sheet of Australian history is overwhelmingly a positive one.'

The Black Armband epithet had been minted three years earlier by the historian Geoffrey Blainey. He used it to characterise what he thought was an excessive emphasis in recent historical writing on past wrongs. This mournful view of Australian history, he suggested, had arisen among a younger generation of historians as a reaction to an earlier 'Three Cheers' view, but the pendulum had swung too far and the Black Armband historians gave an unduly negative account of history's balance sheet.

Mixing Blainey's metaphor further, Howard claimed that 'the balance sheet of Australian history is a very generous and benign one'. While allowing that there were some 'black marks upon our history', he warned of risks if discussion was confined to 'the shortcomings of previous generations'. The risk was increased when 'highly selective views of Australian history' were used for 'endless and agonised navel-gazing about who we are or, as seems to have happened over recent years, as part of a "perpetual seminar" for elite opinion about our national identity'.

The argument moved here from Keating's appropriation of Australian history to the 'elites' who created such tendentiously self-indulgent accounts of the past and the present. The elites provided Howard with a foil for the battlers, whose achievements and sentiments they blackened. It was a nebulous category and an odd term of opprobrium from a man who held the highest national office and who mixed regularly with the wealthy and powerful. These elites variously comprised commentators of progressive sympathy, champions of minority groups, middle-class do-gooders and especially the intellectuals who articulated their concerns.

A synonym, 'the chattering class', became especially popular among the conservative pundits who pontificated incessantly in the op-ed pages of the national press and intoned indignantly on talk-back radio. They demanded to be liberated from political correctness—another catchphrase Howard employed freely as he felt his way into his role—while he purged the nation's institutions of those who dissented from the new orthodoxies.

These heretics had been described earlier as 'whingeing intellectuals, busily manufacturing episodes in the nation's past to complain about', and this activity had created a 'guilt industry' that prosecuted 'a campaign which has been designed above all to delegitimise the settlement of this country'. Howard's former adviser Gerard Henderson asserted in 1993 that 'Much of our history is taught by the alienated and discontented. Australia deserves better. It is time to junk guilt and alienation.' His final rallying-cry, 'Down with the falsification of Australian history', had the ring of a Stalinist ideologue calling down the wrath of the people on dissident intellectuals.

John Howard did not create the anxiety about Australian history but he raised it to a higher level of national prominence. Before he gained office the champions of patriotic history operated as lonely knights errant who challenged the dragons that roamed through the corridors of Australian universities. They sallied forth from conservative fortresses such as *Quadrant* and the *IPA Review*, sometimes cheered on in the press or parliament, only to retire discomfited from the conflict.

They sought in vain a champion who would rid them of the most frightening of the monsters, Manning Clark, who had escaped into the public realm to spread discord and confusion. They welcomed an academic martyr, Geoffrey Blainey, who planted his standard in 1984 at Warrnambool in defence of the old Australia; and they essayed an assault during the Bicentenary of 1988. But the company of the Black Armband held the field, reaching out into the country's schools, its cultural institutions, courts and the public conscience.

Since 1996 the insurgents have enjoyed official patronage. They have been appointed to the governing bodies of the ABC, the National Museum and other public agencies that present history to the public. They are awarded consultancies to advise on school curricula. They have redoubled their campaign to discredit Manning Clark with a reckless assertion that he was an agent of influence for the Soviet Union—the Brisbane *Courier-Mail* ran an eight-page spread just seven weeks after the prime minister denounced the rewriting of history. They publicise their views freely through a sympathetic press, and enjoy favourable publicity as they seek to discredit Aboriginal land claimants, deny that the Stolen Generations were taken from their families, and insist that the European occupation of Australia was remarkably peaceful.

And in all of this they condemn the history profession for its refusal to tell the truth about Australian history. The history departments of the country's universities are said to be dominated by 'tenured radicals' who cling to the discredited liberation struggles of the sixties, who collude in each other's shoddy scholarship, and suppress anyone who challenges their orthodoxies.

Historians are no strangers to political surveillance. In 1953, when Russel Ward began his doctoral research at the new Australian National University, a security file accompanied him to Canberra. Until 1949 he had been a member of the Communist Party and the Australian Security and Intelligence Organisation kept close watch on such intellectuals. 'I am sure that you will readily appreciate', its director-general wrote to the prime minister in 1952, 'the inadvisability of employing, in any University, lecturers who are likely to infest students with subversive doctrines'. He ordered his regional offices to vet all universities: they compiled staff lists, compared them to their own security dossiers and identified all those of suspect loyalty.

These dossiers were compiled on the basis of press clippings, surveillance, phone taps, infiltration and cultivation of informants. Ward's application for a driver's licence went onto the file to provide a record of his handwriting. He was observed to have joined the Fellowship of Australian Writers; to have attended parties at the home of Don Baker, a lecturer in history, while the cars of known communists were parked at the same address; to have visited the house of Bob Gollan, 'the leading Communist in Canberra', and also that of Manning Clark.

A visit to Alec Hope was noteworthy because ASIO believed this eminently conservative poet and professor of English to have had contact with Vladimir Petrov, the defector from the Soviet Embassy. ASIO even noted that Ward visited the home of his supervisor, Laurie Fitzhardinge, who had appeared before the Petrov inquiry.

At the end of 1955, as Ward completed his doctoral thesis, he applied for a lectureship in history at the New South Wales University of Technology. He did so at the invitation of Max Hartwell, the professor of economic history and dean of the Faculty of Humanities; and the selection committee unanimously recommended his appointment. He learned from Hartwell that the vice-chancellor had rejected the appointment on the grounds that Ward 'had been active in seditious circles in Canberra'. He also learned that the chancellor was involved in the decision. The chancellor, Wallace Wurth, was the chairman of the New South Wales Public Service Board.

Hartwell, no sympathiser with Ward's politics, was appalled by this infringement of academic principle, fought it unsuccessfully and resigned to take a post in Oxford. While ASIO denied that it had provided information to the university, it sent the prime minister a report on the matter, kept watch over the ensuing arguments at Kensington and noted that Ward 'was of such character and reputation that no Australian university could or would possibly employ him'.

Ward appealed to leading historians for public support and was advised to go quietly. He returned to high school teaching in New South Wales and ASIO recorded that 'he is very bitter as he considers his Communist background has been held against him in his application for several positions'. The University of New England, to its credit, offered him a post and he accepted it in early 1957. That too was noted by ASIO with no further comment.

The Ward affair came to national attention three years later when Max Hartwell told of it. After criticism in parliament from the Labor Party, Menzies stated that 'the Commonwealth security organisation did not supply any information at all in relation to these matters'. In fact, the director-general of ASIO's minute recorded that 'I don't think we ever vetted Ward for anything. Sometimes Wurth asked us about specially important appointments but I don't think he did so in this case.' For good measure, ASIO recorded that in 1946 Max Hartwell had addressed a meeting of the Sydney University Labour Club.

The Ward affair was an episode in the Cold War. The suspicion attached to his communist past and his continuing association with communists and others of suspect loyalty. The fact that these friendships with Manning Clark, Don Baker, Eric Fry, Bob Gollan, Margaret Kiddle and others arose from shared interests in Australian history seems to have escaped the

ASIO officers, as did the possibility that a visit to the home of Laurie Fitzhardinge might have been a necessary expedient for someone seeking guidance from this notoriously lax supervisor.

Ward's involvement in the progressive Fellowship of Australian Writers was significant along with his membership of the Australian Folk Lore Society because of the radical reputation of such bodies rather than their relevance to his doctoral thesis. There is not a single reference in ASIO's records to Russel Ward's thesis, which he worked into a book in 1958. That book, *The Australian Legend*, would not only reorient Australian history, it would also undermine the whole scheme of values on which the security regime of Menzies and ASIO rested.

Security agencies no longer compile dossiers on historians of suspect loyalty, or if they do the information no longer determines university decisions. Political sympathies are still of concern to government, but they now affect its appointments to councils of museums, libraries, archives and other public bodies that preserve and present the past. The current invigilation of academics is conducted in the media and it goes beyond their political associations to what they write and teach and say about Australian history. It is a public surveillance, without the clandestine character that made Russel Ward so bitter, but no less intimidating. This is the History Wars.

The Wars are not restricted to this country. When Margaret Thatcher set out to restore pride in Britain's past, she took a particular interest in school history. So too did her counterparts in the United States, who reacted with indignation to the appearance of national standards in school history in 1994. The conservative commentator Rush Limbaugh told his radio audience that the standards were part of an America-bashing multicultural agenda, indoctrinating students that 'our country is inherently evil'. By 99 votes to 1, the US Senate condemned the standards. Bob Dole, who was running for the Republican presidential nomination, told the American Legionnaires on Labor Day that a generation of historians were members of 'intellectual elites who seem embarrassed by America'.

The term 'History Wars' gained currency there, and provided the title for a book on a controversy that erupted earlier in 1994 when the Smithsonian Museum prepared an exhibition to mark the fiftieth anniversary of the end of the Pacific War. Its invitation that visitors ponder the moral legitimacy of using the atomic bomb against Japan brought accusations from Newt Gingrich, a historian who had become Republican leader in the House of Representatives, that 'a certain political correctness' was 'seeping in and distorting and prejudicing the Smithsonian's exhibits'. A conservative political commentator wrote that 'the familiar ideology of campus political correctness' had been 'imported whole into our national museum structure'.

That history war was fought over war history, but the term spread across a wide front. The language those who fight the History Wars employ is one of vigilant resolution against a hateful enemy that seeks to denigrate the nation, to infiltrate institutions and corrupt impressionable minds. Those who prosecute the war speak often of killing. The retired Canadian historian, J. L. Granatstein, asked *Who Killed Canadian History?* and answered that the culprits included the politicians, the bureaucrats and his former university colleagues who practised the new modes of social feminist and multicultural history that confused, misled and bored students.

The retired Australian academic, Keith Windschuttle, published a strident polemic in 1994 about *The Killing of History*. He suggested that the discipline and practice of history was suffering a potentially mortal attack from pernicious theorists who asserted that it was impossible to tell the truth about the past, who were hostile to the idea of an objective, knowable

past. The anxiety extends from what historians say about the
past to the methods they employ to say it.

In the dog-days of Labor government in Victoria at the
beginning of the 1990s, after Joan Kirner succeeded John
Cain, a teacher at a private secondary school jumped onto
the conservative bandwagon. He contributed articles to the
Melbourne press alleging that progressive education was
eroding educational standards. Among his bogeys was post-
modernism, a body of theory he could not articulate but
which he portrayed as a form of intellectual nihilism that
threatened to destroy truth and beauty. He was duly rewarded
after Jeffrey Kennett swept into power by appointment as a
consultant to the state's education department, and for good
measure he secured a contract to prepare curriculum materials
in Australian studies.

To develop the materials he turned to a postgraduate
student in the History Department at the University of Melbourne. The early drafts were not to his liking, as they seemed
to employ the very sort of history to which he was opposed.
There was too much gloomy stuff, including a treatment of
the 1930s Depression that explained how deflation allowed
the wealthy to buy more. Discussion proved unproductive and
he turned finally to the whiteboard. Dividing it in two halves,
he labelled one 'Blainey' and the other 'Manning Clark'. The
first was good history, he explained, the other bad.

The hapless researcher reported the incident to me with a
mixture of amusement and alarm. Amusement because he had
a healthy sense of humour and appreciated that Manning
Clark and Geoffrey Blainey, whom Clark had taught, shared
a regard for each other despite their different ways of writing
history. Heightened amusement because it was Geoffrey
Blainey who had explained this effect of the Depression to
him. Alarm because the proposition that different camps of

historical interpretation could be polarised so sharply, the one deemed impermissible and the other obligatory, violated the procedures of scholarship he had learned ever since he began studying history as an undergraduate.

Learning history meant learning to make your own judgements: historians are not used to being told what they should write. Historians reach judgements by consideration of the issues, examination of the evidence, weighing of the arguments. They might well be influenced by an earlier treatment of the subject, particularly if it is provided by an influential historian, and they often undertake the inquiry with their own preferences and expectations. But the inquiry has to be conducted by the procedures of historical scholarship: the relevant literature has to be discussed, the relevant evidence assembled, assessed and set in context, its interpretation justified. These are the procedures that guide the historian. They make it possible for other historians to test the validity of the conclusions, to distinguish history that has warrant from accounts of the past that lack it. The procedures constitute history as a discipline.

If those who commenced the History Wars set out as paladins rescuing the honour of their country, the historians feel themselves the targets in a different kind of warfare. The History Wars opened with a series of pre-emptive strikes launched from conservative think-tanks and their house journals. During the repeated assaults on Manning Clark in the 1970s and early 1980s, the inability of his assailants to find historians who would condemn him confirmed their feeling that the profession was providing safe haven to dangerous radicals. When twenty-three of Geoffrey Blainey's colleagues in the History Department at the University of Melbourne wrote in 1984 to the press to regret his statements on Asian migration, the suspicion mounted. Arguments leading up to the Bicentenary in 1988 heightened accusations of a *trahison des clercs*. In the subsequent campaign against Black Armband history, some fear that the very discipline of history is at risk of collateral damage from its protagonists' weapons of mass destruction.

Historians are ill prepared for such public controversy. They are accustomed to argument—their whole training prepares them to deal with different interpretations of the past—but not to the forms of unilateral assertion that they encounter in the History Wars, where motives are impugned and personal aspersions levelled. Their natural habitat is the seminar, the conference and the academic journal, where the rules of debate are understood and observed. They are less familiar with the media, unused to the polemical style it practises. The press release, the embargo, the immediate deadline and the backgrounding of sympathetic journalists are not part of their repertoire. Since 1996 they have found it increasingly difficult to put their side of the argument in this milieu, so that the prejudices of the columnists and commentators who dominate the national media pass largely unchallenged.

While journalists often ring historians, seeking information (what is the greatest margin of a leadership challenge in federal politics?) or opinion (who were the three greatest prime ministers?) to fill out an interpretive piece, they are much less interested in these historians' research activities. An archaeological discovery is news, as is a scientific breakthrough, but the work of historians is not. It lacks precision and the authority of the experimental finding.

Perhaps it is too familiar, for many feature writers have their own views on what happened in Australian history and see academic historians as making simple and familiar subjects seem complicated and disturbing. The History Warriors, on the other hand, provide good copy. They tell a simple story with great certainty, assuage unease and put the pedants in their place. As the History Wars developed, they became the staple fare of tabloid media and talk-back radio, but they also found a ready outlet in the quality press.

The purpose of this book is to provide a response to the History Wars. It follows the main phases and theatres of the conflict, from the early attempts to discredit Manning Clark to the present efforts to deny frontier massacres and to intervene in the National Museum. Anna Clark contributes a chapter on a particularly contested area, the teaching of Australian history in schools. As we relate each of the campaigns we identify the critics, examine their arguments and evaluate their efforts to rewrite Australian history.

This approach clearly differs from that of John Howard, who complained in 1996 of an attempt to rewrite Australian history in a partisan political cause, and who criticised the historians who contributed to that process of national denigration. The conservative metaphor of the History Wars implies a conflict between adversaries, and it is clear that not all historians are pacifists. In 1970 the young Humphrey McQueen published an attack on the existing historical interpretation of Australian labour history. 'For the next two hundred odd pages', he announced in the Introduction, 'I shout, wave my arms and frantically dash from one battlefield to another'.

McQueen was an unusually pugnacious controversialist but it is undeniable that the historians of his generation did change the understanding of Australian history, as historians before and since have done. It is in the nature of history as a research activity that it should generate additional knowledge and novel interpretations. It is inherent in history as a branch of the humanities that it should respond to changing concerns. The suggestion that rewriting history is a sinister activity rests on a naïve view of the past as something fixed, fully disclosed and final, a record of immanent truth that only malcontents could deny. An account of the History Wars should therefore begin with a consideration of what historians do and how they have shaped the understanding of Australian history.

CHAPTER 2

WHAT DO HISTORIANS DO?

In the course of this year, most Australians will watch a history program on television. Half of them will visit a museum or a historic site. A tiny minority will open a book written by a university-based historian. The academic profession contributes a narrow sliver of information about the past and the crime of which it is accused, rewriting Australian history, would seem to touch lightly on popular interests. Why, then, do John Howard and other opinion-formers wage the History Wars? Why do a scatter of errant academic historians command so much attention?

The reasons are partly to do with the territory under dispute in the History Wars and partly with the way they are conducted. The rewards for coming to terms with the past that Paul Keating offered in his Big Picture included greater tolerance, increased autonomy, a deeper understanding of the land and its original inhabitants, an outward-looking, productive and self-confident nation. The risks of a Black Armband view of Australian history that Geoffrey Blainey identified included intolerance of old Australia, loss of sovereignty, the

14

tying up of productive resources, disunity, pessimism and guilt. Both analyses of the options for Australia invested remarkable significance in the proper interpretation of its past.

Academic historians are prominent in such arguments because they are easy targets. There are not many of them, they are poorly organised, and they have very little political clout. Their academic activities are unfamiliar and their habit of writing for each other in a professional patois lends itself to ridicule and mockery. When they venture beyond the academy they can be blamed for creating the very problems whose complexities they try to explore. You can attack them with impunity.

For similar reasons academic historians are also an elusive target. They are scattered around the country in institutions that do not respond readily to administrative direction and in any case espouse the principle of academic freedom. The observation of that principle came later than is generally understood. Right up to the second half of the last century Australian universities forbade their staff from involvement in public controversy, and the appointment of Russel Ward to a history post at the University of New South Wales was blocked in 1956 because he had been a communist. Freedom of judgement and expression is nevertheless a hallmark of the academic vocation.

The mission of the university, it used to be said, was to pursue knowledge for its own sake and to follow the inquiry wherever it might lead. To this admirable credo might now be added: so long as you can recruit fee-paying students, attract research funding and satisfy an ethics committee. Even so, academic historians enjoy a greater measure of autonomy over what they do than historians working in most other settings.

Academic historians are prominent in the History Wars also because they speak with the authority of the expert. They have been trained in the discipline of history and appointed to university posts because of their expertise. Unaccustomed to media attention, they feel chagrin when interlopers command the headlines and are inclined to respond with professional indignation. After Keith Windschuttle began his challenge to the practitioners of Aboriginal history, one of the less helpful replies was that he had no standing in the field.

Members of the historical profession sometimes regard John Howard's pronouncements on history in much the same way as the medical profession did those of Joh Bjelke-Petersen when the Queensland premier announced a quack cure for cancer. Few professions command the standing of the medical profession, but many Australians would not think that historians can be likened to doctors. A profession possesses esoteric skills, but who is impressed by arcane historiographical allusions? How often does the ABC television news present the findings of a historian with the uncritical admiration it uses for a report of some new cure for cancer?

A profession regulates entry to maintain a monopoly of practice, but the influence of academic historians over the production and consumption of history is probably weaker now than at any time in the past half-century. Australians do not regard history as a form of inaccessible knowledge, nor do they see it as the preserve of experts. These are healthy attitudes—history should not be enclosed, it should be kept as commons—but they leave the role of the history profession unclear. What is it that historians do?

In 2002 the Carlton Football Club announced a record financial deficit. Its autocratic president, John Elliott, finally yielded to criticism and his successor was left to deal with a legacy of debt as well as the penalties the AFL imposed for breach of its player payment rules. In the following year the club announced that it would change the name of the grandstand named after Elliott and introduce a ban on smoking he had resisted so strongly. 'We have ruled a line under the past', the new president insisted, 'and we are moving forward'.

Australians have ambivalent attitudes to history. The Carlton Football Club is proud of its record of sixteen VFL and AFL premierships. Portraits of former players decorate the walls of its social club, along with honour boards recording former officials. The navy-blue jumper worn since 1864, the club song dating back to the Boer War, the recent celebration of Carlton's 'team of the century', all affirm the importance of tradition. The new president, himself a former premiership player, is not ruling a line under that past; rather, he is excising a particular segment of the club's past that is no longer wanted.

History is often treated as dispensable; indeed, the term itself is often used as signifying something that is over and irrelevant. 'He's history' expresses dismissal of someone who no longer matters. This way of thinking about the past is a particular feature of modernity, where change is constant and habitual. With innovation comes obsolescence. Old industries decline, while new industries transform work, consumption and leisure. A country town first loses its rail service and silo. Then the bank closes, medical services disappear and the children are bussed to a school thirty kilometres down the highway. The church is turned into a tourist shop and the football club merges with an old rival in the next town. The farmers who remain are following Chicago commodity prices online in order to decide what crop to plant next. As the familiar landmarks disappear, impermanency becomes a permanent condition.

The English historian J. H. Plumb claimed more than thirty years ago that such radical dislocation was threatening to bring about the death of the past. He drew a contrast between premodern societies, where the past dictated what men and women should do: the weight of tradition was felt in myth and legend, in the sacred books and ceremonies that ensured each generation walked in the footsteps of its predecessor. That idea of an unbroken continuity yielded to the idea of secular time, and of history as a way of understanding change and progress. History thus became a form of knowledge that broke the chains of the past, leaving just remnants of curiosity, nostalgia and sentimentality.

Plumb probably exaggerated the potency of his calling, and he certainly minimised the persistence of the past. The very distinction he drew between the two categories is often breached. There are appeals to history that invoke past events as if they were unproblematic facts that speak for themselves and talk to our innermost feelings. Such appeals strike a chord because they make us part of a compelling story. They tell us who we are, what we have done and what we might do. The words of the national anthem, 'In history's page, let every stage Advance Australia Fair', join us to a binding national past.

The word 'history' comes from the classical Greek word 'to know', with connotations of learning, wisdom and judgement. The writing of history, which goes back two and a half millennia to Herodotus and Thucydides, rests on a distinction between truth and myth. The Athenian's history of the Peloponnesian wars dealt with events that had actually occurred, and it ordered them by means of narrative into a coherent and instructive whole.

The Romans took over the form and used it to create a lineage for their city-state, to record its imperial triumphs and to show the inexorable effects of human passions. From Christianity it acquired a linear notion of time that gave the historical process its sacred purpose and linked all events to the central divine story. From the expansion of Europe, the challenge to Christian faith and the Enlightenment history acquired a sense of the differences between societies, secular progress and the capacity of history to comprehend the forces of change.

History was both an art and a science. It provided knowledge of the past and it employed that knowledge to teach lessons about human conduct. The antiquarian was primarily concerned to create a faithful record or memorial, and employed genealogies and similar devices to do so. The literary historian used imagination and rhetoric to instruct the reader. The two branches came together in the great eighteenth-century histories of Hume and Gibbon, who offered insights into the rise and fall of civilisations that were endowed with the force of art and taught with the authority of the real.

History entered the academy in the nineteenth century as a science, alongside the natural sciences, that would yield objective knowledge of 'the past as it actually occurred'. The phrase 'the past as it actually occurred' was coined by Leopold von Ranke in reaction against the speculative history of Enlightenment radicals, and it was this German professor who codified the disciplinary procedures of a strictly accurate, archivally based scholarship. The records of the past were brought together and arranged in repositories, the historian interrogated the evidence and ascertained its meaning.

History, the academic discipline, formed around these procedures in the universities of Europe. It was a discipline defined by its commitment to the scientific paradigm of research, though that paradigm quickly transformed the teaching function as well. An influential textbook on the study of history, first published in France in 1898 with an English translation in the same year, insisted that it was not 'a summary of ascertained facts', or a speculative exercise in the philosophy of history, but an introduction to 'the method of the historical sciences'.

The authors explained that documents were the raw material, 'the traces which have been left by the thoughts and actions of men of former times'. History was not a science of direct observation and could not conduct laboratory experiments, but it obtained knowledge by chains of reasoning from the sources. The historian applied criticism to establish the provenance, authorship and transmission of the documents, and trained judgement to ascertain their meaning and veracity. Then came the synthesis as the historian determined the pattern of these 'isolated facts' and finally its exposition.

The 'scientific form of exposition' was the monograph, an exhaustive treatment of a particular subject, and the historical profession devised research theses, scholarly books, journals and reviews to disseminate and evaluate its work. The same formats are used today. Then there were auxiliary publications such as calendars of sources, critical editions, handbooks, guides and general works for students; these too continue. The authors of the manual allowed the possibility of popular work for the public, but only on sufferance. 'A populariser is excused from original research.' Those who wrote such works 'abandon themselves . . . to their natural impulses, like the common run of men. They take sides, they censure, they extol; they colour, they embellish; they allow themselves to be influenced by personal, patriotic, moral, or metaphysical considerations.'

We see here the hallmarks of a profession: the claim of esoteric skills that give its possessors, if not a licensed monopoly, then an exclusive authority. It is difficult to know which claim is the more audacious: the assumption that the academic historian is protected by the procedures of the discipline against the natural impulses of humanity, or the belief that the historian's restricted forms of communication can prevail over popular history.

Even when this manual appeared, there were popularisers whose influence far surpassed that of the scientific school. We may think in Britain of J. R. Green, whose *Short History of the English People* (1874) outsold any of the academic histories, or we could go back to the historical novels of Walter Scott that shaped readers' sense of the past with a force that no scholarly article in the *English Historical Review* could approach.

Similar comparisons apply to Australian history. Russel Ward's codification of radical nationalism in *The Australian Legend* sold 40 000 copies in the twenty years after it appeared in 1958, and Geoffrey Blainey's *Tyranny of Distance* has remained constantly in print since it was published in 1966. But two autobiographical works of the 1980s, A. B. Facey's *A Fortunate*

Life and Sally Morgan's *My Place*, comfortably outsold both these outstanding examples of historical scholarship. When historians gather in professional conferences, their conversation soon turns not to sales figures but to the problem of finding a publisher.

Some 350 academics are retained to teach and conduct research in departments of history in Australian universities, and perhaps half of them work on Australian history. A shifting number of part-time and casual employees make up an auxiliary teaching force. There are more freelance historians who earn a living by writing commissioned histories of companies, government and local government bodies, and other organisations. 'Public history' is the name for this activity, adopted from the United States, and with its own professional association. There are more again who write local and family history as a labour of love. They too have their own societies; there are hundreds of local ones and the state peak bodies run up to a thousand members.

In the course of an academic year, possibly 10 000 undergraduates will attend classes in some aspect of Australian history, but the overwhelming majority of young Australians conclude their study of the subject at the end of Year 10 of secondary school. That experience might well be fragmentary, for reasons we shall explore in Chapter 9, and it might have only fleeting connection to the history that is produced in the universities.

Many will form a sense of this country's past by reading novels, since literature has created influential versions of Australian history from well before it was consolidated as an acdemic discipline. Marcus Clarke anticipated the Black Armband in a dark melodrama of a convict serving out *His Natural Life* (1874), and also wrote an early school history. Rolf Boldrewood established the bushranger legend in *Robbery under Arms* and Henry Handel Richardson set down the restlessness of the gold-rush generation and the ambivalences of the migrant experience. More recently, Jean Bedford, Robert

Drewe and Peter Carey have embellished the legend of Ned Kelly, which Sidney Nolan worked so memorably into visual imagery. Drama, verse and art were early and enduring mediums of history.

The first Australian feature-length film told *The Story of the Kelly Gang* in 1906, and the story has been refilmed several times. Clarke, Boldrewood and Richardson were all projected onto the screen, along with a range of films that took up epic events in Australian history, from *Eureka* and *Burke and Wills* to *Gallipoli*. The film *Rabbit-Proof Fence* has reached a wider audience than any of the participants in the History Wars.

Television quickly spawned historical drama series, concentrating initially on the colonial period but moving later into the *Bodyline* cricket crisis, *The Petrov Affair*, *The Dismissal* and *True Believers*. Soap operas such *The Sullivans* are characterised by carefully reconstructed period settings. Historical documentaries range from Peter Luck's newsreel compilation of *This Magnificent Century* to interpretive series such as those presented by Geoffrey Blainey, Robert Hughes and Paul Kelly.

Libraries, galleries and museums were powerful instruments of social memory that preceded the formation of the historical discipline in Australia, collecting, organising and presenting materials deemed worthy of remembrance. The urge to commemorate first raised statues and monuments for individual heroes, such as governors and explorers. Later, most notably in war memorials, it perpetuated the memory of collective heroes. Historical anniversaries, re-enactments and commemorations have become increasingly grand public spectacles: the sums expended by the Australian Bicentennial Authority and the Council for the Centenary of Federation dwarfed the combined budgets of the university history departments over the two decades in which they operated.

History has become a major component of the tourist industry, with centres such as Longreach's Stockmen's Hall of Fame and theme parks such as Ballarat's Sovereign Hill increasingly important to their towns' fortunes. The employment of a historical consultant has become essential to the preparation of a regional authority's strategic plan, the heritage study a condition of permission to redevelop an urban precinct.

How does this proliferation of activity influence popular understandings of the past? A recent American study asked a representative sample of the population whether they had engaged in a history-related activity in the previous twelve months. The researchers found that 81 per cent of respondents had watched a movie or television program about the past, 57 per cent had visited a museum or historical site, 36 per cent worked on family history, and 20 per cent were part of a group studying or preserving the past. This last category encompassed a wide range of activities beyond historical education and research, and if those who pursued a hobby concerned with the past (say, railways) or collected items from the past (perhaps quilts) were added, then it took in two-fifths of the sample. The most popular activity, involving 90 per cent, was looking at photos with family or friends.

Participation in an activity was not always an accurate guide to engagement. The respondents felt most connected to the past when they discussed it with family and friends, or visited a museum or historic site; least connected when in a classroom, reading a book or watching a movie. Respondents also found their grandparents more reliable guides than college professors. 'History is too cold, too analytical', said one. Museums were felt to be more trustworthy because they let 'you come to your own conclusions'.

A striking finding was the small proportion of respondents for whom American history was most important, just 22 per cent. The demographic segment most interested in national history was men aged over 65; the interest fell away sharply among ethnic minorities and others who thought that the history of their own racial, religious or cultural group was most important to them. Yet in discussions with the respondents the researchers discovered this separation was misleading. They found people making connections between personal and public events. A photo of a family member in uniform triggered references to the Second World War; a personal incident in the past would be dated by reference to the assassination of President Kennedy.

More recently, a research group at the University of Technology Sydney has undertaken a similar survey of Australian activities and attitudes. Here again, the most common activities are looking at photos and watching movies or television, with half the sample reporting visits to museums or historic sites and 32 per cent engaged in family history or a history-related hobby. Perhaps surprisingly, Australians are far more interested in their own national history than Americans, and this interest is particularly marked among women. Australian men display greater interest in world and European history, possibly because of their greater interest in war. Women, on the other hand, combine an interest in Australian, Indigenous and ethnic history with genealogy. The researchers suggested that women are the principal custodians of 'the intimate and domestic past'.

As with Americans, most Australians feel the closest connection to the past in family circles or museums and regard museums as the most trustworthy guides to the past, though Aboriginal respondents think them far less so. History teachers come well down the list of reliable sources of information. Academics fare much better, though the researchers warn that this might not be cause for self-congratulation: some of their respondents did not really know what academic historians do.

Nearly fifty years ago a fastidious professor of history at the University of Melbourne surveyed his field at a congress of the Australian and New Zealand Association for the Advancement of Science. He found much to praise as he considered the improvement in the research and writing of Australian history. He rejoiced that the activity had become professional. While allowing that some excellent work was produced outside the academy (he particularly commended that of a young freelance business historian, Geoffrey Blainey), he was insistent: 'If it is "professional", however, its conventions, methods of presentation and standards of evidence are those set in universities'.

The academic history profession that this professor celebrated in 1959 was a recent phenomenon. Before the Second World War there were just five professors of history (with an associate professor in Western Australia) who, with a handful of assistants, conducted the discipline in the country's six small universities. They did not lack students, for history was an integral part of a liberal education, and they lectured and examined in a range of subjects that spanned ancient, European, British, imperial and colonial history.

They professed history as a discipline that yielded an objective account of the past, and some of them even found time to conduct research (usually in Australian history, since its records came readily to hand). Their abler graduates proceeded to further training at Oxford, Cambridge or London University, and some returned to appointments in Australian universities; but with so few positions, that depended upon a vacancy becoming available.

The Second World War convinced government of the national importance of greater expertise and knowledge. Demobilisation brought a dramatic increase in university enrolments, and post-war planning augmented provision further. Funds were provided to enable research, journals and academic presses were established to publish it, libraries were expanded to support it. The Australian universities offered scholarships to graduates wishing to pursue research and introduced the degree of Doctor of Philosophy as a professional credential. As new universities were created, they recruited from this pool.

History shared in this new bounty. In 1954 there were seven departments employing 60 historians; in 1960, ten departments and 150 historians; and by the early 1970s, sixteen departments and 320 full-time lecturing staff. When those in temporary appointments, cognate departments or the colleges of advanced education are included, the academic profession numbered 750. That was the ceiling. When the OPEC oil crisis hit in 1974, an era of sustained economic growth came to an end and the circumstances that had favoured higher education disappeared.

More than a decade later, when the expansion of higher education resumed, its emphases were very different. Under Education Minister John Dawkins the universities were directed to match their activity to the needs of the economy and the labour market, to provide vocational training and produce knowledge for the growth industries of the information economy. History fared poorly in the mergers and reorganisations that followed. When the heads of the country's history departments met in 1989, they reported 451 staff and a subsequent survey in 1995 found 410. The Howard government's funding policies have turned the screws further.

The rapid growth of the profession brought movement into new fields of history, allowed for innovation, fostered esteem and confidence. The subsequent contraction forced the abandonment of some fields, increased staff workloads (since student numbers held up) and made it more difficult to replace those who left. This left an ageing cohort: a survey of staffing in the quarter-century to 1995 found that more than half of all appointments had been made in the years 1970 to 1975. As the opportunities to join the academic profession declined, there was a movement into the new fields of applied history. First, history graduates turned to public history and the heritage industries, then history departments began to offer training and qualifications in these professions. They also began to teach the new forms of history with courses on memory and identity, visual history and film.

Other historians found employment in new university programs in gender studies, cultural studies, Australian, Asian or international studies, tourism, media and communications and the other fields that sprouted as faculties of humanities and social sciences sought to compete with the vocational attractions of professional faculties. Historians are a resilient species, their skills adaptable, and they take their chances where they find them. It is less clear that they are free to carry their discipline into these new activities. Growth areas attract competitors with their own methodologies. After they migrate, historians are under pressure to assimilate.

For all these strains, the discipline retains most of its essential features. History attracts large numbers of undergraduates, excites them with the allure of the past and introduces them to the procedures of historical interpretation. One of the first lessons it teaches is that they must form their own judgements based on their understanding of the subject, their reading of the evidence, their evaluation of the arguments, their capacity for empathy, engagement and lucidity. Students learn how to find the sources that are relevant to their inquiry, and the conventions of citation that ensure it is properly documented and open to inspection. History attracts similarly large cohorts of postgraduates, who apply these methods to the advanced study of a particular topic.

The members of the profession inform their teaching with research. They pursue research in archives and libraries, and this activity remains the primary characteristic of the academic discipline and vocation. It determines both promotion and reputation. Peer assessment, by examination of research theses, refereeing of books and articles, and appraisal of applications for research grants, enforces standards and shapes the topics that are studied. Like other professions, the history profession is also competitive, and the endeavour for originality tempers the tendency to imitation. The research imperative that began with Ranke's school of scientific history continues to drive innovation.

Australia spends heavily on such research. The Commonwealth government allocates hundreds of millions of dollars annually to the activity, and it allows Australian researchers to produce about 2 per cent of the world's research literature. The Australian Research Council is the principal agency that allocates research grants across the full range of academic disciplines and it is able to fund just one in four of the more than 3000 applications it receives each year. Historians might pick up twenty-five or thirty of those grants. Towards the end of the year, when the minister approves the council's recommendations and a press release goes out, there is a good chance that it will be a history project that attracts attention. The pattern was set some years ago when Labor was in office and an Opposition 'waste watch committee' seized on a grant to support a research project on family life in ancient Rome.

The choice is instructive. Few question the public funding of research since the creation of new knowledge is the mainspring of the information economy. Ridicule is never directed at projects in the biological or physical sciences. No-one queries the merits of a grant that allows economists to buy a data set from the Australian Bureau of Statistics in order to apply some econometric model in the American literature. But research in the humanities is both familiar and puzzling. It seems to labour over questions where the answer is obvious, and to couch the investigation in terms that provide philistines with an irresistible target.

John Howard's denunciation of the rewriting of Australian history draws on this suspicion. He appeals to a history that is given rather than made, and needs to be defended from those who would tamper with it. Commenting in 2000 on the anniversary of Gallipoli, the prime minister regretted the way that the 'issues' raised by historians distracted attention from a proper appreciation of 'exactly what happened'. In defending the national past from rewriting by revisionists, he upholds the facts against interpretation.

The appeal to history as a record of 'exactly what happened' attests to the force of Ranke's dictum: 'the past as it actually occurred'. But Ranke was the authority who insisted that this knowledge had to be retrieved and the scholar who laid down the procedures of historical research that would create it. History is a reconstruction of the past that seeks a particular kind of fidelity within which the facts acquire their authority. Of all its devices, the narrative is the most compelling for it creates a sequence of factual events and connects them with a dramatic momentum that carries the history forward from starting point to conclusion.

That is not how life is lived. Human life is a swirl of divergent impulses, failed beginnings and unexpected outcomes that are as surprising as humanity is rich and complex. Life is lived in the present without the benefit of a grand narrator. It is the historian who enjoys the advantage of hindsight to select particular events and arrange them into a coherent pattern. The facts do not exist prior to the interpretation that establishes their significance. Rather, historical research involves a continuous dialogue between the two.

The historian goes to the archives with hypotheses—without them it would be impossible to know what to look for—that are entangled with sympathies and expectations. But you never find precisely what you are looking for, or if you do it bodes ill for the project. The sharpest excitement comes when you open a file and are confronted by some unexpected evidence. That is when you revise the argument and reorient the inquiry. The interaction between what you are looking for and what you find is continuous. It carries over into the process of writing, which is the most taxing and the most rewarding aspect of historical discovery.

History is also a discipline. In academic parlance, a discipline refers to a branch of knowledge, but it also reminds practitioners of the rules that govern their activity. If historians create history, they are not free to invent or falsify it. The discipline defines the standards historians are expected to observe. They include familiarity (the ability to situate the subject within a substantial body of relevant material), comparative judgement (the capacity to absorb and appraise different, sometimes conflicting sources), appreciation of authority (acknowledgement of earlier accounts and proper consideration of them), awareness of manifold truth (the ability to understand why those with different views are bound to know the past differently) and honesty (a fidelity to what is found).

These are the attributes that enable historians to contribute to the history that is practised outside the university and to shape the understanding of Australian history. Their adherence to such standards is one of the issues at stake in the History Wars.

CHAPTER 3

WHAT DO THEY SAY?

The first Australian histories were not histories of Australia. They were histories of British settlement in the antipodes. They were published in London as well as locally, and directed to British as well as Australian readers. William Charles Wentworth, John Dunmore Lang, Henry Melville, James Macarthur and John West wrote history as a medium of debate about the burning issues of the day, seeking to inform public opinion and persuade those in Whitehall who determined colonial policy.

Were the convicts a help or a hindrance? Did the governors abuse their authority? Had the rights of the Indigenous inhabitants been respected? Were the colonies ready for self-government? These questions were answered in narratives that related the course of events since settlement to demonstrate the pernicious effects of bad policy and the welcome results of good. They were polemical histories, as sharply political in content and purpose as any mentioned in the History Wars.

The advent of self-government in the 1850s did not end these tendencies. Colonial governments commissioned historians who boosted their achievements and prospects to attract migrants and investment from Britain. Conservative critics such as G. W. Rusden and H. G. Turner traced the ruinous consequences of departing from British custom. Rusden offered another reason for his three-volume *History of Australia* (1883). 'The actors in what has been called the heroic work of civilization are rapidly passing away', he explained, and a definitive record was needed to keep their memory alive. As the new society grew, consolidated its prosperity and threw up new buildings in place of earlier ones, it threatened to efface its origins. Memoirs, reminiscences, and the collection and publication of records served the impulse to record the foundations and honour the pioneers.

Commemorative history continued to divide opinion. All the Australian colonies joined the rest of the empire in 1887 to honour the fiftieth anniversary of the reign of Queen Victoria. The wily premier of New South Wales, Sir Henry Parkes, seized control of what he called 'our 100th birthday' in 1888. Parkes wanted a grand edifice that would be both a museum of the nation's past and a mausoleum for its heroes, but had to settle for a bare Centennial Park and a week of champagne and speeches. The weekly *Bulletin* magazine, radical and nationalist, saw nothing worth celebrating in 'the day we were lagged'. It suggested Australia's national day should be not 26 January but 3 December, the anniversary of the Eureka rebellion when 'Australia set her teeth in the face of the British Lion'.

The federation of the colonies into the Commonwealth of Australia at the end of the century augmented national sentiment. It brought a national flag, a coat of arms supported by an emu and kangaroo, widespread use of Australian flora as well as fauna for national symbols and decorative motifs, and the adoption of Wattle Day by schools. It also brought Empire Day, when these young Australian citizens were reminded of their heritage. Australian history was installed in the schools 'to foster love of home, country and race, and to elevate morally the coming man and woman'.

The first academics to practise the discipline of history in Australia, similarly, were not historians of Australia. They were teachers of European, British, imperial and colonial history. Australian history appeared in this curriculum as an aspect of European and British expansion. It was taught comparatively, so that Australia and New Zealand (they were often joined together as Australasian history) were considered along with other societies formed by British settlement. And it was taught sequentially so that the student understood the colonial society as an offspring of the parent, inheriting its traditions, reproducing its institutions and upholding its ideals.

The University of Sydney catches this understanding of cultural transfer in its motto: 'The same spirit under new skies'. It is said that the course taught there on Australian history gave such faithful attention to British origins that the First Fleet was often yet to leave Portsmouth when the first term's lectures ended. At the University of Melbourne until the 1960s, no student could enrol in Australian history without first completing British history.

Two of the professors who shaped this education in history were English by origin, the rest Australian. Arnold Wood was appointed to the new chair of history at Sydney in 1891, a recent graduate of Manchester and Oxford, and held it for twenty-seven years. One of his earliest students, George Henderson, had gone on to Oxford, and took up a chair at Adelaide in 1902. Melbourne appointed Ernest Scott to its chair in 1913. He was an English immigrant and his student Stephen Roberts succeeded Wood at Sydney in 1929 after further study at the London School of Economics.

Another of Scott's students, Keith Hancock, returned from Oxford to succeed Henderson at Adelaide in 1926. When Hancock returned to England in 1933, he was replaced by

Wood's student G. V. Portus, who also had an Oxford degree. The Melbourne graduate Edward Shann taught briefly at the University of Queensland after study at the London School of Economics before appointment in 1913 as foundation professor of history and economics at the University of Western Australia, with Scott's student Fred Alexander as his assistant and successor. Finally, Wood's student Max Crawford succeeded Scott at Melbourne in 1937 after the inevitable Oxford interlude.

The lineages are so closely entwined as to threaten some genetic defect of inbreeding. To this can be added the powerful influence of the environment in which these professors operated. They were influential public figures. They controlled the school curriculum as well as that of the university; they were prominent in the state historical societies, active in the library and cultural institutions of their city, contributors to the press. They mixed freely with the governing class and most of them were members of the Round Table, a network of discussion circles formed in Britain and the Dominions to 1910 to foster the imperial ideal.

These academics established the historical discipline in Australia. They instructed their students in the methods of historical research and put advanced students to work on local material. Both Wood and Scott concentrated initially on the European exploration of Australia and the early period of settlement. Henderson and Roberts published original research on colonial policy in the Pacific, and Roberts later wrote on land settlement. Their successors moved further afield but almost all of them were pressed into service for the Australian volume of the *Cambridge History of the British Empire*, edited by Scott and published in 1933.

This was conceived as an authoritative account of Australian history and Scott liked to think it would 'probably be used all over the world for a century to come'. The English general editors suggested in the preface to the volume and its New Zealand companion volume that 'The history of both

Dominions takes a special character from this comparatively free development of English life transplanted to coasts and islands on the other side of the world'. The Australian contributors reinforced this interpretation. Roberts presented the growth of the wool industry as 'a perfect example of the process of Empire development'. Portus treated the gold rush as a magnet for the better type of British migrant, and dismissed the idea that 'the Eureka riots' had been more than a passing disturbance. Others traced the transfer of British freedoms and the application of British institutions of self-government. Hancock's chapter on the early Commonwealth and Alexander's on post-war politics both warned against nationalist excess.

Nothing appears as ridiculous as an obsolete orthodoxy. The imperial interpretation of Australian history has passed so completely that we find it almost incomprehensible, except as an object of mockery—hence the jibes of Paul Keating about local Tories tugging their forelocks and dreaming of the Land of Hope and Glory. Politicians are licensed to employ such rhetoric. The duty of the historian is to understand how an earlier age might have held such views.

The loyalty that these Australians felt for the empire did not imply a lack of attachment to their own country. On the contrary, their patriotism was at once national and imperial in the same way that someone today can be a Queenslander as well as an Australian. It was an attachment based on shrewd calculation of self-interest and instinctive feeling, a sentiment of shared blood, traditions and ideals. Alfred Deakin, a fervent imperial loyalist, caught the combination of loyalties when he called himself an Independent Australian Briton.

Nor did these imperialists think Britain was superior to Australia and that we should defer to the Mother Country. When Deakin went to London as a representative of his country, he was appalled by the class prejudice, poverty and squalor, the arrogance of the British ruling class and its condescension to the colonials. The Australian members of the

Round Table worried that Britain was neglectful of its imperial responsibilities, and they frequently asserted an Australian point of view.

They set down their imperial interpretation of Australian history at a time when the relationship was coming under growing strain. The First World War cost 60 000 Australian lives. It divided the country over the issue of conscription, embittered many Irish Australians when the British Army put down a rebellion in their homeland, and alarmed many empire loyalists when the majority of Australians rejected conscription. It depleted Britain, weakened its economy and left Australia with a large debt on war loans raised in London. The writings of the imperial historians turned after the war to contemporary concerns. Edward Shann's *Economic History of Australia* (1930) argued that Australia had prospered as an exporter of commodities to Britain, and suffered when governments interfered with the market to protect domestic industries and living standards.

Keith Hancock incorporated Shann's affirmation of the imperial economic relationship into his extremely influential *Australia* (published in the same year). He saw Australians as 'transplanted British' invigorated by their new environment, and he noted the emergence of a self-assertive national sentiment, while insisting on its limits: 'Among the Australians pride of race counted for more than love of country'. The British had posed no obstacle to self-government, so that Australia was content, 'while accepting the privileges of nationhood, to deny herself some heroics . . . and some responsibilities'.

Settler societies such as Australia were characterised by what Hancock called a 'distaste for the past'. A nation of restless and acquisitive individuals freed from the constraints of the Old World, they pressed their demands upon government so that 'Australian democracy has come to look upon the State as a vast public utility, whose duty it is to provide the greatest happiness for the greatest number'. They established a White Australia, they built tariff walls to protect local industries, they regulated wage levels and they borrowed recklessly to sustain profligate public agencies.

In the very year these two books appeared, an officer of the Bank of England came to Australia to curb such immature extravagance. The Depression had struck, the prices for Australian exports collapsed, the capital market closed and the country was hard pressed to maintain interest payments on the external public debt. The British banker insisted that Australia reduce public outlays, cut wages and accept the hardship of mass unemployment. The arrival two years later of an English cricket team and the employment of bodyline tactics by its unbending, upper-class captain, Douglas Jardine, strained imperial relations further.

In such circumstances it was hardly surprising that the imperial interpretation should come under challenge. Bert Evatt, who wrote Australian history while a member of the High Court, objected to the patrician tone struck by the members of the Melbourne branch of the Round Table who contributed to the *Cambridge History of the British Empire*: it seemed to him as if 'every important event in our history must, in some mysterious way, have revealed its true importance to a Melbourne coterie exclusively'.

A freelance Melbourne historian, Brian Fitzpatrick, took issue with Shann's account of Australian economic development and Hancock's condescending treatment of Australian nationalism. Fitzpatrick was one of Ernest Scott's few dissatisfied students and retained an aversion for the pedantry of academic history. 'The origins of the people are not in the library', he would declare to a gathering of the profession. In any case, his radical politics and erratic lifestyle disqualified him from an academic career. He turned to journalism and later became the driving force of the Australian Council for Civil Liberties.

In two substantial books of economic history published in 1939 and 1941, Fitzpatrick argued that Australia's settlement and subsequent development had been shaped by the economic interests of Britain. It was a field for investment and a source of dividends, a provider of raw materials and a market for British products. The growth of Australian industry and the rise of an Australian labour movement were autonomous forces, but at critical moments—the depressions of the 1890s and 1930s—the continuing dependence on foreign capital became clear, along with the persistence of economic, cultural and political servility.

Fitzpatrick was a nationalist and he was also a radical. 'I have taken the view', he wrote in one of his more popular general works, 'that the history of the Australian people is amongst other things the history of a struggle between the organised rich and the organised poor'. He identified the efforts of the labour movement to secure social justice with the impulse towards Australian independence. His radical nationalism affirmed the efforts of ordinary men and women to share the wealth of the country. 'The Australian people made heroes of none', he concluded one of his general surveys, 'and raised no idols, except perhaps an outlaw, Ned Kelly, and Carbine, a horse'. But they had fought nature as well as their own taskmasters, and 'made of Australia a home good enough for men of modest report to live in, calling their souls their own'.

The radical nationalist interpretation of Australian history caught the national mood as the Second World War spread to the Pacific. After the fall of Singapore, when it was clear that Australia could no longer expect Britain to guarantee its security, a Labor government mobilised the people for national defence and a new post-war order. Wartime service shaped a new generation of historians: it broadened their experience, turned them into fully independent Australians, drew them to schemes of millenarian change. A number became communists (at least until 1956 when they realised the truth about Stalin), and most of the others supported the Labor Party. The post-war expansion of the universities enabled them to find academic posts, after they had completed their studies, where they could teach, research and write.

The story they told was one of protest against oppression and exploitation, struggle to realise popular aspirations and progress towards a free, democratic and independent nationhood. Russel Ward showed in *The Australian Legend* how the experience of the convicts, bushrangers, gold-diggers, drovers and shearers in the bush interior gave rise to a national ethos that was practical, laconic, suspicious of authority, impatient with affectation, sympathetic to the underdog.

The radical nationalist tradition was explored in studies of literature, art and popular culture. Other historians traced its extension into politics. Bob Gollan showed in *Radical and Working Class Politics* how the labour movement emerged out of earlier efforts to extend democracy. Ian Turner examined the growing militancy of the unions in *Industrial Labour and Politics*, and many of the radical nationalists concentrated on labour history to emphasise the leading role of the working class in this democratic advance.

Not all historians accepted the radical nationalist interpretation. Some preferred to study religion, education, high culture and other received forms of European civilisation. Some argued for the contribution of business, the influence of the middle class and the creative role of non-Labor politics. John Ward at Sydney continued to work in the more conservative imperial tradition. Manning Clark posed the sharpest challenge to the radical nationalists with his call in 1954 for historians to drop the 'great Australian illusion' of a radical past that could inspire and instruct endeavours. Those who persisted with this understanding of Australian history, he insisted, were clinging to the exhausted creed of secular humanism and a naïve faith in progress.

The appearance in 1962 of the first volume of his *History of Australia* signalled a different way of writing history as epic. Clark's theme was how Europeans had brought the great systems of belief—Catholicism, Protestantism and the Enlightenment—and tried to establish them here. He related a clash of ideas embodied in heroes who failed nobly in this endeavour, partly because of their own fatal flaws and partly because the land and spirit of Australia defeated them.

This was a history that borrowed freely from the Bible, the Book of Common Prayer and the great works of nineteenth-century European literature. Like his hero Dostoevsky, Clark wanted to be there 'when everyone suddenly understands what it has all been for'. He broke with both the conservative and the radical versions of academic history to seek a different kind of understanding—the story-teller as seer—and those in both camps were not sure what to make of it. He transcended both the imperial and national schools with his insistence that the great questions of human existence could be pursued in Australian history. Clark had few imitators and the successive volumes had much greater impact on the public than the profession.

Yet it was Manning Clark who had farewelled his former student Geoffrey Serle to further study at Oxford with the injunction, taken from Henry Lawson, that he should 'Call no biped lord or sir and touch your hat to no man'. The influence of radicalism ebbed with the onset of the Cold War and the supremacy of Menzies. Nationalism lingered as the country's growth and prosperity enlarged its capacity, leaving an increasing confidence in national achievement that was apparent in textbooks such as R. M. Crawford's *Australia* (1952), Gordon Greenwood's *Australia: A Social and Political History* (1955), Crawford's subsequent *An Australian Perspective* (1960) and Douglas Pike's aptly named *Australia: The Quiet Continent* (1962).

Then came the Vietnam War and a new generation of student radicals turned on the radical nationalist faith of their predecessors. Humphrey McQueen's one-man assault in *A New Britannia* in 1970 accused the makers of the Australian legend of romanticising the past. The convicts were not innocent victims but professional criminals. The gold rush had not fostered mateship and rebellion but acquisitive individualism. Bush poets such as Henry Lawson were not harbingers of radical nationalism but racist versifiers. The labour movement was complicit in imperialism, militarism, xenophobia and careerism.

The Cold War orthodoxies no longer held, and many students caught up in the anti-war movement turned to the study of national liberation movements in Asia and other parts of the third world. Those who worked on Australian history looked for similar signs of radical potential here. They employed Marxist theory to analyse the class structure and the forces that shaped it.

They also followed the directions of the social history that had emerged in Britain and America, shifting the emphasis from those who exercised power to those who resisted it. They experimented with new forms of history, no longer as an authoritative account of decision-making written from the official record but as the lived experience of ordinary people, fusing oral history with new ways of using archives to piece together the everyday forms of earlier ways of life. This 'history from below' was conceived as an emancipation of those previously excluded from the historical record, and sometimes involved them in collective projects designed to help local communities tell their own story.

Labour history pioneered that activity. Women's history quickly supplemented and challenged it. In 1976 Miriam Dixson, who had previously written labour history from the radical nationalist perspective, published *The Real Matilda*, an account of how women had suffered particularly harsh oppression in Australia. Her argument turned Russel Ward on his head, suggesting that *The Australian Legend* enshrined a misogynist mateship. Anne Summers, similarly, took two early characterisations of women as *Damned Whores and God's Police* (1975) as a formative dichotomy of the roles assigned to women.

Women's history grew rapidly both in response to the feminist movement and as an important aspect of it. It generated a large literature on the lives and activities of earlier generations of women that spoke to female interests while it guided feminist endeavours. It was in fact the first branch of the discipline where the practitioners were both the subject and object of their own historical knowledge, the first form of identity history.

Other social movements formed around sexuality, race and ethnicity and it is hardly surprising that they should generate their own forms of knowledge. Each seeks to know more about the earlier experience of predecessors who had no place in the older Australian history: hence the move into multicultural history that re-establishes the presence of national minorities. Each seeks recognition by demonstrating its lineage: hence the reconstitution of a gay subculture that goes back to the early colonial period. Such identity history has been practised widely over the past two decades.

In itself this pluralism causes little offence, except to monocultural moral conservatives. The problem arises when its practitioners go beyond what the feminists called 'contribution history', and seek to challenge the larger patterns of conventional history. In 1994 four women's historians published a new national history, *Creating a Nation*. They assembled much of the recent research and brought it to bear on the familiar narrative, but their work was much more than an exercise in adding women to men's history. Rather, they asserted 'the agency and creativity of women in the process of national generation'.

The intrusion of gender relations into the national story shifted its axis from the public activity of purposeful men. It yielded a more intimate, differentiated account of the traditional narrative landmarks, of convicts, gold, federation, the wars, depression and industrialisation. It also brought criticism from a traditional male historian who insisted that women were less important than men in 'defining the nation, ruling the nation and defending the nation'.

The revival of Aboriginal history has been even more disturbing to the traditionalists. Revival, because the interaction between settlers and the Indigenous peoples was a prominent feature of the history that was written in the colonial period. Nineteenth-century newspapers had reported frontier encounters, pioneers had recalled them in memoirs, and colonial historians such as Melville, West and Rusden had responded with moral indignation to the violent expropriation of the original inhabitants.

Indigenous people were written out of Australian history following the establishment of the nation-state at the end of the nineteenth century. The new Commonwealth sought racial purity. It deprived Aboriginals of voting rights, excluded them from the body politic and joined with the states to confine them on reserves. Ernest Scott's *Short History of Australia* (1916) presented them as 'hapless children of nature', incapable of absorption or adaptation to civilisation, though he conceded that the manner of their dispossession 'was very grim and hateful'. Forty years later the professorial survey of the academic discipline observed that 'the Australian aboriginal is noticed in our history only in a melancholy anthropological footnote'. And in 1962 Manning Clark opened his *History* with the statement: 'Civilisation did not begin in Australia until the last quarter of the eighteenth century'.

The anthropologist Bill Stanner spoke in his 1968 Boyer lectures of a 'great Australian silence' about the relationship between 'ourselves and the Aborigines'. The relationship was already changing when he suggested that the inattention amounted to 'a cult of forgetfulness practised on a national scale'. The Commonwealth had restored voting rights, the states had recently repealed much of their discriminatory legislation, the Yolngu had sent a bark petition to Canberra in 1963 to protest at the incursion of a mine on their land, the Gurindji had struck in 1966 for decent wages and land rights, and in 1967 Australians voted overwhelmingly in favour of a referendum to give the national government greater responsibility for Aboriginal affairs.

As part of this awakening, scholars turned to Aboriginal history. Charles Rowley's *The Destruction of Aboriginal Society* (1970) was the first of three volumes that set out a record of repressive government policy and institutionalised racism. Many similar studies followed, while the establishment of the journal *Aboriginal History* provided an outlet for the growing body of research by anthropologists and linguists as well as historians. Such scholarship assumed increasing significance from the late 1970s when land rights legislation required claimants to demonstrate traditional ownership. Equally, the research undertaken by the historian Peter Read on Aboriginal children who had been taken from their parents had direct implications for public policy. He coined the term 'Stolen Generations' in a report published by the New South Wales government in 1982.

By the 1980s attention was shifting from the treatment of Aboriginals to their own strategies of treating Europeans. In *The Other Side of the Frontier* Henry Reynolds used the colonial sources to show how Indigenous peoples would have perceived the arrival of these strange newcomers and how they would have responded. He discerned a variety of strategies, from co-operation and assistance to violent resistance. Using a number of regional studies, Reynolds estimated that they would have killed somewhere between 2000 and 2500 Europeans in the fighting that occurred across the continent over 150 years from the First Fleet to the final imposition of control in northern and western Australia. Given the disparity of force between spears and guns, he thought it was 'reasonable to suppose that at least 20,000 Aborigines were killed as a direct result of conflict with the settlers'.

This is the figure that arouses such fierce criticism from Keith Windschuttle and his school of historical revisionists. He moved to discredit it in articles published in *Quadrant* in 2000, and now in a series of volumes on *The Fabrication of Australian History*, because he sees it as legitimating the claim that Australia was the site of genocide. Similarly, other revisionists have cast doubt on the validity of Aboriginal claims over sacred sites, and have condemned the findings of the Human Rights and Equal Opportunity Commission's major inquiry into the Stolen Generations. They see such Aboriginal history as romanticising the 'noble savage', blackening the national reputation, encouraging present-day Aboriginals in a futile separatism and fostering 'the break-up of Australia'.

Theirs is a remarkably flattering view of the historian's influence but it is also ill informed. Reynolds has continued to reach a large audience with books on frontier dispossession, but he has also written of Aboriginal adaptation to European settlers and European attempts to reach some lasting accommodation. Other historians have largely moved on from frontier history and from the conquest–resistance model of the frontier to ones that allow a greater capacity to Aboriginal peoples.

The revisionist condemnation of academics engaged by Aboriginal history is also patronising. When Windschuttle accuses them of 'white vanity' and presuming to 'play God', he dismisses the significance of Aboriginal memory. His view is that 'Aboriginal oral history, when uncorroborated by original documents, is completely unreliable, just like the oral history of white people'.

Just like the oral history of white people? Historians have relied on memory ever since Thucydides drew on his own recollection and the recollection of others to relate the history of the Peloponnesian war. No-one recorded the speeches given by the Athenian leader Pericles on the values and aspirations of his city-state, and the version given to us by Thucydides is an early example of oral history. Would Windschuttle have us set this oratory aside as uncorroborated by original documents? If so, he would leave a gaping hole in western tradition of civic patriotism. The same is true of the New Testament gospels: all of them are products of oral history.

Nor are the original documents that Windschuttle takes as the bedrock of historical knowledge uncontaminated by human frailty. Official documents, private correspondence, personal diaries, memoirs and recollections are all grist to the historian's mill and all of them are partial and incomplete. Observation and memory form a continuum of historical testimony that the historian has to appraise. Windschuttle's distinction is specious.

Memory has an augmented significance in a society that has no written records. It enters into Aboriginal narratives, life stories, fiction and painting that expand our awareness of a living tradition. Historians sensitive to the qualities of such oral history use it to extend the boundaries of conventional historical knowledge.

Indigenous history, finally, raises questions about control of the past. Academic research rests on the principle of open inquiry. Historians sometimes encountered restrictions on access to records. Working in the Tasmanian archives sixty years ago, a young historian was surprised to receive an invitation to morning tea with the governor—His Excellency wanted to be sure that the researcher was not delving into convict origins. For that matter, restrictions have been imposed more recently on identifying individuals with a criminal record. Government records are not available to historians until thirty years have elapsed, and ASIO continues to withhold many older ones on grounds of security. Many private organisations deposit their records in archives on condition that the historian submit a draft of any research before publication.

Further restrictions are imposed by university ethics committees. Australian universities established these ethics committees during the 1980s because the national body that funds medical research made it a condition of its grants; by an unethical act of aggrandisement it extended their ambit to all forms of research. Hence any historian who proposes to conduct research involving 'human experimentation' is required to obtain approval, so before engaging in oral history the researcher needs to demonstrate that all interviewees provide their informed consent.

Research on Aboriginal subjects is bound by further protocols. Fieldwork in a number of areas requires the permission of the Aboriginal land council. Some archaeologists have been required to surrender their artefacts. The reasons for such sensitivity are powerful. Aboriginal people were long treated as an object of study and with good reason they resented what was written about them. Well into the twentieth century, ethnologists and medical researchers collected Aboriginal remains as if they were zoological specimens.

Beyond this, Aboriginal people aspire to hold onto their history. Like feminists and other identity groups before them, they see it as a precious resource. It records their own experience, enshrines their own customs and traditions, sustains their own values. It tells them who they are. We may well sympathise with the Aboriginal protesters who said that the two hundredth anniversary of British settlement had a special significance for them. We can understand the actions of those who threw a copy of the authorised Bicentennial history into Sydney Harbour when Bob Hawke launched it there in 1988.

But a claim for exclusive ownership of the past is another matter. This is the very claim that the curators of the Smithsonian Museum encountered in 1994, when the veterans' associations insisted on control of the exhibit on the bombing of Hiroshima. It is the claim the Japanese ministry of education asserts when it refuses to allow textbooks that acknowledge Japanese military atrocities. Speaking in 1993 to students at the Central European University in Budapest, the historian Eric Hobsbawm observed the perils of such uses of the past: 'history is the raw material for nationalist or ethnic or fundamentalist ideologies, as poppies are the raw material for heroin addiction'. He allowed the tug of human feelings but insisted that the duty of the historian was 'to stand aside from the passions of identity politics'.

The claim to control your own history is, in any case, self-defeating. Left to themselves, such autohistories do little more than comfort those who create them. It is only when they are shared that they can influence others, and only when they are open to criticism and evaluation that they acquire persuasive authority. Far from protesting against the rewriting of Australian history, the prime minister ought to have welcomed the process as a necessary part of the conversation about the past that keeps it alive.

That conversation began, as we have seen, as soon as Europeans arrived with their particular awareness of time and change, their techniques of recording events and interpreting them. It developed when their universities adopted the disciplinary practices of historical research, and it has continued to take new turns. The transience of historical understanding, the repeated changes of interpretation, might seem to undermine the status of history as an evidence-based disciplinary form of knowledge. How can there be such dramatic changes in accounts of what happened in the past?

The answer lies partly in the availability of new evidence. The National Archives holds millions of files of the Commonwealth government in its Canberra and regional repositories, and most of them remain unrequested to this day. There is also the impact of new techniques. Historians argued at length on the character of the convicts: were they innocent victims of a harsh penal system, or hardened criminals? It was only with the advent of quantitative history in the 1960s that we learned precisely what offences they had committed, only the advent of women's history in the 1970s that gave us the female convict both as damned whore and mother of the nation, only econometric history in the 1980s that told us of their work skills, only the cultural history of the 1990s that showed us the convict body.

Here and more widely, we understand the past in the terms available to us. Historians reach new conclusions because they ask new questions, in response to new interests and concerns. The dialogue between past and present is an uneven one. The past cannot speak for itself—there are only its mute remains and the historian has to attend to them with utmost care. The past cannot defend itself from judgement by the standards of the present—the historian must guard against the dangers of anachronism, mindful that a future generation will find ours as ignorant and insensitive as any we deride.

CHAPTER 4

THE HISTORIAN UNDER FIRE: MANNING CLARK

Rising in the House of Representatives, Bob Hawke moved 'That this House expresses its deep regret at the death, on 23 May 1991, of Emeritus Professor Manning Clark, AC, and tenders its profound sympathy to his family in their bereavement'. Paul Keating, Neal Blewett, John Dawkins, Ros Kelly and Andrew Theophanous spoke from the government side in support of the motion. John Hewson, the Opposition leader, suggested that Clark might have taken an unduly tragic view of Australian history; David Kemp observed that he had neglected the market economy and rejected the British heritage. Both joined with Jim Carlton in expressing their deep respect for his art and his vision. The members of the House stood to affirm the prime minister's motion.

Five years later a new prime minister, John Howard, said that he had always had 'a less than rapturous view of the Manning Clark view of Australian history', and found the 'cultural rapture of the Left' for it 'rather nauseating'. 'It's too negative', he explained, and accused Clark of trying to generate 'pessimism about Australia' through 'his black armband view'. Howard was speaking to the *Courier-Mail* after that newspaper published an eight-page feature accusing Clark of having been awarded the Order of Lenin for services as a Soviet agent. Three years earlier, Clark's publisher made a remarkable attack on an author whose friendship he had enjoyed. He alleged that *A History of Australia* was a fraud and Clark himself 'partly a mountebank'.

The summary of Manning Clark's career that Bob Hawke read to the parliament after he died gave little hint of such turmoil. Born in 1915, the son of an Anglican clergyman, Clark had attended Melbourne Grammar and Trinity College at the University of Melbourne, then pursued further study at Oxford before returning to Australia and teaching at Geelong Grammar. He lectured at Melbourne University, was the foundation professor of history at the Australian National University and the first holder of the visiting chair of Australian Studies at Harvard. He was made a Companion of the Order of Australia in 1975, the country's highest honour, and named Australian of the Year in 1981.

This was hardly the pedigree of a rebel, though Clark never assimilated into his establishment background. At school, where he was a scholarship boy, he stood 'a pace or two apart' from the hearties. At Oxford, where he was a colonial, 'England soon became one of my many lost illusions'. In the Cold War he recoiled from 'the spiritual bullies', and the dismissal of the Whitlam government stirred him into protest. The guardians of the establishment, to which he had been born and in which he had acquired such eminence, looked on him as a class traitor. And if someone was prepared to betray his class, why would he stop at betraying his country?

Yet Clark's nonconformity did not stop here. While still young he lost his Christian faith, and the inability to find comfort in religion tormented him. It was the decline of religious authority and the loss of the promise of eternal life that made ours 'an age of ruins' and shaped his tragic view of history. Clark despaired not about Australians but about the human condition. He wanted desperately to believe, and for a time was drawn to the secular faith of the left, but could not share its conviction in human perfectibility and corresponding inability to realise the human capacity for evil.

For similar reasons, he rejected the conventional forms of academic history. At Melbourne, where he embarked on Australian history, he had been a gifted teacher and a difficult colleague—especially when in his cups. Canberra gave him greater freedom. In the address he delivered there in 1954, when he declared that the 'belief in a radical tradition distorts and warps our writing of Australian history', he also expressed his dissatisfaction with the discipline. There was an urgent need for a rewriting of Australian history but he did 'not believe that this rewriting will come from the universities' because they were the most persistent defenders of 'the bankrupt liberal ideal'. It would not come from the measurers, 'for they hold the terrible belief that measuring will show there is no mystery'. History must have something to say, 'some great theme to lighten our darkness', some sense of the mysteries of life and death.

Manning Clark broke with both political and academic orthodoxy. His rewriting of Australian history was utterly different from John Howard's understanding of that activity. It served no partisan purpose, nor did it seek to blacken the national past, for it was singular, prophetic and deeply reverential. Yet controversy pursued Manning Clark throughout his career and after his death.

Clark came to the attention of the authorities as a lecturer at the University of Melbourne immediately after the Second World War. He was a peripheral target in the Cold War, caught up when a conservative member of the Victorian parliament attacked the professor of history for involvement in a

Soviet friendship society. After the parliamentarian denounced the 'pink professors and puce pedagogues' who were subverting impressionable young minds, Clark appeared on a radio program in 1947 to debate the question 'Is Communism White-Anting Our Educational System?'. Introducing himself as a lecturer who was 'not a communist, never having been one, and with no intention of becoming one', Clark affirmed the duty of the teacher to ensure students could reach their own judgements. The national security agency duly noted his views.

Two years later, when the Canberra University College (it was yet to become part of the Australian National University) proposed to appoint Clark to its new chair of history, it asked for a security report. The newly formed Australian Security and Intelligence Organisation combed through the files it had inherited and determined that Clark had definite 'leftist tendencies' but was not a communist. The appointment was therefore approved. The college at this time was essentially a night school for public servants, and as part of his duties Clark helped to select and teach the annual intake of trainee diplomats for the Department of External Affairs.

In 1953 he participated in a peace conference and ASIO again reviewed the file. This time it found further cause for concern. Clark and his family had moved into a Canberra house previously occupied by an Australian diplomat suspected of espionage; he planned to dedicate a volume of historical documents he was compiling to a former student who had been a communist. The Department of External Affairs accordingly terminated his teaching. A letter to the press in 1954, in which he joined three other public figures in urging Australia not to intervene in Vietnam, brought public condemnation in parliament from the prominent anti-communist W. C. Wentworth.

In 1958 Clark and two other members of the Fellowship of Australian Writers went on a delegation to the Soviet Union. Learning of this arrangement, ASIO once more described

Clark as 'believed to be a communist sympathiser', but then amended the assessment to 'believed to have been a communist sympathiser in the immediate post-war years'. Clark went to Moscow an incessant traveller, a lover of Russian literature and a scholar of history who wished to gauge the emancipation of communism from Stalinism.

His hosts were anxious to ensure a favourable assessment. Judah Waten, the communist writer who was part of the Australian delegation, worried that Clark was a 'fence sitter', too often prepared to accept 'right-wing-views' and when pressed to praise Soviet achievement inclined to take refuge in quotations from Dostoevsky. In the three weeks the Australians spent in Russia, Clark did form a favourable view of the Soviet achievement in raising living standards, pursuing equality and fraternity, 'bringing culture to the masses'. It was the narrow dogmatism, the grey conformity and the spiritual nullity that oppressed him. He had hoped to find some sign of revival of the grand ideals of 1917, and he encountered only monuments to Lenin. 'Why', he asked, 'did Lenin—a man who seems to have been Christ-like, at least in his compassion—have to die and this other one take over from him?'

Clark's account of *Meeting Soviet Man* (1960) angered both right and left. Douglas Stewart in the *Bulletin* thought the book displayed 'too much sentimental goodwill and too much of the desire to excuse or explain away'. Donald Horne depicted Clark in the equally anti-communist *Observer* as a dupe of Intourist propaganda, one of those intellectuals who sublimated their guilt towards their own society with 'adulation of another's'. Judah Waten, on the other hand, wrote in the communist weekly *Tribune* that Clark had repeated 'many anti-Soviet clichés and half-truths'. Judged by the insistent standards of the Cold War, Clark was either a fellow-traveller and apologist for communist tyranny or a timid capitulator to reactionary pressures.

These judgements arose out of Clark's extra-curricular activity, his engagement in public life and contemporary issues. A parallel argument was building over his work as a historian.

In the 1954 lecture Clark had foreshadowed a rewriting of Australian history to replace the radical nationalist interpretation. This prospect attracted members of the Australian Association for Cultural Freedom, which was established in the same year to rally the anti-communist intelligentsia. (It was the Australian arm of an international organisation funded, through various intermediaries, by the CIA, as an ideological front in the Cold War.) Clark knew James McAuley, the poet and founding editor of its journal *Quadrant*, whose fervent religious hostility to secular humanism made a deep impression on him. Peter Coleman, another of the association's cultural impresarios, took up Clark's inaugural lecture as heralding a 'Counter-Revolution in Australian History' and included an essay by Clark on 'Faith' in his 1962 symposium on *Australian Civilization*.

Clark had been working on his *History of Australia* since 1956. Initially it was to consist of two volumes and be 'an academic work characterised by caution, judiciousness and balance'. Then he cast caution aside and embarked on a literary epic. Successive drafts of the first volume grew to more than 200 000 words and took the story only to the first decades of colonial settlement. The book appeared late in 1962 and a reprint was necessary within a week.

Academic historians were not sure what to make of a work that violated their expectations of orthodox historical scholarship. Some pointed to factual inaccuracies, some to the way that Clark pursued his systems of belief through a constant search for fatal flaws in those emblematic individuals who embodied them—the polymath Oskar Spate remarked that 'Clark pictures all his people, all the time, as wrought up to a state of moral hypertension'.

The most hostile review came from Malcolm Ellis, a *Bulletin* journalist and the author of biographies of Macquarie,

Macarthur and Greenway. Ellis was a cantankerous conservative (he had written two substantial anti-communist tracts) with an animus against the profession, but he and Clark had previously reviewed each other's work favourably. They fell out when Keith Hancock appointed them joint editors of the *Australian Dictionary of Biography* in 1959, a remarkable failure of judgement that ended in both men vacating the post, and Ellis seized on this opportunity to settle accounts. His lengthy review, 'History without Facts', cited a long list of Clark's errors and finished with the charge that 'The physical, the adventurous, the toil of men have little appeal to Manning Clark. He is obsessed with the little things of the mind and spirit.'

This onslaught did not assist Peter Coleman's endeavour to claim Clark for his counter-revolution, and in 1963 he convened a seminar under the auspices of the Association for Cultural Freedom. The thirty participants included Clark and Ellis, but the meeting did not repair the rift. Clark explained the purpose of his *History*. A number of historians offered their various appraisals of it. Ellis renewed his criticism, and was followed by a solicitor with expertise in the European exploration of the Pacific who had claimed in the *Bulletin* that Clark's treatment of it was riddled with mistranslations, misunderstandings and mistakes. (Dymphna Clark, Manning's wife, was a gifted linguist and had helped him by translating the records of a number of the European voyages.)

The expert on exploration had brought a large manuscript entitled 'Clio Etwas Gebuckt' to the seminar, but before he could read from it, Clark challenged him: 'You say that my wife doesn't read Dutch!' The critic faltered, Clark repeated the accusation more insistently, and the unfortunate man abandoned the platform. After others contributed their views, Clark said that his critics made him wonder if any human being could ever communicate anything, but there were moments when he dared to hope he had said something. He remained silent throughout the rest of the seminar.

Clark's second volume appeared in 1968 and the third in 1973, to increasing acclaim. His academic colleagues were no longer surprised by the treatment of Australian history as a moral drama, less inclined to dwell on its departure from convention, more ready to recognise its literary force. Radical nationalists such as Russel Ward and Ian Turner responded to Clark's deep feeling for Australia and the depiction of Australian history as a contest between competing forces. Conservatives recognised that his insistence on the complexity of human nature, the strength of tradition and the frailty of all projects for redemption affirmed a tragic view of life that was deeply conservative.

Peter Coleman disagreed. In a review of the second volume of the *History*, he acknowledged that 'Manning Clark is the man who brought Pessimism into the writing of Australian history'. Coleman welcomed pessimism as an antidote to the progressive orthodoxy propagated by the left, but worried the cure was now threatening to harm the patient. Clark had slighted the pioneers, failed to recognise the nation's 'physical, commercial and managerial achievements'. With mock reluctance, Coleman concluded that 'I now think there is something in Ellis's phrase about "the little things of the mind"'.

With this jibe, the right parted company with Clark. Henceforth *Quadrant* would treat him as a suspect, an unreliable intellectual who traduced his country's history. The break is indicative of a shift in the right, since Clark had not altered his own position and indeed kept up his membership of the Association for Cultural Freedom. The second volume of the *History* was no different from the first: Clark pursued the same themes of high aspiration and tragic grandeur.

It was rather that the right was shifting its own stance. In fighting the Cold War it had taken a pessimistic view of human nature against the naïve optimism of the secular humanists, and a cautionary view of Australian civilisation against the millenarian schemes of the radical nationalists. Now, as the Cold War faded, the right was more confident and affirmative of the national achievement. Its polemicists abandoned Clark and conservatism.

Yet Clark's singular treatment of Australian history appealed to an increasing audience. Barry Humphries, who had regarded the subject from school as unspeakably dull, told Peter Coleman that the first volume was 'wonderfully and passionately written'. Patrick White hailed Clark as a kindred spirit. In 1968, when the literary editors of leading newspapers asked prominent Australians to identify the books published in that year which had most impressed them, Patrick White, Leonie Kramer, Henry Mayer, Stephen Murray-Smith and Gough Whitlam selected the second volume of Clark's *History*.

Clark responded in turn to Gough Whitlam's modernising leadership of the Labor Party. In an article published in 1973 he characterised the previous quarter-century as 'the years of unleavened bread'. The hope of better things offered by Curtin, Chifley and Evatt had died. Australia had become affluent and timorous, backward looking in its defence of economic privilege and the supremacy of the white man. 'The great Australian dream of social equality and mateship was bleeding to death in the jungles and paddy-fields of Vietnam.' Then Whitlam showed the way forward. He would extricate Australia from Vietnam, shake off the vestiges of colonialism, provide justice for Aboriginal people. Listening to his election speech at Queanbeyan in 1972, Clark believed that 'at long last we had a teacher to lead us out of the darkness into the light, always provided THEY did not cut him down . . .'.

In 1975 they did cut him down and Clark was at Parliament House on 11 November to hear Whitlam's denunciation of the governor-general. He reacted to Labor's subsequent electoral defeat with an elegy for its 'three, halcyon, golden years' in office—bringing an Australian honours system, support for the arts, protection of the environment, assistance to Aboriginals, liberation of women—and concluded that 'history will probably be kinder than the people'. He spoke at a meeting in the Sydney Town Hall to call for a republic which would rescue democracy from those who had conspired to bring down an elected government.

As the result of such appearances Manning Clark became a celebrity, instantly recognisable for his grave countenance and allusive utterances, the sober suit set off with a broad-brimmed hat and thick leather belt. A mild-mannered professor, he made apocalyptic predictions. On the day of the Dismissal he warned of a resort to 'violent political change' if Whitlam was not restored to office. When Fraser secured a mandate for his actions, he wondered if 'we can only march forward by destroying our old corrupt society root and branch'. Speaking in the Melbourne Town Hall on the first anniversary of the Dismissal, he warned again of the danger of 'a violent explosion, ripening into a revolutionary situation'.

In every one of these predictions, it should be noted, Clark was not advocating such desperate measures. Rather, he was prophesying the possible consequences of the resort by 'the forces of reaction' to a constitutional coup. The same was true of another of his commentaries at this time: 'Are We a Nation of Bastards?' Clark was not proposing that description, he was responding to its use by an outraged Xavier Herbert, and he answered the question in the negative.

Members of the new government made it seem he had coined the epithet. They also pounced on a passage in this article, where Clark imagined that some people's government of Australia a hundred years hence might judge the governor-general harshly and not even allow historians to defend his actions, as if Clark was endorsing such censorship. On the contrary, he was observing how the victors control history and deploring the demands they imposed on historians.

The ABC's invitation to Clark to deliver the 1976 Boyer lectures aroused particular fury. 'Can a guarantee be given', a Liberal senator asked, 'that Professor Manning Clark will not use his power to stop other historians from getting paper, to have their pencils broken so that they can not write, and have them sent to a leftist fascist Gulag Archipelago?' The government leader in the Senate could give no guarantee and observed that Clark's recent activities showed he was 'a political partisan and apologist for the Labor Party'.

The Boyer lectures offered an account of how one man had discovered 'one way of writing the history of Australia'. Standing at the mid-point of that project (the fourth volume would appear in the following year), they clarified what he was trying to do. 'My purpose was to tell the story of what had happened when a great civilization was transplanted to our ancient land.'

He was conscious of the limitations of telling that story through the lives and thoughts of its most purposeful and articulate actors. He would try increasingly to incorporate the subjects that a new generation of historians was bringing to prominence: Aboriginals, women, class. But these subjects were less amenable to his technique of personification; they became a more prominent part of his story but as victims rather than active agents. Clark would regret that he 'never found the answers to the relationship between the characters in the front of the stage and the backdrop. I was weak on backdrop.'

The lectures also enabled him to affirm his faith. 'Everything a historian writes should be a celebration of life, a hymn of praise to life. It should come up from inside a man who knows all about that horror of the darkness when a man returns to the dust from whence he came, a man who has looked into the heart of that great darkness, but has both a tenderness for everyone, and yet, paradoxically, a melancholy, a sadness, and a compassion because what matters most in life is never likely to happen.'

The reception of his work from this time was marked by an insistence that Clark was consumed by hatred of his own country. Historians praised the fourth volume of the *History* while conservatives criticised its excessive gloom. An offshoot that appeared six weeks later, *In Search of Henry Lawson*, incurred the wrath of Emeritus Professor Colin Roderick, the jealous custodian of Lawsoniana. He described it as a' tangled thicket of factual errors' and alleged Clark read Lawson's life 'in an extreme totalitarian leftist fashion'. This was grist to the media mill and both the Murdoch and Fairfax presses ran with further condemnation.

The publication of the fifth volume in 1981 brought a new round of hostilities. It was a 'bitter and cynical' history written by 'a man who hates his own society'. Several of the critics took the opportunity to review all five volumes, and a writer for the *Australian* pronounced it 'a labour of hatred and distress, nurtured by bitterness and sustained by repugnance'. A reviewer for the same newspaper widened the criticism: Clark's *History* raised 'profoundly disturbing questions' about 'the closed shop of professional historians'. He expressed his deepest sympathy for the students who would be compelled to read it.

This was an unlikely allegation. Clark had retired from the Australian National University in 1975 and continued to emphasise his dissatisfaction with the 'Mr Dry-as-Dusts' who professed history. Some academics resented his celebrity, some carped at his grandiosity and some pounced on his factual errors. The assumption that they were prescribing his *History* as compulsory reading for undergraduate courses in Australian history betrayed an ignorance of how such courses were constructed: they consisted of close examinations of particular topics, and Clark's sweeping narrative defied such segmentation.

There is a widespread view that the country's history departments were filled with Clark's disciples who taught his history as binding orthodoxy. Nothing could be further from the truth. He had little interest in academic politics, except as a source of gossip, and he was notorious for the fragmentary form of his testimonials. Most academics promote the academic careers of their former students, and furnish selection committees with exhaustive letters of recommendation that trumpet the applicant's accomplishments. When Manning Clark was asked to provide a reference, it was likely to say merely that 'Dr Smith is a good historian and you should appoint her'; sometimes he used a postcard.

There was no Manning Clark school of history. Even in his own department at the Australian National University he appointed a widely disparate group of colleagues. He had his admirers and he also had his critics. Manning Clark's celebrity was as unusual as his appearance, manner and prose: it defied imitation. But when editors searched the universities for historians to assist an assault on the integrity of a colleague, it was hardly surprising that they should refuse to join the witch-hunt. It was this refusal that brought the condemnation of a closed shop.

Needs must where the devil drives. *Quadrant* turned of necessity to the Sociology Department at La Trobe University, where Professor Claudio Veliz presided over seminars to which he invited some of Melbourne's like-minded opinion-makers. These *conversazioni*, as he styled them, invoked western tradition as a defence against levelling democracy. Veliz lauded English constitutionalism for its refusal of the dangerous enthusiasms of his native Latin America, and he now came forward with an appraisal of the fifth volume of the *History*. Veliz condemned Clark for the presentiments of revolution that hung over his treatment of the 1890s and his failure to appreciate Australia's good fortune to have enjoyed a remarkable tranquillity. Veliz's colleague, John Carroll, sniped from the sidelines.

Clark made no response. He was working on his sixth and final volume, struggling with aneurism of the heart and, after 1983, coping with a new Labor government that claimed him as its historian laureate. He accepted too many of the invitations he now received to launch books, write forewords and offer public commentary. The *History* was completed in 1987, and two volumes of autobiography followed. A musical based on the *History* opened and closed in 1988.

The shrewd realism of the Hawke ministry did not excite him, and he pined for the excitement of Whitlam's sweeping change. Like many historians, Clark was fascinated by politics. Like a good number of them, he took the Labor side. But he had little interest in the party process or the business of government. Rather, he was drawn to the drama of political combat and intrigued by those whom it consumed. He recalled how he stood a pace or two apart at the Canberra cemetery in 1965 for the burial of Bert Evatt, the most tragically flawed of all the Labor leaders, and watched while Robert Menzies gazed down at the open grave. He thought he saw a shadow of doubt pass over the prime minister's face as he wondered how posterity would remember his rival and himself.

Clark's political heroes were the risk-takers, complex and creative leaders who enlarged life. He thought he saw those qualities in Paul Keating when the impatient treasurer turned his sights on the Lodge; but the historian died in May 1991, before Keating's second challenge succeeded. The new prime minister and his speechwriter drew on Clark's telling of the Australian story, but there was more to their own story than Clark. The Morphy Richards toaster and the slippers, the fall of Singapore and Australia's place in Asia did not come from the *History*. They were reference points that Paul Keating drew from his own childhood, distilled from Labor lore and conjured from his convictions.

The prime minister had an instinct for such story-telling; his speechwriter gave it historical definition. Together they built up a narrative of exile, tribulation and redemption that affirmed the national capacity for creative renewal. Theirs was an epic version of Australian history that vexed conservatives, yet also perplexed historians with its polemical thrust. In the absence of alternative corroboration, Clark was pressed into service. I delivered a memorial lecture in his name at the Australian Labor Party's 1994 national conference. Through-out his celebrity as a national prophet, Manning Clark had employed his gnomic phrases to keep a pace or two apart from the tribal loyalties of party politics. In death he was attached far more closely to the Labor side, and a reckoning was inevitable.

Manning Clark endured greater public obloquy than any other Australian historian. His vulnerability to criticism made his courage in enduring it all the greater. But he needed reas-surance. He had a habit of ringing his publisher at Melbourne University Press, Peter Ryan, who would give him the latest gossip and ease his anxiety. Ryan had been a student of Clark and a drinking companion when he lectured at the University of Melbourne in the 1940s, and their subsequent professional relationship was close. Clark's *History* outsold any other book the Press published and kept doing so year after year.

At some point in this relationship—we are reliant on Ryan's retrospective testimony—the publisher began to flag in his admiration. He says he sent Claudio Veliz's hostile review of volume five to Clark and received no reply (but surely he sent copies of all reviews of every volume, for I used MUP's file some years later when writing an article about Clark's reception and it was comprehensive). He stayed away from the launch of volume six (but he had told Clark's wife, Dymphna, that 'booksellers were baying' for it). He began writing regu-larly for *Quadrant* and learned that it received 'five sheepish refusals' from historians it asked for a review of volume five.

Quadrant's editor relates that Ryan proposed in May 1991 to write a highly critical essay on Clark, but held back when Clark died shortly after. He therefore published the essay two years later without ever revealing his antagonism to Clark, without even paying the widow who had so often given him hospitality the courtesy of an explanation for turning on her late husband.

The editor of *Quadrant* was Robert Manne, who was then part of Veliz's circle at La Trobe, though ostensibly unaware of his journal's long vendetta against Clark (he said that *Quadrant* had published only two significant criticisms in the twelve years before he became editor, and seems not to have followed the frequent attacks of the 1970s). Manne appeared on radio to promote Ryan's contribution and called it an act 'of great civic courage'. I replied that it was an act of 'personal cowardice'. Manne said that Ryan was aware that his denunciation of an 'old friend' would bring ostracism from Clark's network of friends and admirers, but his essay gives no hint of regret or remorse.

He relates the long decline of a historian betrayed by the fatal flaw of vanity. The story begins with a gifted young teacher who even then was susceptible to striking poses, scarred by rebuffs and soured by envy. The success of his *History* turned his head. He adopted the trappings of a character, gave free rein to his clichés, indulged himself in long-windedness and self-pity. From anecdotes and intimacies, Ryan builds a portrait of a man who was guilty of bad faith and wrote bad history. The volumes were riddled with factual inaccuracy, filled with unwarranted gloom, mired in cliché, 'an artefact of disingenuous contrivance'.

Such an assault on a national figure created a predictable controversy, especially when Paul Keating affirmed Clark's achievement. Russel Ward declared that 'to say Ryan must be off his head is the kindest thing I could say'. Robert Hughes said Ryan played 'dirty pool'. I called Ryan a coward, Don Watson called him a cannibal. The propriety of a publisher turning on an author, the morality of waiting for a friend to die before betraying him, were aspects of the affair that disturbed many.

Robert Manne claimed subsequently that *Quadrant* intended no more than a long-overdue reappraisal of Clark's historical reputation. Ryan, who had introduced his essay as an exercise in cutting down a tall poppy, claimed afterwards that the main consideration was the value of Clark's *History* and the failure of the historical profession to offer an honest appraisal of it. Both invoked a recent assessment of Clark's work by John Hirst, an accomplished and strikingly original historian working at La Trobe. Hirst had suggested in *Quadrant* that Clark abandoned the high scholarly standards of his early work in the 'loosely organised chronicles' of the *History*, and also surrendered his original understanding of the working out of European civilisation in Australia to become a 'barracker' for radical nationalism. While Hirst concluded that 'the whole game escaped him', he did not anathemise Clark. He retained sufficient respect to assist an abridgement of the six volumes that appeared at this time.

All this was incidental to Ryan's original essay. It mounted an *ad hominem* argument with the additional force of personal intimacy, for as Peter Craven observed, Ryan affected the candour of a close companion who had eaten and drunk with Clark over four decades in order to relate his follies. To the objection that this was an unwarranted intrusion into private life, he insisted that 'the drive of Manning's life was to be a public citizen'. It was the extension of the historian into public affairs that justified the attack on his person and his standing as a historian.

The defence of Clark by members of the historical profession brought a further extension. By this time Ryan had retired from Melbourne University Press and was using his newspaper column to criticise the academics he had once served for their privileged laziness. In his reply to his critics he singled out 'the tenured plump and middle aged' historians for their acceptance of Clark's work. The profession was a 'disappointing and unproductive lot', frightened to voice its reservations, and 'a good spring cleaning of the house of history is overdue in Australia'.

When Peter Ryan's pursuit of Clark's fatal flaw of vanity appeared in 1993, another *Quadrant* reader was pursuing a different trail. Peter Kelly was a retired journalist of strongly anti-communist reflexes—on the few occasions that I figure in the press, you can rely on him reminding its readers that I was a communist and recalled that experience warmly in the preface to my history of the Communist Party of Australia.

Kelly had been a friend of Geoffrey Fairbairn, a conservative colleague and friend of Manning Clark, and he recalled Fairbairn telling him that he had seen Clark wearing the Order of Lenin at a function at the Soviet Embassy in Canberra. Fairbairn had died in 1980 but Kelly heard in the early 1990s that the poet Les Murray was telling people he too had seen Clark wearing the Order of Lenin. In 1993 he contacted Chris Mitchell, a family friend who worked at the *Australian*. That newspaper made some investigations but did not pursue the matter. Then Mitchell went to Brisbane to become editor of the *Courier-Mail*, and he assigned a journalist to work with Kelly on the story. He seems to have worried that the investigation would leak if it involved the newsroom and therefore chose his sports writer, Wayne Smith.

The subsequent investigation was conducted as if it were a security inquiry. Smith and Kelly obtained a copy of Clark's ASIO files and made three trips to Canberra. They travelled to England to consult the records of security agencies there—for Clark had been at Oxford in the 1930s and his career suggested ominous parallels with the notorious Burgess, Maclean, Philby and Blunt, who were recruited to Soviet espionage while at Cambridge in the same decade. The investigators compiled their dossier and they asked international experts on espionage, including a former KGB officer, to assess it.

They pursued all possible sources of information except one. They did not ask Dymphna Clark. Chris Mitchell would later claim that this was because her son Andrew Clark was the editor of the Sydney *Sun-Herald* and might have scooped the *Courier-Mail*; he subsequently altered this unlikely explanation to fear that the Clark family would take out an injunction to prevent him publishing the story.

The *Courier-Mail* broke the story in its weekend edition on 24 August 1996. Eight pages of commentary and background accompanied Wayne Smith's lead story, 'By Order of Lenin'. It claimed that 'Charles Manning Hope Clark was indeed a communist', and more than this, was 'an undiscovered member of the communist world's elite' as the holder of the Soviet Union's highest honour, the Order of Lenin.

What had he done to earn it? Smith said it was not known if he had stolen documents or used secret codes, but 'his enduring influence surely was in his ability to influence people and policy'. He quoted one KGB expert that such an award, under secrecy, indicated Clark was 'not only an extremely significant agent of influence but possibly something more—"a very important agent"'. The newspaper also reported a retired KGB colonel saying of the Order of Lenin, 'if it is kept secret, then it's got nothing to do with agent of influence; it's got to do with spy'.

The *Courier-Mail* provided the context for its allegations. The Coalition had been elected to office, John Howard had indicated his determination to reclaim the 'historical battle-ground' from the Black Armband historians, and Alexander Downer had recently refused to present a set of Clark's *History* to Georgetown University in Washington. 'History is a very, very powerful weapon', the newspaper quoted the minister for foreign affairs.

While the *Courier-Mail* offered the story to other newspapers in the Murdoch chain, few accepted it. Most simply reported the allegations as a news story after they appeared. The Melbourne *Herald-Sun* ran with part of the *Courier-Mail's* contents and explained that 'While no-one has set out to upset his family, Australians are entitled to know whether the historian had a hidden agenda behind his overt left-wing espousals'. Howard adopted a similar stance when asked his opinion about the claims. After saying he did not have one, he expressed his distaste for Clark's view of history and declared the *Courier-Mail's* treatment to be 'all part of the process'.

The case presented by the *Courier-Mail* quickly began to collapse. The testimony of Geoffrey Fairbairn's widow had to be retracted. Les Murray was unsure if he had seen an Order of Lenin. Dymphna Clark suggested and the Russian ambassador later confirmed that the medal he might have seen was a commemorative medal issued in 1970, the centenary of Lenin's birth, to thousands of visitors to Moscow in that year. It also emerged that the portrait of Clark used by the *Courier-Mail* had been altered without permission of the photographer to give him a sinister visage, a peasant smock and a sneering expression.

Within a few days the *Courier-Mail* was denying it had ever suggested Clark was a Soviet spy (it had removed that accusation from later editions of the original story) and sticking grimly to claims he was an agent of influence. The editor was already complaining that he, rather than Clark, was the victim of vilification. A colleague accused the sceptical *Sydney Morning Herald* of 'playing the man', while Wayne Smith would claim that his newspaper had tried to 'depersonalise the debate by simply laying the facts before the Australian public'. Fifteen prominent Australians complained to the Press Council. At the end of the year the council found that the *Courier-Mail* had too little evidence for its assertion that Clark had been a communist, awarded the Order of Lenin or a Soviet agent.

The *Courier-Mail* appealed, unsuccessfully, then pursued a new tack. It demanded answers to a number of questions arising from ASIO's surveillance of Clark. In particular, it asked questions about his four visits to the Soviet Union. He had in fact made only three, in 1958, 1970 and 1973. The last of them, with Dymphna, was to travel on the Trans-Siberian railway, but in 1958 and 1970 he had gone as an official guest. (The 1970 visit was to deliver lectures on the bicentenary of Cook's voyage to Australia and the centenary of the birth of Lenin.) Passages from *Meeting Soviet Man* were now exhumed, along with the text of the speech he gave on Lenin. He was reported as saying that Lenin's beliefs were being verified by life; his daughter Katerina, a professor of Russian literature, noted that the correct translation was not 'verified by life' but 'put to the test'.

Alongside its reports of Clark's views on the Soviet Union, the *Courier-Mail* quoted Robert Manne's assessment that they were 'disgraceful' and Gerard Henderson's that they were 'inexcusable'. Similar judgements appeared in other papers from Cold War veterans such as Paddy O'Brien, and younger recruits to the History Wars such as Christopher Pearson (who was Howard's speechwriter) and Imre Saluzinsky (a Newcastle academic who aspired to a career in the media). B. A. Santamaria, an undergraduate contemporary of Clark and creator of the anti-communist movement, broke a lifetime of cordial relations to condemn him. The charge that Clark was an apologist for communism had augmented force after the ignominious collapse of the Soviet empire.

This is apparent in Robert Manne's treatment of the controversy. By 1996 Manne was uncomfortable with the extremism of some of his *Quadrant* colleagues, and in the course of the year he refused to publish a particularly unpleasant article that purported to reveal Manning Clark as an anti-Semite. He now rejected the *Courier-Mail*'s allegations and accepted that Clark was by no means an uncritical admirer of Soviet communism; but this left his gloomy portrait of his own country and his romantic fantasies of a revolutionary alternative.

That was a long way removed from the continuing campaign of vilification. After the *Adelaide Review* published the article that Manne had refused to publish, accusing Clark of anti-Semitism, Dymphna Clark rang to complain and was told to wait until the *Review* showed him to be a bisexual. Christopher Mitchell pronounced Clark 'a David Irving of the Left', and announced the *Courier-Mail* was pursuing its investigation in archives in Moscow, Berlin, Prague and Washington.

He also said the newspaper had obtained Australian rights for the full records of the Communist International. They were already available on microfilm in the felicitously named Mitchell Library in Sydney. I read them there in the early 1990s and Clark's name does not appear. Since the Communist International was dissolved in 1943, this source is not likely to assist Mitchell. But we should not expect that to get in the way of further onslaughts.

The treatment of Manning Clark suggests the perils of the historian who leaves the safety of the study. In this case, a historian who was dissatisfied with the limitations of conventional history achieved remarkable influence, but that in turn exposed him to remarkable hostility. His work as a historian was a secondary consideration in the posthumous attacks on his reputation; the quality of that work and its validity as an interpretation of Australian history were less important than the public figure who came to stand for a highly politicised view of the national past.

His stature as a historian entered into the controversy because it afforded him a particular authority to speak about the past, but it was contested along lines that had little to do with the discipline. The historians who joined the argument became part of it, while those who remained silent were damned. A similar fate had already overtaken Geoffrey Blainey and his colleagues.

CHAPTER 5

THE HISTORIAN BETRAYED: GEOFFREY BLAINEY

'I have been under very heavy pressure from intellectuals who I believe to be liberal not to speak on this issue.' Early in 1984, when Geoffrey Blainey voiced misgivings about immigration to a gathering of Rotary International at the Victorian country town of Warrnambool, he did not expect his remarks to arouse controversy. He had made similar comments before and in more prominent forums. This address, however, was recorded by an alert local journalist and taken up by the metropolitan press. On the morning it appeared, Blainey's phone kept ringing.

His comments on current immigration policy came at the end of an explanation of how Australia had changed for the better—indeed, he wrote the final passages at the breakfast table just before he went to Warrnambool as he searched for an apt conclusion to an address he had prepared. The address provided a historical perspective on the theme of multiculturalism. It reminded listeners that ours was a migrant society made up of waves of newcomers, and that Aboriginal and colonial Australia had been more multicultural than the present. It related the dismantling of the White Australia Policy that had operated for much of the twentieth century, and welcomed the growth of diversity and tolerance.

Only in the improvised conclusion did Blainey strike a cautionary note. There was a danger of pressing too far ahead of public opinion, he suggested, especially at a time of unemployment. An increasing number of Australians seemed to be resentful of the large number of Vietnamese and other South-East Asian settlers who, through no fault of their own, were unable to find work and lived here at the taxpayers' expense. The old White Australia Policy had been arrogant and insensitive to the people of our region. The present one was arrogant and insensitive to a large section of the Australian population.

The publication of these comments drew criticism from representatives of immigrant and ethnic organisations. Blainey responded the next day by calling them 'naïve in the extreme' and rejecting 'the view widely held in the Federal Cabinet that some kind of slow Asian takeover of Australia is inevitable'. Members of the government condemned his statement. Within a fortnight Blainey was warning of the danger of race riots and the shadow minister for immigration and ethnic affairs was calling for a review of immigration.

In 1984 Geoffrey Blainey was a widely respected historian and public figure, the dean of the Faculty of Arts at the University of Melbourne, the chairman of the Australia–China Council and a former chair of the Australia Council. He had written some of the most original books on Australian history with a verve and grace that made them best-sellers. A journalist suggested at the outset of the controversy that 'since history is his speciality, Geoffrey Blainey's doubts must carry weight'.

He was also a remarkably undogmatic man, unassuming and even diffident in manner, yet obstinate under attack. Both the misrepresentation of his views and the vehemence with which they were condemned strengthened his resolution. Rather than let the media tire of the dispute, he pursued it in articles, interviews, speeches and statements. Instead of clarifying his claims, he pushed them further.

The storm of criticism that broke on Geoffrey Blainey in 1984 distressed many of his friends; some were uncomfortable with his stand. Twenty-three colleagues in the History Department at the University of Melbourne wrote to the press two months after the controversy began to dissociate themselves from his views on immigration policy. A month later some protesters picketed a class he taught at the university and there was violent disruption of a lecture at Sydney. 'I have made a careful note', he commented, 'of the people who have defended free speech and it does not need a very large piece of paper'.

He believed that an open discussion of Asian immigration was needed. Upon coming to office in 1983 the Labor government inherited an immigration policy that took in refugees, and accepted other applicants from Asian countries under its skilled worker, business and family reunion programs. The Hawke government sought closer links. This was a period when the 'tiger economies' of South-East Asia were booming and pundits predicted they would soon outstrip the old economies. 'Asianisation' was the term used to promote Australia's participation in this future, and the last thing the government wanted was talk of an Asian takeover.

Blainey refused to accept this logic. He alleged that the government refused parliamentary debate of its policy (he would later claim it kept the policy secret and falsified the statistics) because it feared a public backlash. He was convinced that he spoke for a wide body of opinion and regarded the argument conducted in the press, and on radio and television, as a necessary substitute for the failure of the national institutions. Those who urged him to desist were in his opinion mistaken. It was better to argue the matter out than stifle discussion. 'The distrust of free speech', he noted, 'has been especially noticeable amongst a small scatter of academics'.

This aspect of his public vilification was particularly distressing. Beyond expressing 'intense disappointment' in the actions of the colleagues who had written to the press, he was loath to discuss it. Others were only too happy to do so. Two senior academics at the University of Melbourne suggested that the members of the History Department had seized the opportunity to denigrate their most distinguished member out of an envy that they cloaked in 'refined hypocrisy'. Peter Ryan accused them of 'intellectual totalitarianism'. John Stone, the former head of Treasury on his way to a brief career in the Senate, described the historians who contributed to a book dealing with Geoffrey Blainey and Asian immigration as 'jackals' and 'intellectual brown-shirts'.

The debate over Asian immigration lasted for the best part of a year. The effects of Blainey's Warrnambool speech lasted much longer. He moved on to other topics of controversy—Aboriginal land rights, the environment, the monarchy, trade unions, judicial activism, Black Armband history—because he had become a controversialist, and at the end of 1988 he resigned from the university to become a freelance writer and commentator. For many, what Blainey had said in 1984 was less important than his right to say it. The controversy left him and others with deep scars, but as recollection of the precise arguments faded, John Stone's claim persisted that he was 'a brave man set upon by various political and intellectual thugs'.

In 1954 the professor of history at the University of Melbourne described his former student as an able man with some unusual qualities. Upon graduation three years earlier, he had 'decided against academic work of the usual kind' and travelled to the wild west coast of Tasmania to undertake a commissioned history of the Mount Lyell mine. Still only twenty-four, he was now applying to write the centenary history of his own university, for he was set on a career as a freelance historian. In supporting Blainey's application, the professor noted 'his independence of mind and his adventurousness'. He described Blainey as an 'individualist'.

The same qualities had struck Manning Clark when he taught Australian history in 1949. Clark recalled a shy second-year student who looked wise but didn't say a word in class until he submitted by far the most impressive essay at the end of first term. His teacher had to ask 'Who is Mr Blainey?' Clark would head north at the end of the year and Blainey upon graduation would go south, but the two retained a friendship and respect for each other's accomplishments.

For ten years Geoffrey Blainey earned a living by his pen. He produced eight books, mostly company histories, and he acquired an understanding of the world of business that remained mysterious to most historians. He was fascinated with technology and its power to shape history. As Graeme Davison has observed, Blainey has an unusual ability to explain how things work, and a tendency to use technology as a metaphor, or even a model, of historical processes—hence his fondness for springs and levers, swings and see-saws. It enabled him to bring complex and abstract problems vividly to the reader's imagination, to strip problems down to their components and show how they worked.

Writing for a living also fostered a strongly practical approach to his craft. When Blainey subsequently advised postgraduate students who were embarking on historical research, he emphasised the importance of writing early and often. Not for him the tortured genius waiting for the romantic glow of literary inspiration: he told them of the work habits of the novelist Anthony Trollope, who sat down each morning at his desk and did not rise until he had completed his regular instalment.

Plying his own trade as a freelance historian, Blainey worked alongside men of action—at the pitface and on the shopfloor as well as in the boardroom—and his writing captured their rhythms of speech. He created vivid narratives in which nouns and verbs do most of the work. His prose prefers the particular to the abstract, eschews the passive voice, avoids words like eschew.

He dispensed with much of the scholarly paraphernalia whereby historians discuss each other's interpretations and fortify their own with entanglements of learned references. He was also sparing in his use of quotation, for his histories are populated by characters who are chiefly memorable for what they did. His mining histories tell of resourceful, determined individuals who pit their energy and their fortune against the impersonal forces of geology, climate, distance and markets. They are realised by description of their appearance, brought to life in deft sketches of their impulses and mannerisms, made memorable by their accomplishments—but they seldom reflect.

In 1960 Geoffrey Blainey filled a temporary vacancy in history at the University of Adelaide. In 1961 he returned to the University of Melbourne as a lecturer in economic history and in 1968 he became professor. Working in a Faculty of Economics and Commerce until 1977, when he crossed to the History Department, he became more interested in patterns of historical change.

Economists employed models of human behaviour to explain the outcomes or predict the consequences of a given course of action with mathematical precision. Blainey was drawn to such determinism himself, though he was conscious that any particular event involved a multiplicity of forces and in most cases they were closely balanced. He used the words 'perhaps', 'possibly' and 'probably' in his own bold hypotheses, probably more often than any other historian. He was not hedging his bets: the hesitancy accompanied the boldness like the bracken that grows alongside nests of bull-ants, its sap salving the sting of his discoveries. He had great faith in the discipline of history, both to explain past events and predict future ones, and he believed that nearly every argument of consequence in public life rested on an appeal to history. He regretted that historians were too cautious and timid to contribute to their public discussion.

While working in a department of economic history, Blainey did not follow the dwindling trail of mathematical abstraction as its practitioners turned to the construction of statistical time series for analysis by the application of economic models. His major works during this period were far more adventurous. They offered an explanation of mineral discovery, an exploration of the theme of distance in Australian history, an analysis of the causes of war over the past 250 years, an evaluation of Aboriginal life before the European arrival, and a study of the swings between optimism and pessimism in western society.

He searched constantly for new ways of thinking about familiar subjects. Historians too often relied on stock responses, he suggested, and needed to be more adventurous. One of their stock responses was to 'reverence all primary sources' and assume that they provided direct access to the past. Here he challenged a paradigm that went back to Ranke's foundation of the discipline of history. To the claim 'My historical technique is to stand completely aside and let the documents simply speak for themselves', he rejoined that 'this assumes a historical document was born a robot, oblivious of its audience'. Some documents, he observed, 'omit vital information because it was too obvious to be worth stating'. In his own work, he had often studied the evidence for a historical problem and found the vital clue only as a buried assumption. 'I constantly search for the obvious.'

That search paid little attention to the work of other historians, except as a point of departure. Blainey ranged freely across their fields of expertise, confounding them with the novelty of the obvious and leaving them to puzzle over its deceptive simplicity while he moved on to a new investigation. He differed from Manning Clark in this versatility, and he proposed no grand theme, but he was just as distinctive in his artistry.

Writing in 1979, Rob Pascoe described Blainey as 'the solitary prospector who searches in magpie fashion across the terrain of Australian history looking for a pattern in the landscape which others have missed'. In *The Rush That Never Ended* (1963) he found such a pattern of mineral discovery and in doing so overturned the conventional version of the Eureka rebellion as a political protest by showing the effects of an indiscriminate tax on a high-risk enterprise. In *The Tyranny of Distance* (1966) he set out to write a history of transport and then turned that subject upside down to explain how distance had shaped Australian history. In *The Causes of War* (1973) he suggested that the challenge was not to explain the occurrence of conflict but the outbreak of peace. And in *The Triumph of the Nomads* (1975) he argued that Aboriginal civilisation sustained a higher standard of living than that of the European peasantry.

His academic colleagues admired the ingenuity of these strikingly original books and cavilled over their conclusions. One reviewer of *The Rush That Never Ended* lamented that Blainey 'sometimes pretends he isn't an academic, and refrains from plying his readers with footnotes and statistics'. Another reviewer praised the vigour and colour of *The Tyranny of Distance* but regretted the 'over-simplification, the use of pictures rather than statistics' and the 'quixotic note of controversy'.

Specialists took issue with his peremptory despatch of their orthodoxies. The argument in *The Tyranny of Distance* that the British settled Australia not as a dumping ground for convicts but as a naval base and a source of naval supplies occasioned a lengthy debate in the academic journals. Those who objected to the paucity of documentary evidence for this claim were disconcerted by Blainey's reluctance to concede ground and unsettled by the liveliness of his rejoinders. 'Knockabout controversies are amusing', one complained, but when the controversialist's 'experience of the period and its problems is less well grounded in original research', his 'straining after novelty' was unhelpful.

I first came to know Geoffrey Blainey when I returned to Melbourne in 1980. As a young lecturer, I was pressed into service as secretary of the Victorian branch of the Business Archives Council, a body he promoted. It joined historians with executives and trade unionists to encourage the preservation of business and labour records. One of the executives was Sir Thomas Ramsay, the chairman of the Kiwi Polish Company, and keen book-collector and amateur historian. He was generous enough to offer me encouragement: 'Just write like Geoffrey Blainey'.

The advice was well-meant but utterly impractical. How could I explain that Blainey was inimitable? I already knew him as a senior colleague who was approachable, supportive, entirely without affectation, yet only partly with us. Since his habit was to begin writing in the small hours of the morning, it was small wonder that when he arrived at the university to teach, confer and attend to his many outside commitments, he was often preoccupied.

An academic adviser might not have offered the same counsel. Blainey had little regard for the measures that universities were applying to academic performance. He was not interested in chasing research grants because he conducted his own research and in any case followed hunches that no research plan could predict. Like Manning Clark, he practised scholarship as an art. Both were individualists. Neither, apart from Blainey when he wrote the history of his school and his university, ever worked with anyone else. Each followed his own drum.

In 1980 a journalist prepared a feature article on this increasingly celebrated historian. 'Geoffrey Blainey is an unspectacular and shy man, peering up from under at a world much nastier than himself.' The journalist detected a modesty and 'a sort of farm-boy innocence' in a man who said that he wrote simply 'to impose some kind of shape of things' and was not wholly satisfied with any of his books but then added: 'I'll defend them strongly if they are attacked'.

Historians who see things differently are sometimes accused of bias. Writing of Brian Fitzpatrick's radical nationalist history of British imperialism in Australia, Blainey observed that 'When a historian lacks the orthodox assumptions of his times, the complaint is loud that he is biased or that his methods are odd. This merely means that so many writers share a common bias that they have ceased to realise that it is a bias.' The emphasis here is on the transience of orthodoxies, and the rewriting of history to challenge them.

But that did not mean exchanging one bias for another. Speaking at a forum on history, Blainey observed that an older belief in objective history had given way to the view that bias was inevitable since all historians were prisoners of their experience and their preferences. On the contrary, he sometimes found himself studying a problem, examining the evidence and reaching a conclusion at variance with his own predilections. Such was the discipline of history that he could pick up what he had written and say to himself, 'Well, I wish I hadn't said that'.

Geoffrey Blainey offered these reflections just three weeks after the Warrnambool controversy broke but there was little evidence that he regretted having said the things there that had whipped up such a storm. While he conjured up the spectre of racial conflict, he was not proposing it—rather, like Manning Clark's intimations of political violence in 1975, he warned of ominous portents. He saw himself as a voice of commonsense drowned out by extremists. 'The strangest thing', he suggested more than three months into the controversy, 'is that all along I believe I've occupied the middle ground. But apparently I'm the only person occupying it.'

Others undoubtedly contributed to the polarisation of opinion. Labor ministers were quick to condemn Blainey's questioning of immigration policy and to blame him for the shadow minister's threat to campaign against it. No sooner had the Coalition drawn back to confirm a bipartisan position on such a sensitive issue than the shadow minister predicted it would bring his party substantial gains at the next election. The prime minister then criticised Blainey and the Coalition again fell into line. But Bill Hayden, the minister for foreign affairs, once more attacked Blainey, albeit after press reports that the National Party was courting him to stand for parliament. He had resigned from the last of his official positions (the council of the proposed National Museum) after the minister had accused him of 'deliberately distorting' the immigration issue 'to attack the Labor Government'.

The conflagration had long since breached the safety-lines that existed when Blainey spoke at Warrnambool, yet he continued to light new fires. There he had suggested that the government, perhaps inadvertently, was straining community acceptance. A fortnight later he accused his critics and the government of surrendering Australia. He had originally expressed support for multiculturalism but was now lamenting that it put Australians second.

The appearance of his book, *All for Australia*, at the beginning of October brought a further escalation of the argument. He had begun writing it midway through the year to set out his arguments against the present immigration policy and started by explaining how the controversy had arisen. The opening chapters emphasised his moderation and his intention from the outset to persuade the government to fall back into step with public opinion.

But the very title of the book was provocative. It harked back to the All For Australia League that was created during a political crisis in the Depression of the 1930s as a conservative mobilisation against a Labor government. Moreover, the preface declared that a number of fundamental ideas—democracy, race, free speech and national independence—were 'at war in this controversy'.

While Blainey made it clear that he had no animosity towards Asians and supported Asian immigration, the closing chapters of the book presented an alarmist report of racial hostility. A chapter entitled 'The Front Line is the Neighbourhood' drew from the testimony of 'residents in the invaded suburbs' to describe 'pavements now spotted with phlegm and spit', and skies 'filled with greasy smoke and the smell of goat's meat', of 'old Australians' who were frightened to say what they think, and of divided schools and bullied children.

Blainey's criticism of immigration policy drew him here into rash charges. He had previously argued that the method of selecting immigrants, ostensibly without any reference to their racial origin, in fact gave preference to Asians by manipulating the criteria. In *All for Australia* he likened the operation of the selection process to a cricket scoreboard where the government was constantly changing the rules, so that the underarm bowling of the Lebanese was rewarded while the overarm bowling of the Dutch was penalised.

Blainey had a talent for metaphors but on this occasion it failed him. Inside the scoreboard, he suggested, there was a secret room where immigration officers rigged the scores to achieve their desired increase of Asian immigrants. The public did not know of this secret room, and parliament probably was unaware of it, but it was certainly known to the minister for immigration. The rules that governed its operation were also secret, and not even the Freedom of Information Act provided access to the back door of the secret room, but Blainey claimed to have seen one of its secret policy documents.

This passage of the book aroused particular interest and journalists who asked Blainey to justify it reported him saying that 'he had all the documents necessary to prove his point despite the secrecy . . . and refusal to requests under freedom of information legislation'. Jack Waterford immediately challenged these claims. He was a Canberra journalist with an unrivalled knowledge of public administration, and had already obtained policy documents from the department. He rang Blainey, who said he had been misquoted and had not in fact made a freedom of information request. The journalist pressed him further. Was Blainey aware that the documents were in fact available? No. Would he pursue them? 'I might have a look at it. I'm not infallible.'

That was an unusual concession in a heated debate where insult and accusation too often displaced measured argument. The mode of the debate as a media controversy did not help for the disputants became engaged in a form of combat by press release, each burst of rhetoric bringing an immediate and equally polemical response.

The lack of opportunity to explore differences in a less confrontational manner was particularly regretted by Blainey's colleagues, who would read his latest philippic in the newspaper but had no chance to express their misgivings. He was out of the History Department while dean, frequently caught up with media engagements and absent overseas when they wrote their own letter to the press. I then persuaded him to meet with us and see if we could clarify our differences, but that meeting was fatally handicapped by reciprocal resentment.

We met in the departmental common room where, before he became dean in 1982, he had been a regular participant in the conversations over morning tea. Some of us tried to explain the concerns that had caused us to sign the letter, especially the way that his title as professor of history was invariably attached to his statements on such a sensitive contemporary issue. He replied that those statements were based on his historical expertise. Could he not see the damage he was doing to race relations? Could we not see that he was entitled to state his views? It was a wretched occasion and hardly surprising that Geoffrey Blainey avoided subsequent academic forums on the issue.

What was the issue? For some it was his introduction of race into discussion of immigration policy, or rather his re-introduction of race after it had been removed tacitly in the

1960s and emphatically by the Whitlam government in the early 1970s. In his Warrnambool speech he had cautioned that it was difficult to absorb migrants in periods of high unemployment (the unemployment rate reached a post-war peak of 9.8 per cent in 1983, though it was already falling in 1984), but he had singled out Asian migrants in his warnings of discord. His subsequent criticism of ethnic enclaves bringing degradation, resentment and animosity was directed at this new presence in Australian society.

Blainey is not a racist and he was understandably indignant when accused of racial prejudice. Racism takes race as an innate characteristic that defines capacity, character and worth, and Blainey made it clear that 'all peoples, all races, are worthy of respect'. Nor was he prejudiced against Asians. He had a longstanding interest in East Asia and a particular respect for its peoples. He had welcomed the abandonment of the White Australia Policy and he supported immigration from Asia, only in reduced numbers and with altered expectations. He did not propose exclusion on grounds of race but, rather, was concerned with the incorporation of immigrants into the host society.

As he pursued his argument, he came to the conclusion that some migrants were less able and less inclined to make this adaptation, not because of their race but because their culture was less compatible with the Australian way of life. He also reached the judgement that the government's policy of multiculturalism impeded their incorporation. The groups he identified came from Asian countries but it was not their racial status that caused the difficulty (for he acknowledged that Chinese professionals lived harmoniously in Australia). Rather, Asian origin served as a marker of cultural difference. But the multicultural orthodoxy suppressed all discussion of race, turning it into 'a weapon of indignation and a word of fear'.

Blainey had begun to express misgivings about multiculturalism before he gave his Warrnambool speech. Speaking at the National Press Club in 1983, he had said that Asian immigrants should come on our terms. As the controversy proceeded, he became more critical. Multiculturalism had ceased to be a harmless platitude for a diverse and tolerant society, 'mostly words, packaging, oratory, pork barrelling and folk dancing', and was beginning 'to sweep into every corner of national life like a tide at full moon'. It was being imposed from above by politicians, ethnic leaders and academics far removed from the realities of the invaded suburbs. Blainey now supported multiculturalism only if it was 'moderate, tolerant and articulate rather than rabid and woolly and divisive'.

Some sought to lower the emotional temperature by returning to the issue of migration. Peter Shergold, who is now the head of the Department of Prime Minister and Cabinet but was then a senior lecturer in economic history at the University of New South Wales (and himself an immigrant from England), offered a number of corrections to Blainey. The migrant quota had been cut back with the onset of the 1983 recession. All applicants were assessed by the same criteria, and the claim that Europeans suffered discrimination was 'a dangerous nonsense'. There had been more settlers from the United Kingdom and Ireland in the previous year than from Asia (a geographical category that stretched from Turkey to Korea), and a much higher proportion of British and Irish applicants were successful.

Contrary to fears of a rapid increase in Asian numbers, Shergold calculated that Australians of Asian descent constituted 2 per cent of the population and were likely to increase to 4 per cent early in the next century. They made up some small enclaves, as earlier groups of migrants had done in the past, but were just as likely to dissipate. Recent public opinion polls revealed no greater antagonism than before. In a final flourish he said that 'We need to learn from our past, not forget or distort it'.

Such questioning of his expertise affronted Blainey. When he commented on the letter written by members of the Melbourne History Department, he said 'they were acting in a political way rather than in a historian's way'. When he met with them in the strained meeting that followed, he observed their great surprise when he said that his arguments on Asian immigration were based on his knowledge of Australian history. Geoffrey Bolton, a close contemporary and himself a distinguished historian, provoked an unusual outburst when he said that Geoffrey Blainey did not have specialist knowledge of Asian immigration. 'How long do I have to live, what else do I have to do, to become qualified?', he demanded.

The history he affirmed was one of British settlement and endeavour. When he accused his critics of advocating a Surrender Australia policy, he insisted that 'This land is not a rich prize which Australians have stumbled upon. It is a prize they have developed, often at great pain and against great obstacles.' Those who chanted the slogan that 'Australia is part of Asia' were putting geography before history. They treated 'the long phase of British Australia' running from 1788 well into the twentieth century as 'not a very significant phase of Australian history' and ignored its precious legacy of democracy, freedom of speech and freedom to worship—vital characteristics that were uncommon in Asia and the third world.

With the surrender of Australia went a 'disowning of our past', expressed in arguments that the country was a bonanza snatched from the Aboriginals and 'attempts to depict Australian history as mainly a story of exploitation, of racial violence, of oppressions and conflict'. Many Australians had come to see their compatriots as almost uniquely racist. Against this pessimistic view (Blainey had yet to call it Black Armband history), he thought the record was 'not very impressive' in the nineteenth century and first half of the twentieth, though far from the worst in the world. Since then the level of toleration had improved rapidly and Australia had conducted a more successful immigration program than any other. All of this, he argued, was now put at risk by a government that was breaking with the past and telling a people proud of their accomplishments they had travelled the wrong path.

This aspect of Blainey's argument received little attention while argument raged over issues of race, migration and multi-culturalism. The controversy raised contemporary issues rather than historical ones, but when his university colleagues published their letter in May it also became a controversy over historians. A public statement of disavowal appeared to many as an act of betrayal. For twenty-three members of Blainey's department (the press counted twenty-four but they double-counted one of them who had a named chair) to put their names to the letter seemed a case of ganging up to impose censorship.

The letter specifically disavowed any suppression of free speech: 'We do not wish to limit debate and discussion by Professor Blainey'. Its primary purpose was to declare that he spoke for himself and not for us—over the preceding two months he had been regularly identified as a Professor of History at Melbourne University and Dean of the Faculty of Arts. There is a loose convention that academics should reserve use of their university title to commentary on matters of professional expertise and our letter therefore said that he spoke as an individual. But the further statement that he did not speak 'as a representative of historians at this university' was unnecessarily provocative, for he had never claimed to do so and the very idea of a representative position on such a subject carried implications of collective orthodoxy.

The second paragraph of the letter went further to regret the discussion of immigration policy in racial terms. 'However much it is couched in the language of reason', we said, it invited less responsible groups to incite feelings of racial hatred against ethnic groups. Members of the department felt very strongly on the issue of race—like most collective letters, this one had to straddle a range of feelings—and some were already experiencing racial animosity either personally or through family members. Even so, the admonition qualified the letter's affirmation of free speech.

Academics found it hard to see how they could be accused of suppressing Blainey's freedom of speech. They observed that he had ready access to press, radio and television, while several newspapers had declined to publish the letter from the twenty-three members of the Melbourne History Department. His articles were frequently accompanied by line drawings that showed a quizzical, popular figure, while they were portrayed as a baying mob. This aspect of the controversy soon became an issue in itself. In August a poll asked respondents whether Blainey had been treated unfairly by academics: 39 per cent said yes and 43 per cent didn't know.

The issue of free speech was magnified by attempts to prevent Blainey from speaking and even teaching. In June an off-campus 'Stop the Racists Committee' announced its intention of picketing a class that Blainey was teaching. The university employed a security service to protect access to the building where the class was conducted, but some of the thirty demonstrators gained entry and Blainey cancelled two talks he had planned to give on campus because he feared that further violence would damage the university's reputation.

Both he and others seemed to lose their judgement. After Blainey heard an organiser of the 'Stop the Racists Committee' claim on radio that the History Department supported its views, he wrote to David Philips, a member of the department whom he thought was the organiser of the letter and demanded to know why he was accused of racism. Philips assured him he had not organised the letter, had nothing to do with the demonstration and had not accused him of racism, yet he subsequently accused Blainey of 'paranoid fantasy'. In a review of *All for Australia* he said that Professor Blainey 'seems to have publicly abandoned' sound historical method and that if the book had been submitted as a first-year essay he would have sent it back for further research and rewriting.

Another colleague condemned the 'baloney view' of history at a student meeting and suggested that Blainey should pay back the salary he had drawn as dean of the Faculty of Arts while conducting a political campaign. Blainey had a faculty officer write to him requesting an explanation of his proposal as a matter of urgency so it could be considered by the faculty's budget committee, which the dean chaired. He seemed oblivious of the conflict of interest in such point scoring.

Geoffrey Blainey described the experience as 'traumatic' and there is no doubt that he was deeply wounded. Already running the gauntlet of public criticism, he had not expected it would spread to his own workplace. A widely respected and extremely popular man whose door had always been open, he was disconcerted by hostility on campus just as others were distressed by the breakdown of tolerance and civility.

Some of the friends who sprang to his defence only increased the recrimination. His staunchest supporter was Dinny O'Hearn, the sub-dean of the Faculty of Arts and a legendary rough diamond. Dinny knew that I disagreed with Geoffrey Blainey. He argued with me but never allowed it to affect our friendship. He assumed that I would not allow my disagreement to spill over into personal antagonism for such a fine and decent scholar, and I owe much to his example.

The issue of free speech and academic criticism revived in 1985 with the publication of a book of essays on Geoffrey Blainey and the immigration controversy. Its two editors from the History Department at Monash University set the scene by describing the growing unease with his statements during the previous year and the reservations about the scholarship on which he based his claims.

Other contributors then cast back over Blainey's earlier work to suggest how it anticipated the views he had expressed. They found a flawed paradigm in *The Tyranny of Distance*, a growing antagonism to the Chinese presence in his writing on the gold rush, an exaggeration of Aboriginal violence in the *Triumph of the Nomads* and an avoidance of frontier conflict in other writings. With pardonable exaggeration, one sceptical reader of their book suggested these historians made Blainey's views appear to run in a straight line from Mount Lyell to the Warrnambool Rotary Club.

It was hardly surprising that John Stone should denounce these historians as thugs, nor that Bruce Ruxton should add his denunciation of 'those pinkies in their ivory towers'. A newspaper editorial described them as a 'lynch-mob' and in the *Age* Peter Nicholson drew Geoffrey Blainey bound to a stake and tormented by mean-spirited academics.

The bill of charges laid against Blainey was remarkably similar to that brought against Manning Clark. He too preferred the eye-catching episode or example to the more prosaic but substantial evidence, employed imagination at the cost of 'misconceptions, misunderstandings and faulty judgements'. Clark had been accused of excessive gloom, while Blainey was castigated for evoking a golden age that historians found 'somewhat sanitised and idealised'.

Blainey, like Clark, was an unconventional historian. The criticisms levelled at both of them, imagination and error, passion and bias, drew attention to the qualities that made them influential figures in public life. Both were superb teachers but both retired early with much of their writing still to come. Both were mavericks who dispensed with the constrictive conventions of the academic profession to reach a wider audience. Their tribulations fuelled suspicion of the historical profession. In Clark's case it was the failure of the academics to denounce him that caused the suspicion; in Blainey's it was their readiness to do so that aroused ire. Out of these two episodes a case of intellectual bias was building.

Geoffrey Blainey was elected to a second term as dean and completed it at the end of 1987. His failure to secure a third term briefly revived accusations of persecution—B. A. Santamaria blamed it on 'the feminist influence' and the 'liberal intelligentsia'—but six years was as long as anyone had held the office and most felt it was time for a change. He returned to the History Department and taught during 1988, but decided to take early retirement. His colleagues farewelled him at a dinner and paid him tribute. The allegation that he was hounded out of the university persisted in conservative circles, encouraged from time to time by Peter Ryan who invariably gets the most elementary historical facts wrong. On the only occasion that I had a conversation with John Howard, he raised this charge, listened to me and acknowledged that he was mistaken.

The issue of Asian immigration fell away until John Howard took it up in 1988, encountered general condemnation and retreated. There it rested until Pauline Hanson was elected to the Commonwealth parliament in 1996. In her maiden speech she paid tribute to the courageous Australians 'who were prepared to take on the priests of political correctness' before she did, and noted that 'in 1984 Professor Geoffrey Blainey delivered a speech to a Rotary club in rural Victoria, in which he made a reasoned call for a debate on the levels of Asian immigration'.

CHAPTER 6

BICENTENARY BATTLES

Manning Clark and Geoffrey Blainey were drawn to controversy as moths to a flame. Their desire to bring history to bear on contemporary issues, their authority as interpreters of national destiny, capacity to coin arresting phrases and celebrity as public figures ensured that those controversies were highly personal. Argument over their motives, repute and integrity became inseparable from argument over the issues they raised, and overshadowed consideration of the history they deployed.

The historical profession figured in these media controversies either as accomplice or accuser. From the late 1970s, when Clark contested the legitimacy of the Fraser government, historians were castigated for their failure to repudiate him. From 1984, as Blainey widened his campaign against the policies of the Hawke government, historians were accused of betraying him. In contrast to its two most prominent practitioners, the rest of the historical profession remained an obscure clerisy. Clark and Blainey were familiar figures, instantly recognisable in appearance and mannerisms, while their colleagues constituted an anonymous collectivity. Their fields of expertise were scarcely acknowledged, the nature of their activities ignored.

After 1984, arguments over Australian history broadened beyond the positions occupied by its two most eminent practitioners. In the wake of the immigration controversy, attention turned to the impending celebration of the two hundredth anniversary of British settlement, and in 1985 an acrimonious debate broke out over how it should be celebrated. Historians were already engaged on a number of projects timed for publication in the anniversary year of 1988, for the Australian Bicentenary presented them with an unprecedented opportunity to reach a popular audience. The history profession made up only one small company in the battles fought over the Bicentenary, but it was a battle conducted on their field of history.

Historians were therefore able to bring their knowledge and their disciplinary expertise to bear on this new controversy. History itself was now the subject of debate and two previously separate versions of Australian history, that of the academics and that presented in the popular media, came together. The methods of academic history, its interrogation of the evidence and commitment to critical inquiry, met the commemorative impulse with its attachment to binding tradition. Out of this encounter a group of ideologues constructed a charge of treason. Historians were no longer lacking in personal judgement, they were part of a conspiracy to denigrate the national past and replace pride with guilt.

Prime Minister Malcolm Fraser announced the establishment of the Australian Bicentennial Authority in April 1979. 'Deep in any human community', he said, 'is a consciousness of its origins and identity and its hopes and resolutions for the future'. National anniversaries allowed expression of these impulses. The Bicentenary would therefore 'be a time for calling to mind the achievements throughout this country and by its people over two centuries' as well as 'a time to reflect upon our developing and changing national identity'.

Here already a particular kind of history was indicated, one that would join origins to change, achievement to resolution, in order to strengthen the nation's consciousness of itself. Fraser nominated the influx of immigrants from an increasing diversity of countries over the past thirty years as a particular agent of change, since he was a champion of multiculturalism, but did not attempt to prescribe the content of the Bicentenary beyond indicating there would 'no doubt be a strong emphasis on history'.

The form of the anniversary, its program of activities and commemorative themes, would be determined by the Authority, which was established as a company to give it appropriate autonomy and flexibility. Its board would consist of seven members nominated by the six states and the Northern Territory, seven more representing the Commonwealth, with an additional nominee of the prime minister and the leader of the Opposition. There would be state councils and local committees for every one of the country's 839 local government authorities.

The elaborate structure signalled the importance of the occasion. The Centenary of the British colonisation of Australia had been an improvised affair when New South Wales entertained dignitaries from the other colonies for a week of festivities. The Sesquicentenary, in 1938, was again controlled by the government of New South Wales, which created a 150th Anniversary Celebrations Council in 1935 with a host of committees to organise a re-enactment of the landing of the First Fleet, arrange a procession through the city of Sydney, stage a 'Gala Night' at the Sydney showground and co-ordinate a range of other activities that stretched over three months.

The Bicentenary was to occupy a full year and extend into every part of the country. It would have a budget of $200 million, not to mention the projects attached to it such as a national road-building program worth $2.5 billion and the construction of a new Parliament House in Canberra that eventually cost another $1 billion.

The Australian Bicentenary, like the two hundredth anniversary of the American Revolution in 1976 from which it took many of its ideas, was a massive undertaking requiring a full decade of preparation. It was a national festival on a grand scale that exhibited the nation to the rest of the world, created spectacle and entertainment, assisted tourism and commerce, stimulated patriotism and protest. The emphasis on popular participation required that the Bicentenary encompass local forms and voluntary activity. The celebration of national origins would have to include newcomers to the national community who felt no attachment to its foundational history. Such a commemoration was bound to be contentious.

One of the tasks of the Authority would be to make the original landing at Sydney Cove on 26 January 1788 a truly national event for Australians living in other states. Western Australians were more aware of the Dutch ships that came aground on their coast long before British navigators began to explore the eastern one. South Australians took pride in the foundation of a free province, that had nothing to do with the convict colonies. A further challenge would be to prise the Bicentenary from the tenacious grip of the Premier State. New South Wales would retain control of the centrepiece of the Bicentennial program, in Sydney on 26 January 1988. It would also spend $70 million augmenting its share of the Commonwealth funds to put its stamp on the event.

The chairman of the Australian Bicentennial Authority was John Reid, a Melbourne businessman, and its chief executive officer was David Armstrong, formerly the director of a college of advanced education in Melbourne. Since the Authority was based in Sydney—it first occupied offices in Chifley Square and later moved to the Rocks, the historic precinct built into the sandstone cliffs on the western side of Sydney

Cove—that seemed an appropriate compromise. Reid and Armstrong began with a remarkable freedom to shape the Bicentenary. The prime minister expected the Authority 'to draw upon the ideas of highly imaginative and creative people' to recommend an appropriate theme, and laid down few expectations other than that it should 'encourage initiatives at the grass roots of Australian society'.

Accordingly the Authority encouraged Phillip Adams, an advertising agency executive and newspaper columnist of considerable imagination and creativity, to convene preliminary discussions of the great and the good: Talbot Duckmanton of the ABC, Jean Battersby of the Australia Council, Bob Hawke of the ACTU, Gus Nossal of the Walter and Eliza Hall Institute, the conservationist Harry Butler, the playwright David Williamson, the actor Graeme Blundell and a score or so others. The grass roots and the historians were conspicuously absent from these formative discussions.

Out of them came the Bicentenary's initial goals. It should be an occasion for national stocktaking, for reflection on Australian history and possibly for changing national symbols such as the Australian flag and the national anthem. 'A warts and all approach should be adopted, showing our achievements and identifying problems.' Among the problems, 'the issues of racism, materialism and philistinism should be addressed'. There was considerable discussion of an appropriate theme before multiculturalism prevailed and the phrase 'Living Together' was chosen.

The board accepted Living Together as the theme—and it also established the nomenclature of Bicentenary the noun and Bicentennial the adjective, along with the Authority's exclusive right to every imaginable variant on the Bicentennial vocabulary. Living Together signalled an inclusiveness which, along with the 'warts and all approach', was designed to allay early sensitivities. Following Malcolm Fraser, the Authority was already referring to the Bicentenary as the anniversary of European settlement rather than British colonisation or white occupation of Australia. Critics had already alleged that the event marked the destruction of Aboriginal society and the Uniting Church had called for a boycott of the Bicentenary unless Aboriginal rights were restored.

David Armstrong replied immediately that 'we know Aborigines were murdered, driven off their lands and decimated by introduced disease'; and 'anyone would be a fool not to recognise their rights'. This was much more than a tactical response. Armstrong embraced the 'warts and all approach', for his own style was ruggedly earnest and he wanted a program that would be 'serious and broadly educational and cultural in nature'.

Speaking as the ABC's Guest of Honour shortly after appointment, he said that 'The Bicentenary presents a unique, once-in-a-lifetime opportunity for us to *celebrate* Australia'. He used celebration in what he called 'the theological sense' of remembering things past, reaffirming our best values and 're-dedicating ourselves to the immense task of solving the problems that still confront us as a people—racism, philistinism, materialism, lack of national pride, widespread inequalities of opportunity, desecrated historic sites, polluted streams, ignorance of our collective past—the agenda is a long one'.

It certainly was, though it was some way ahead of what the prime minister had in mind when he had called for grass-roots initiatives. The Authority was encouraging the formation of local committees, but the need to orchestrate their inchoate impulses into a coherent program was inherent in the very nature of a participatory national anniversary. Only a quarter of Australians, in 1981, were able to identify the Bicentennial year.

The grass roots that particularly perturbed Malcolm Fraser were the prickly thickets of Commonwealth–state relations. Under his policy of New Federalism, the Commonwealth was drawing back from his predecessor's profligate centralism to devolve responsibilities back to the states. Yet he had created an Authority in which state nominees made up nearly half of a governing body that would allocate the expenditure of

Commonwealth funds. At the end of 1981 he signalled that his government would not write cheques for every activity it devised and would expect others to contribute.

He was also unimpressed by the theme of Living Together, which all the states with the conspicuous exception of the Western Australian premier, Sir Charles Court—an unbending conservative—had endorsed. It was not that the prime minister disagreed with the sentiment. Rather, he was unimpressed by the Authority's claim that it had conducted extensive research to formulate the phrase (he probably suspected that this research consisted of offering sandwiches to the *illuminati* who suggested it) and, as he later put it, thought such a slogan 'inadequate, hollow and a little bit pathetic'.

In place of Living Together, Fraser imposed 'The Australian Achievement'. He wanted a celebration of 'positive achievements and triumph over adversity and social problems', and specifically the role of democracy, free enterprise and trade unionism, educational, intellectual and technical achievements, the multicultural society and the contributions of Aboriginal people, and sport. This was a broad canvas, but David Armstrong remained resistant to what he described as 'tremendous pressure from some groups to mount a safe Bicentenary'. He said he was not interested in 'staging a wank'; and in response to concerns about Aboriginal participation, he told journalists that 'if it is going to be a white wank I want nothing to do with it'.

Armstrong had a weakness for such imagery. When a new survey in 1984 showed that still only 37 per cent of respondents knew when the Bicentenary would occur, he said that the Authority was 'anxious to avoid a premature ejaculation'. It had created no less than nineteen task groups in a wide variety of fields—in addition to those nominated by the prime minister, they included the environment, religion, women and youth, the arts, and history—to compile components of a national program that Fraser unveiled on Australia Day 1983.

Six weeks later he lost office. The new Labor government requested the Authority to revise the program and give greater emphasis to women and Aboriginals. It scrapped the slogan of The Australian Achievement in favour of the original Living Together, and it also altered the Bicentenary's corporate colours from blue and gold to the national green and gold.

These changes in turn drew criticism from the right. *Quadrant* had maintained a watching brief over the work of the Authority, and conservative commentators had long looked with suspicion on the impulsive David Armstrong. Now Ken Baker, a research fellow of the Institute of Public Affairs, a business think-tank, argued that the revised Bicentenary program was sacrificing tradition to 'the fashionable concerns of a minority' and slighting 'the core values and sources of pride of most Australians'. He singled out 'the neglect of the Christian and British foundations of Australia' and condemned the Authority for using its own logo in place of the Australian flag.

The press quickly reported Baker's criticisms with headlines such as 'Bicentenary Plans Slated' and 'Birthday Plan "Not Dinkum"'. Such adverse publicity disturbed a government that had come to office to unite the nation and a prime minister who was conducting a romance with the Australian people. Bob Hawke was in any case unhappy with the extravagance and inefficiency of an Authority whose administrative costs and fondness for overseas travel came under media scrutiny by 1985. He therefore had its chairman arrange the resignation of the chief executive officer, and after the size of that termination package brought further criticism, replaced the chairman as well.

The new chairman and chief executive officer was Jim Kirk, a Sydney businessman with safe hands. Kirk tightened the administration, printed new stationery that put the Australian flag alongside the Authority's logo, and kept careful watch on all controversy. He censored contributions to the Authority's magazine from Michael Kirby, who had drawn attention to discrimination against Aboriginal people, and from the New South Wales parliamentarian Franca Arena, who called for a republic. The Authority 'is not the forum for such debate', Kirk insisted. So, too, the naturalist Harry Butler was omitted from a television advertisement because he opposed the World Heritage listing of the second stage of Kakadu National Park.

That advertisement was commissioned by the Authority to promote its new theme, Celebration of a Nation. It flew sixty celebrities into the red centre so that they could form a chorus line with Uluru in the background and sing an anodyne jingle:

> The celebration of a nation,
> Give us a hand!
> Celebration of a nation, let's make it grand!
> Let's make it great in '88,
> C'mon give us hand.

The song was performed on television and radio, the slogan appeared in the press, on buses, trams and billboards. If recognition of the Bicentennial year increased, the mass marketing abandoned the lofty ideals that had shaped the program.

Kirk's Authority added a Heritage 200 component to placate allegations that the program neglected Australian achievement (it would select 200 individuals for commemoration as *The People Who Made Australia Great*) and commissioned Time-Life to prepare a series of books on *Australians at War* to counter complaints that the Bicentenary was neglecting the Anzac tradition. Similarly, it endorsed a celebratory scheme for a chain of beacons to be lit around the continent. This had been proposed by Claudio Veliz of La Trobe University and was taken up by a Melbourne group, with corporate sponsorship; among the group was Geoffrey Blainey.

The strategy of the Authority might be characterised as repressive tolerance. It controlled the national program and had sole control of the Bicentennial label. While excluding those elements it judged to be politically contentious, it defused accusations of bias by allowing most interest groups to join the roll-call of achievement. This strategy did not silence the clamour—the cattlemen, for example, complained that an early publicity exercise showed too many sheep—but it returned the Bicentenary to a familiar political pattern of 'me too'. So too did the distribution of largesse for local projects and major facilities such as the Stockmen's Hall of Fame at Longreach.

The Bicentenary began on 1 January 1988 with a national television program incorporating more than seventy satellite link-ups to traverse the country. Meaghan Morris described it as 'a four hour tourist brochure for international, including Australian, consumption'. The anniversary itself remained closely tied to a particular time and place. On 26 January somewhere between one and two million people gathered on the shores of Sydney Harbour while ten thousand boats speckled its surface. There were speeches at Bennelong Point (the Prince of Wales delivered the most accomplished), music, balloons, a flypast and fireworks.

These were familiar entertainments on a familiar public holiday. Two further attractions defined the occasion. One was the assembly of 200 sailing vessels from all around the world as an international tribute to Australia's birthday. The other was the appearance of eleven square-rigged ships that had retraced the original voyage from England of the First Fleet. The first of the flotilla mimicking the First Fleet came through the Heads with a spinnaker that advertised Coca-Cola, for it was a private venture that had no place in the Authority's planning. Much of the argument over the Bicentenary was conducted around this naval venture.

The re-enactment of the First Fleet was the brainchild of Jonathan King, who traced his descent from Phillip Gidley King, an officer of the First Fleet and later governor of New

South Wales. As a young, unemployed journalist, King had visited his ancestor's neglected grave in London in 1974. In the following year he stumbled on Lieutenant King's journals in Sydney's Mitchell Library and conceived the idea of re-creating the voyage. He found encouragement from both Manning Clark and Geoffrey Blainey: in his Canberra eyrie, the former stroked his beard and said it would teach Australians a great deal about themselves; in Melbourne, the latter brushed locks of tousled hair off his forehead and said it would remind them of their British lineage.

These atmospheric recollections come from King's subsequent account of *The Battle for the Bicentenary*, which pits a visionary idealist against a devious and obstructive bureaucracy. King portrays the Authority as an organisation in denial of history, turning its back on the country's British origins to embrace new political priorities, and redefining Australia as 'a nation ashamed of its past'. He presents himself as an innocent who was slow to recognise the Authority's duplicity, and an enthusiast convinced that his project will assist Australians to come to terms with the ghosts of the past. He advertises his progressive sympathies and allows for his impulsive blunders. At the outset he gets his reckoning wrong and calculates 1978 as the bicentennial year. He attracts patrons and then alienates them, makes agreements and breaks them, for he is a man caught in the spell of the past.

At every turn King found the government obstructing his plans. He could only understand resistance to the First Fleet re-enactment as a misguided fear of the past. From 1979 he and his friends dressed up in period costume to come ashore at Sydney Cove on Australia Day and claim possession of Australia. These annual masquerades created publicity for his project but they also attracted Aboriginal protest. The Authority worried that a full re-enactment of the British colonisation of Australia would highlight the usurpation of its original inhabitants, while emphasis on an imperial venture would estrange those who had settled here more recently and given their allegiance to an independent nation. The Authority preferred the more inclusive commemoration of a country of immigrants and followed the United States in inviting countries from all round the world to send their Tall Ships.

Jonathan King described this as 'rewriting history' but the Authority felt that his own mimicry was bound to appear artificial and inauthentic. Australians were uncomfortable with fancy dress and overblown ritual. It would cost too much to assemble a replica First Fleet and bring it on a voyage lasting eight months (the Authority's own Tall Ships were provided by other countries and cost little) and King's proposed fund-raising program would cut across the Authority's own sponsorship campaign. There were further concerns about safety and predictions of limited media interest.

In November 1981 the Authority announced that it would neither support nor endorse the proposal of King's First Fleet Re-enactment Committee. The historical resonances of re-enactment were certainly unwelcome but, as a journalist observed, it was 'torpedoed by those essential twin tools of twentieth-century management—the cost-benefit analysis and the feasibility study'.

King was never going to let those objections defeat him and pressed ahead with the assistance of powerful patrons. Sir Donald Trescowthick and Sir Robert Southey had extensive business interests, Sir David Fairbairn brought further connections to the Liberal Party, Sir James Hardy conferred nautical prestige, Lady Mary Fairfax provided connections to the press. Later, as the project took on a more commercial character, King formed a business partnership with Hoyts–Michael Edgley International. But he had progressive supporters, such as Tom Keneally, and several Aboriginal activists—Pat O'Shane, Reg Blow and Burnum Burnum—also came aboard. Burnum Burnum would stage his own ceremony on 26 January 1988 by planting the Aboriginal flag on Dover Beach and laying claim to England on behalf of his people.

The History Warriors quickly embraced the First Fleet Re-enactment. In 1981 *Quadrant* called it a 'brilliant and challenging idea' and condemned its 'shabby treatment' by the Authority. Geoffrey Blainey counselled King to let the Authority think it had snuffed out the project but go on developing it. Blainey's former student, Tim Duncan, took the lack of support for the re-enactment as emblematic of the failings of the Authority. Writing in the *Bulletin* under the headline 'Bicentennial Blues Spoil the Party', he said it had 'ignored many of the very things that most Australians view as central to the unity and identity of the nation'. As government ministers condemned the project—John Dawkins called it a 'tasteless and insensitive farce'—Coalition parliamentarians protested that 'If we are going to put blank pages into the history books for the benefit of some people's feelings we will lead ourselves into terrible error'.

In the end, it was a Labor politician who breathed wind into the sails of the becalmed First Fleet Re-enactment. Neville Wran liked the idea and as premier of New South Wales he determined that it would be part of the program at Sydney on 26 January 1988. Once this was determined, Jim Kirk as chair of the Authority agreed to endorse the First Fleet project providing it replaced 'Re-enactment' in the title with 'Commemorative' and accepted that there would be no landing. An earlier re-enactment, in 1938, had trucked in Aboriginals from western New South Wales to retire brandishing their spears as Governor Phillip came ashore to take possession of Australia. There was general agreement that any such ceremony in 1988 would be deeply offensive, for many Aboriginal people objected to the burlesque version of the landing that Jonathan King and his friends staged each year during the 1980s, so in the Bicentennial year he finally abandoned the provocation.

Even with funding from New South Wales and a loan from the Authority, he struggled to enact the commemorative voyage. Suitable ships were hard to find and expensive to lease: just ten set sail from Portsmouth, the fleet was down to seven as it crossed the Atlantic from Rio to Cape Town; it made up the full complement of eleven only in Australian waters. Early bookings were slow and King resorted to a mock flogging with tomato sauce effects to drum up trade in London. The second First Fleet departed England in April 1977 to a royal farewell and Aboriginal objections. There were further demonstrations whenever the ships put into port and an unseemly brawl between some crew members and Aboriginals when the fleet made its last (unhistorical) stopover at the New South Wales town of Eden.

Some of those present in Sydney on 26 January 1988 might have felt, along with Geoffrey Blainey, that the arrival of the fleet was 'the most moving event' of the entire commemoration. Few would have agreed with him that the red banner of an American soft-drink company was 'another sign' of the success of 'this most courageous and imaginative of ventures'. He reported the gathering around the harbour as 'the triumph of the silent majority' over the politicians, bureaucrats and the Authority with its 'lickspittle slogan'. He interpreted the First Fleet as an act of homage, but the mood was one of light-hearted revelry.

Jonathan King had a particularly reverential attachment to the past. Previously a writer of impressionistic Australian histories, he turned during the 1980s to minute documentation of the First Fleet. During the voyage he held discussion groups, using the original First Fleet journals, and regularly began his pep-talks with the words 'Two hundred years ago today . . .' As King retraced the path of his own ancestor, he sometimes gave the impression that he had sailed this course once before and could speak on behalf of the original expedition as well as the commemorative one.

He showed little interest in what historians had written about the First Fleet, and seemed curiously unaware of the historical argument (to which Geoffrey Blainey had contributed) over its original purpose. He placed his faith in the original sources and was particularly excited when he discovered a letter in the Public Record Office in London written in 1783 by James Matra, a former midshipman in the Royal Navy, proposing that the British settle Australia. 'I held in my hands', he proclaimed, 'Australia's Magna Carta. Yet who had ever heard of Matra?'

The answer is that every historian who worked on the subject was aware of Matra, and his proposal to the British government was central to every serious discussion of the subject. But this did not stop King from claiming to reveal the document for the first time. Similarly, he used Australia Day in 2003 to lament the neglect of the First Fleet in Australian history lessons and attributed to Governor Phillip a visionary speech that in fact had been invented for the Sesquicentenary in the 1930s. His was a kind of ersatz verisimilitude that served the commemorative impulse.

Conservatives took up King's project as part of their argument against the early directions of the Bicentenary. Ken Baker had set out that argument in the *IPA Review* at the beginning of 1985 when he claimed that the Authority's draft program substituted apology for celebration, and he subsequently orchestrated the campaign to restore a proper reverence for national traditions. The battle for the Bicentenary emerged out of a growing unease among conservatives about the intellectual culture.

This unease was explained in a collection of essays edited by Robert Manne that appeared in 1982 under the title of *The New Conservatism in Australia*. Manne acknowledged that a 'new conservatism' sounded like an oxymoron, but used the term to indicate that the older forms of Anglophile traditionalism represented by Robert Menzies no longer held. Ever since the Vietnam War those values had been cast aside by the opinion formers who had imposed a left-wing orthodoxy.

Here the Australian new conservatives borrowed from their American counterparts, who were known as neo-conservatives. Encouraged by Ronald Reagan's assertion of national strength and resolution after the humiliations of the Carter administration, the neo-conservatives had opened an offensive against liberal progressivism. They blamed the malady on the tertiary-educated professionals whom they saw as constituting a 'new class' of privileged, disaffected parasites.

In applying the neo-conservative theory of the new class to Australia, Manne explained that the rapid growth of universities had provided a home for the student radicals of the 1960s who now dominated the humanities and social sciences. Their students in turn moved into careers in teaching, journalism, broadcasting and public service, 'where the core values of our civilization were defined and shaped and passed onto the young'. Another contributor to the collection was John Carroll, who argued that this generation was infected by 'a paranoid hatred of authority' expressed 'in direct attacks on the society's leading values and institutions'. Rejecting the Puritanism of the old and failing culture, they had created a remissive culture of hedonism, hatred and ideological treason.

Ken Baker carried these ideas to the Institute of Public Affairs. He was a postgraduate student in sociology at La Trobe University. John Carroll, his supervisor, and Rod Kemp, the director of the Victorian branch of the think-tank, had been students at Ormond College in the University of Melbourne during the 1960s when the new class was incubated. Carroll's ideas crystallised in Baker's initial criticism of the Bicentennial program, which he suggested was undermining the legitimacy and authority of Australia's traditions. The Bicentenary presented an opportunity to affirm the values that gave meaning and purpose to the nation, and failure to do so risked 'producing a generation of rootless, purposeless individ-

ualism full of resentments against the society that has disin-
herited them'.

Baker solicited further contributions to the *IPA Review*
that developed these themes. John Carroll claimed that the
Authority's 'denigration of Australia's British links' betrayed a
'self-hatred' among the intellectuals whose rejection of authority had created a collective guilt that they sought to escape
by exorcising the British past. Hugh Morgan, the mining
executive, accused church leaders, journalists and Labor politicians of joining the academics to create a 'guilt industry' that
denigrated the settlement of Australia in order to further their
own careers.

A covey of commentators rose to prominence by spreading
these claims in the popular press. In 1985 Michael Barnard
wrote in the *Age* that the Bicentennial Authority 'has not only
failed to maintain unity but also seems more intent on rewriting history than on celebrating it'. Anthony McAdam
lamented in the Melbourne *Herald* that left-wing radicalism
had captured the Bicentenary: 'The new totems to be worshipped are clearly multiculturalism, republicanism (at least
implicitly), and a patronising "noble savage" mystique of the
Australian Aboriginal which fully caters to white guilt and
black vengeance'. John Howard, as leader of the Opposition,
followed with demands that the Bicentenary should not
'apologise in any way for Australia's European Christian
origin'. He condemned the 'guilt inducing' destruction of
national pride.

Geoffrey Blainey, as always, imparted a novel twist. At the
beginning of 1985 he suggested that 26 January might not be
the most appropriate date for commemoration since it was an
anniversary of the officials and the bureaucrats who first raised
the Union Jack on these shores. A better Australia Day might
be 18 January when the First Fleet reached Botany Bay, or
perhaps 3 January when it first sighted land. Those who found
the commemoration repugnant because of the Aboriginal loss
that followed had 'some justice', but many more lives were

saved by the white enterprise that followed; since 'the Aboriginals, not through their own fault, had sat on rich resources and been unable to use them'. Productivity salved the conscience of those who would now celebrate the founding of white Australia.

Later in the same year, when the Authority unveiled its program, Blainey was far more polemical. The Bicentenary 'was trying to write the British contribution out of Australian history the way the Russians omitted the contribution the Tsars had made to Russian history'. It was subservient to three minority interests: the Aboriginals, the multicultural lobby, and 'a certain form of socialism' that was entrenched in parliament, several newspapers, 'not unknown in the ABC and busy in some classrooms and university departments'. This was the habitat of the new class with a deep sense of grievance, and Blainey noted that it saw 'Australia's history as largely the story of violence, exploitation, repression, racism, sexism, capitalism, colonialism, and a few other "isms". Some of their books on Australian history appear now in thundering prose, delivered from a moral height.'

Thereafter he was a constant critic. Jonathan King relates how Blainey rang him at an awkward moment in the First Fleet Re-enactment project to report that the general manager of the Bicentennial Authority had offered to change the theme from Living Together to Celebration of a Nation if only the professor would stop attacking its work. If such an offer was made it was disingenuous, for the celebratory slogan was adopted despite Blainey's continuation of his campaign, but the story captures the way that critics of the Bicentenary misunderstood its political complexities. The prime minister had put the Authority on a short rein, determined that it should avoid further controversy. Aboriginals, ethnic groups and academics all felt unhappy about their marginal role in the Bicentenary, yet the neo-conservatives were convinced that government was dancing to the tune of special interest groups.

These neo-conservative ideologues, all of them located within the very new class they identified, somehow escaped its strictures. They too were aggrieved, despite their privileges and influence. They also wanted to set the world to rights, and many of them were former radicals who applied the same ideological zeal to the vindication of the existing order. They were unencumbered by guilt or bad faith because they represented the people. The people, whom the adversaries of the new class constantly invoked, carried no markers of difference. They were unaffected by gender, ethnicity, class, age, religion, or any of the other forms of social identity. They were just ordinary people.

'The people' is hardly a sophisticated tool of political analysis. Taken at face value, it seems to embrace everyone, for are we not all people? But the populist movements that have invoked the people over the past 150 years have invariably discriminated. They have demanded that the people be released from the bondage of those who exploit and degrade them. Sometimes they have excluded the financiers, sometimes the Jews, sometimes aliens, sometimes Bolsheviks, sometimes simply the enemies of the people. Conservatives traditionally avoided populist ideology, for they upheld a customary social hierarchy and were suspicious of the levelling implications of popular idolatry. Neo-conservatives brushed aside such cautionary inhibitions. They were as unsettling in their ideological fervour as the radicals they denounced.

Any questioning, any note of dissent, challenged the virtue of the people. One of the principal programs of the Bicentenary was a travelling exhibition with thematic displays of the Australian past, present and future. It included a display that showed Australians 'Living Today' with a giant shopping trolley full of oversize products. Professor Leonie Kramer of the University of Sydney and a leading conservative was a member of the exhibition's reference panel and she objected to this alarming depiction of mass consumerism. When the Authority had appointed the board, it was conscious of the list of 'core values' that Ken Baker had published in the *IPA Review* (Christian traditions, British heritage, alliance with America, the work ethic, the family, private enterprise, and the monarchy were just some of them) and specified that 'Ken Baker's ideas be taken into account in the Exhibition'.

Any sign of conflict was an affront. One of the principal challenges of the Bicentennial Authority was to seek Aboriginal participation in an event they had no reason to celebrate. The Commonwealth government had hoped to reach some new accommodation with the Indigenous people by 1988, for it appreciated that the Bicentenary would direct international attention to their aspirations. Yet a remark by the minister responsible for the Bicentenary that Aboriginal people could not be expected to do handsprings down Martin Place in 1988 only fuelled accusations of guilt, while John Pilger raised a storm of condemnation with his television documentary, *The Secret Country*, which drew attention to their plight.

There was an Aboriginal on the board of the Authority, and an Aboriginal program that funded a large number of projects, but many remained unreconciled. The slogan '200 years of lies' appeared on the Authority's offices in the Rocks, and a protest was arranged for 26 January 1988. It was preceded by alarmist media predictions of violent confrontation, but in fact the March for Freedom, Justice and Hope proved remarkably good-humoured.

Here was a vivid reminder of the pluralism of the people, yet this peaceful demonstration of difference only fed accusations of betrayal. 'Guilt-ridden Canberra egg-heads are trying to make Australians despise their achievements, riches, history', was the verdict of the English conservative, Paul Johnson. Geoffrey Blainey saw the day differently, only to reach a similar conclusion: 'This Australia Day marked the triumph of the people and their quiet sense of national pride over all those politicians and bureaucrats who had earlier done all they could to turn it into a very different day'. Canberra had wanted a day of contrition and had used 'all the propaganda resources of the nation' in 'wagging the finger at the Australian people', but their own patriotism had prevailed.

The effect of the Bicentenary was therefore to open a gulf, in the new conservative mentality, between the people and those who tried to tell the people what to think. Whether the people enjoyed the bread and circuses or treated the Bicentenary with indifference, the intellectuals were at fault. Hence Robert Manne's conclusion that 'When historians look back on the Bicentenary, their most challenging task will be to explain the mood of cultural pessimism which, during this year, took hold of the intellectual class and cast its shadow across our celebrations'.

The historians were meanwhile dealing with their own controversies. Five days before Australia Day, the prime minister had launched *The Penguin Bicentennial History of Australia* on the path that runs alongside Farm Cove, when an Aboriginal protester seized the book and launched it further—into the waters. The book was written by John Molony, professor of history at the Australian National University, who also chaired the taskforce of the Authority that advised on the Bicentennial history program. Molony took as his brief 'to write of the land and its white peopling' and said little about Aboriginal history—other than an apologetic 'sorry mate'—on the grounds that 'I am not one of them' and therefore could not tell their story. However well-intentioned, a history that omitted their story was liable to such a response when it bore the Bicentennial imprint.

Apart from its war history series, the Authority commissioned nearly a score of books. The most expensive was an encyclopedia of *The Australian People*, modelled on a similar

Encyclopedia of American Ethnic Groups produced in 1976 for the American bicentenary. With 300 contributors, this one ran to a million words and cost a million dollars. Its editor, Jim Jupp, adopted the ingenious device of arranging the entries for each ethnic group—there were over a hundred—alphabetically but weighting them to reflect their presence in Australia. Hence the Serbs received more space than the Welsh, but the sub-entries for the English exceeded many of the entries for other nationalities.

James Jupp was an English immigrant of multicultural sympathies and one of his objects, 'to write the English back into the script', provided a riposte to those who claimed multiculturalism slighted Australia's British heritage. The book's launch by the prime minister in September 1988 co-incided with another round in the immigration controversy, so Bob Hawke took the opportunity to declare that the work provided 'the clearest possible evidence of Australia's multi-cultural identity'.

The Authority contributed just $20 000 to another history project and it proved the most contentious. This was a stage production of *Manning Clark's History of Australia—The Musical.* Manning Clark was a ubiquitous figure in the Bicentenary, forever writing or speaking on its meaning—one commen-tator suggested that he served as the national intellectual who articulated the nation to itself—and he had his own exhibit in the travelling exhibition where he announced that 'we are now all citizens in the Kingdom of Nothingness'. Clark's leading article in the Bicentennial edition of *Time Australia* declared that Australians were beginning to take the blinkers off their eyes, 'to face the truth about the past' and see that the coming of the British brought 'three great evils': the violence against the original inhabitants, the violence against the convicts, and the violence done to the land itself.

The musical was an ambitious attempt to dramatise his six-volume history, and did so by making him a character in the

story. Thus the young Manning encounters imperial condescension while playing cricket at Oxford; later he sets out with
Dymphna in their baby Austin car to discover the real Australia and finds Ned Kelly in a hotted-up FJ Holden, Henry
Lawson in the pub and Nellie Melba as a chirpy barmaid.

The musical opened in Melbourne on 16 January. The hot
weather, poor publicity, a limited number of singable tunes
and some uneven performances contributed to its closure after
six weeks. The production attracted venomous criticism,
partly settling old scores against the 'Carlton push', since the
production involved members of the circle associated with the
agitprop theatre of Melbourne's Pram Factory, and this allowed
critics to portray the musical as an anachronistic blend of
radicalism and rough red. Beyond this, it provided an opportunity to pursue the allegation that the new class had turned
the Bicentenary into an exercise in guilt. Melbourne's tabloid
Sun condemned the musical as 'Left-wing cant that spews over
the footlights in the name of history' in 'another whinge by
the revisionist of the Left'. Its evening stablemate, the *Herald*,
put the business commentator, Terry McCrann, to work on
the finances of the production and later had an investigative
journalist suggest that the Labor government used taxpayers'
money to stage it.

Apart from these histories commissioned or supported by
the Authority, there were a number of other works pitched at
the Bicentennial market. The most successful was Robert
Hughes' *The Fatal Shore*, which appeared in 1987 and became
an international best-seller. Here was an epic of Australia's
origins as a convict colony, related with a literary force that
evoked the trauma of the penal system. Writing against the
grain of recent historical research, which had lifted the stigma
from the convicts to incorporate them into the national story
and suggest how they flourished within it, Hughes dwelt on
the horrors of these fatal shores as places of exile, punishment
and death—Australia, on the eve of its Bicentenary, was

revealed as a gulag. Curiously, this dark and sonorous *tour de force* drew greater criticism from the historians than from the guardians of national honour.

A large part of the history profession was engaged on its own effort to reach a popular audience. Ken Inglis, a professor at the Australian National University, had floated the enterprise more than a decade in advance and suggested it provided the opportunity to produce essential reference works as well as new ways of thinking about Australian history. The reference volumes were a historical atlas, a historical dictionary, a guide to sources, a handbook of events and places, and a compendium of historical statistics.

These allowed for collaboration but the organisers were reluctant to attempt a similarly collaborative exercise in narrative history, where one specialist would carry the baton for a short distance before handing it on to the next. Instead they hit upon the idea of assembling teams to take a single year and reconstruct how people lived. The 'slices' would cover the years 1838, 1888 and 1938: to acknowledge prior Aboriginal occupancy, the first volume would run up to 1788, and the fifth would cover the period after 1938. The slice approach was meant to break from the familiar landmarks of narrative history, or what one of its general editors called the 'traditional Australian catechism—convicts, squatters, gold, Land Acts, the Kelly Gang, the Anzacs, the Depression, World War II etc.'.

'Slicing' suspended the usual convention of narrative history that carried the reader towards a predetermined conclusion—in this case the modern Australian nation—by breaking the illusion of an unbroken thread leading from past to present. We would understand these people better, said Inglis, 'by grasping the truth that the future that beckoned or alarmed them was not necessarily our past' but a 'hidden destiny' of probabilities and uncertainties. This was an approach that seemed to sever the links that commemorative history affirmed, and it was perhaps surprising the invigilators of the Bicentenary did not notice its subversive implications.

The working groups of the slice and reference volumes involved hundreds of scholars. Several of them generated regular journals. They received no support from the Bicentennial Authority but relied on research grants and university support. A publishing arrangement encouraged the historians to make extensive use of illustrations, charts, graphs and maps (there were 3000 of them in the full series), placed a premium on clear and accessible prose (the editors created a readability formula), imposed strict deadlines and possibly tempered iconoclastic tendencies. The massacre of Aboriginals at Myall Creek pervaded the 1838 volume, and one commentator suggested it exhibited 'an accumulating and brooding guilt', but publication aroused no great controversy. One reason, perhaps, was that the volumes were so large and handsome. Marketed as heritage items, their design, production values and cost placed them beyond such scrutiny.

Another collaborative project was conceived as an anti-Bicentennial history, explicitly opposed to the celebration of 'the British invasion of 1788'. This was the *People's History of Australia since 1788*, told in four thematic volumes and edited by two young Melbourne historians. It was 'critical not celebratory' and started from 'a recognition that Australian settler society was built on invasion and dispossession'. But the editors repudiated the idea of national guilt just as they rejected the conceit of national pride, for their history told of patterns of inequality that imprisoned the convict shepherd as tightly as it did the Aboriginals whose land he occupied.

The aim of the *People's History* was 'to encourage people to think critically about the imagined community of the Australian nation'. The aim of another project was to Australianise just about every form of knowledge. *Windows onto Worlds* was the report of a committee established by the Authority's educational program to review Australian studies in tertiary education. Its authors were progressive nationalists who refused to surrender patriotism to the conservatives. Taking love of one's country as entailing a concern for its heritage and environment, a pride in its independence and respect for others, they proposed to insert Australian studies into almost every field of study and training, from engineering to hairdressing.

But these and other contributions to the Bicentenary appeared years after the conservatives had set the terms of debate. The initial hopes for reflection, and a measured assessment of achievements and failures had quickly been snuffed out. The Bicentennial horse bolted long before the anniversary year and the historians, who waited, were left behind. At the end of 1988 the *IPA Review* published a special issue on 'The Rewriting of Australian History'. Ken Baker offered the epigraph 'He who controls the past, controls the future' for his rapid catalogue of the failures of their publications. These historians who divided and demoralised the people sometimes claimed to speak on their behalf but their values 'could not be more alien to the values of ordinary Australians'. Introducing a new epithet, he accused them of being elitist.

John Hirst of La Trobe University, in a hostile review of the *People's History*, also coined a new charge. Earlier historians, of both the left and the right, had acknowledged that Australians had striven for improvement, but these new radicals put black spots on their picture of the past and then proceeded to fill the whole canvas with it. He called this 'The Blackening of Our Past'. The Bicentenary had cast historians as part the new class, and accused them of spreading guilt. Geoffrey Blainey would improve on Hirst's metaphor to press home the intellectual offensive.

CHAPTER 7

'RELAXED AND COMFORTABLE'

My only discussion with John Howard occurred ten years ago, in the autumn of 1993. I was then a member of the Council of the National Library, which published the war diaries of Sir Robert Menzies. They were to be launched by Menzies' daughter and invitations to the launch had gone to former colleagues, members of the public service, officers of the Liberal Party and its parliamentary representatives past and present. A good many were present but just one serving parliamentarian bothered to attend.

John Howard was in a sombre mood. Just a few weeks earlier, the Coalition had lost a federal election it should have won. Worse, it had lost to Paul Keating, a dark and baleful enemy. Howard carried little responsibility for the defeat, since he had been replaced as Liberal leader four years earlier, but he was entitled to think that he would not have wasted the lead the Coalition enjoyed going into the campaign and he might well have wondered if he would ever be back in office—Labor had governed for a decade and he was approaching fifty-four years of age.

Another member of the Library Council, Rodney Cavalier, was a former Labor minister from New South Wales, familiar with Howard, and he could not resist asking him, 'Where are all the others?' Howard responded with frank comments about the lack of respect for tradition among his absent colleagues and especially the Liberal leader, John Hewson. The launch concluded and we drifted up to the Lobby restaurant for a meal, where Howard joined us over coffee. When I was introduced as a professor of history at the University of Melbourne, he bridled and remarked that I was one of those who had driven Geoffrey Blainey out of office. I challenged him to justify that claim, and set out the circumstances of Blainey's return to the department after a second term as dean. Howard conceded he had not been aware of those circumstances.

Our conversation then turned to history. He told me of his respect for our British heritage and reminded me of his name, John Winston Howard. Many Australian boys born after 1940 were named after Winston Churchill, just as those born twenty years earlier (including two prominent left-wing historians, Robin Allenby Gollan and Ian Alexander Hamilton Turner) were named after British military commanders, but I remarked that it was unusual to find someone christened Winston who was born in mid-1939. At that time Churchill was on the Opposition benches, unheeded in his warnings of the danger of appeasing Hitler. Churchill's warnings were soon realised and he was recalled to lead his country in its fight for survival. It did not occur to me that Howard would also return from the political wilderness.

How could it? By 1993 the Liberal Party was at the lowest ebb in its fifty-year history. In the 1940s Menzies had furnished it with a program and a philosophy of broad national appeal that made it the natural party of government for the next quarter-century. Such was its authority that the Coalition survived six years of inept leadership after Menzies retired in

1966. Whitlam captured the middle ground in 1972 but soon estranged it, so that Fraser restored the Coalition to office at the end of 1975. But his defeat in 1983 left the Liberals in disarray. The Labor government bound the unions into an Accord, seized the initiative with a modernising program of economic reform, softened its social effects with renovated welfare programs, and through Bob Hawke projected an emotional, sometimes testy, message of inclusiveness and national affirmation.

Howard gained the Liberal leadership in 1985, only to be brought down by internal dissension. He was the first leader to embrace the doctrines of the New Right that Margaret Thatcher and Ronald Reagan were practising, a mixture of economic radicalism and moral conservatism, stern self-reliance and patriotic duty. Economic radicalism was taking root in business think-tanks such as the Institute for Public Affairs and called for a dismantling of the barriers to the operation of the market; but Labor had already floated the dollar, reduced financial controls, cut tariffs and would soon embark on privatisation of public enterprises. Moral conservatism found a champion in the Lutheran premier of Queensland, Joh Bjelke-Petersen, and a quixotic campaign to install him as prime minister wrecked Howard's election campaign in 1987. (Howard was not helped when Geoffrey Blainey hailed the self-knighted Sir Joh as 'one of the quiet giants in our political history'.)

To revive his leadership, in the Bicentennial year Howard released a comprehensive statement of *Future Directions* that amalgamated the economic and social elements of a new conservatism. The Liberals would remove government control over people's lives, restore individual freedom, strengthen the family, give greater personal incentive and rebuild 'One Australia'. The cover of the policy statement, showing an ideal white couple with two children outside an ideal home with a white picket fence, presented Keating with ample opportunity to suggest that Howard would lead Australia backwards to an insular, inefficient, irretrievable past.

Future Directions also fought the History Wars. It deprecated the 'professional purveyors of guilt' who taught Australians 'to be ashamed of their past'. 'One Australia' was ambiguous about multiculturalism and Geoffrey Blainey had recently renewed the allegation that the policy was turning Australia into 'a cluster of tribes' who threatened its very survival. Howard was pressed for his views and asked if *Future Directions* would mean a reduction of Asian immigration. 'It could', he replied, and later on the same day said that it would be appropriate to slow the influx of Asian immigrants to preserve social cohesion.

Nick Greiner and Jeff Kennett, Liberal premiers of the two states with the largest immigrant populations, both rejected Howard's statement. So did Malcolm Fraser, while Howard's shadow minister for finance, John Stone, made matters worse when he declared 'Asian immigration has to be slowed. It's no use dancing round the bushes.' Hawke exploited the division by introducing a parliamentary motion to affirm the non-discriminatory principle and four senior Liberals crossed the floor to support it.

Howard never recovered from this debacle and lost the leadership in the following year. He believed, sincerely, that he had been misrepresented: 'I'm being kicked from one end of the country for being a bigot or racist', he said the day after his blunder. He was not a racist, though he was prepared to use racial prejudice for political advantage, and in this instance he had been lured beyond the carefully formulated signals given in *Future Directions* by a weakness for improvisation.

The effect was to harden his antagonism to multicultural-ism, so that several months later he would suggest that 'in effect' the policy made it 'impossible to have a common Australian culture' and 'I think that is hopeless'. It also strengthened his predisposition to feel victimised. He thought of himself, like Blainey, as the defender of old Australia. He presented himself as the victim of an intolerant leftist orthodoxy.

Howard was challenged and defeated by Andrew Peacock, who lost the 1990 election and gave way to John Hewson, a merchant banker. Hewson staked his all on *Fightback!*, a program of further economic reform that was so dry as to make the eyes water. The centrepiece was a new tax system, but it promised a further round of blood, toil, tears and sweat to a nation that longed for respite. Most of all, it offered no hint of the Australia that would emerge from further upheaval.

Hewson gave the impression that people did nothing other than buy, sell and calculate profit margins; that all forms of human interaction could be expressed as a utility calculus. In place of society, with its lived reality of friends and neighbours, and its further calls of empathy and conscience, *Fightback!* proposed a market within which all individuals would provide for their own needs. As Keating, the new Labor leader, applied the blowtorch, Hewson blinked and was gone. Alexander Downer lasted long enough to demonstrate he was no leader and then, their options exhausted, the Liberals turned in 1995 once more to Howard.

For the six years from 1989 to 1995, then, the Liberals surrendered the ground that Menzies had made their own— the articulation of values that bound people together and gave purpose to their lives. Economic rationalism allowed no place for tradition, ignored the stories that defined the nation. During this interregnum, economics vied with history as an alternative source of understanding but failed miserably to provide the reassurance the electors craved. Keating, the former treasurer who entered the Lodge in 1991, set up shop in history and profited accordingly.

He was assisted by Don Watson, his speechwriter and a historian of rare eloquence. Most political speechwriters traffic in history, for the past provides reference points for a policy statement, defines its place in the life of the nation that makes the occasion momentous, and offers words and phrases that give an address persuasive force. Some speechwriters, like Don Watson and Gerard Henderson (who worked closely with Howard during his first term as Opposition leader), are trained historians; and some, like Graham Freudenberg (who performed the function for Gough Whitlam), simply live and breathe it.

Watson began working for Keating at the beginning of 1992, just a few weeks after Keating overthrew Hawke. He had been one of the writers of *Manning Clark's History of Australia—the Musical*, and was close to Clark, who had died in the previous year. Clark's influence was apparent in a skirmish that followed a royal visit to Australia in February 1992, when Keating had the temerity to guide the Queen with his arm. Hewson tried to use the press uproar in Fleet Street against 'the Lizard of Oz', and Keating responded with a broadside against the Liberals for their lack of national pride and failure to learn from history. The British had left Australia to defend itself against the Japanese advance in 1942, he said, yet these local Tories remained British to their bootstraps.

This and later statements pursued the claim that Labor had always championed the national interest while the conservatives still clung to an outmoded imperial past, or—to use the metaphor that Clark took from Henry Lawson's 'Song of the Republic'—that he nurtured the Young Tree Green and his opponents served the Old Dead Tree of British philistinism. Keating's rejection of the dead British past served his push for an Australian republic, while the Liberals' monarchism illustrated their role as 'good little horatios' who 'held the bridge against national progress'.

It was Robert Menzies who had declared himself to be British to his bootstraps, and much of Keating's assault was directed at that Liberal heyday when the country had missed its opportunities, timorously shielding itself from a changing post-war order behind the tariff wall and the White Australia Policy. During the argument arising from the royal visit, the prime minister suggested that Howard and Hewson should be placed in the Old Parliament House museum, along with those other icons of the 1950s, the toaster, lawnmower, television and 'a pair of heavily protected slippers'. As for himself, he had acquired self-respect and regard for Australia, and learned not to cringe to Britain. 'Even as it walked out on you and joined the Common Market', he concluded with a final thrust at the Menzies era, 'you were still looking for your MBEs and your knighthoods and all the rest of the regalia that goes with it'.

This version of history transferred the evils of colonialism to the imperial master. It was the British who had claimed possession of Australia and disregarded the rights of its original inhabitants, who worked the land with convict labour and planted it with exotic species of flora and fauna regardless of the damage to the native environment. It was the British again who encouraged the deferential attitudes that still persisted in the conservative ranks.

Only the colour-blind could accuse Paul Keating of a gloomy view of Australian history. His Big Picture employed bright colours of suffering and endurance, emancipation and triumph. It painted a story of redemption, not guilt, because it attributed the evils to them, not us. To his refusal of guilt there was a conspicuous exception: 'We took the traditional lands and smashed the original way of life. We brought the diseases. The alcohol. We committed the murders. We took the children from their mothers. We practised discrimination and exclusion. It was our ignorance and our prejudice.'

When Keating delivered this speech at Redfern Park in December 1992, the Aboriginal audience was barely attentive. An undercurrent of conversation is audible in the recording. As he reached this passage, a hush fell as if the listeners could scarcely believe their ears, and when he finished the confession they burst into applause. Here was a frank acknowledgement of the past, for Keating insisted that 'there is nothing to fear or to lose in the recognition of historical truth'.

The speech was delivered six months after the High Court handed down its decision in a case that had begun a decade earlier, when Eddie Mabo and other Torres Strait Islanders sought recognition of native title to their islands and the surrounding waters. The court decided that the application of the doctrine of *terra nullius* by the British Crown when it assumed sovereignty over these islands 'depended on a discriminatory denigration of indigenous inhabitants' and did not extinguish their native title. Two of the judges went further and referred to 'a national legacy of unutterable shame'. The judges emphasised that they were not attributing moral guilt, but rather basing their judgement on the 'full facts' of Aboriginal dispossession; among the sources they used was the research of the historian Henry Reynolds.

The Mabo decision aroused strong fears within the mining and pastoral industries. It provoked alarmist talk of Aboriginal claimants taking over people's homes, and outrage that the High Court should tamper with the doctrine of *terra nullius* on which the traditional understanding of Australian history and nationhood rested. Liberal and National Party parliamentarians joined state premiers in warning of the damaging economic effects of judicial activism, but Hewson was illequipped to tap the deep emotional resonances of the Mabo case. He had little interest in history and was in any case preoccupied with fighting the imminent 1993 election with the economic reform program of *Fightback!*. He treated Keating's uses of history as a distraction, even a sign of weakness, and kept to his economic script.

The History Warriors therefore lacked a general. They resisted Keating's sallies and they contested what they saw as the High Court's attack on the nation's legal and moral legitimacy, but in the absence of a coherent strategy they were fighting a disjointed rearguard action. Before the 1993 election Hugh Morgan criticised the Opposition's apparent acceptance of Mabo, and he redoubled his criticism after it. Geoffrey Blainey told the Western Australian Chamber of Mines that the Mabo issue was twenty times more significant for Australian sovereignty than the republican issue.

For others the republic was vital. The Monash historian, Bruce Knox, condemned Keating's falsification of history at the inaugural conference of the monarchist Samuel Griffith Society in 1992. Griffith, the first chief justice of the High Court, was just one of the neglected figures of the past whose names were now attached to conservative causes.

Another was H. R. Nicholls, the editor of the Hobart *Mercury*, who was charged with contempt in 1911 for calling the president of the Arbitration Court a 'political judge'. Businessmen, lawyers and New Right politicians formed an association in 1986 to wage war on industrial arbitration, and named it the H. R. Nicholls Society for his defiance of the 'industrial relations club'. Their history was poor: when Griffith dismissed the charge of contempt, he noted that Nicholls had already apologised for his slur. The critics of arbitration pressed this dubious martyr into service, nevertheless, to dignify their assault on a national institution.

Most conservatives are highly selective in their attachment to the past. Many of the notables who clung to the trappings of the British Crown were setting at naught a device that had been invented by the new nation to affirm its commitment to a fair go. They lamented the disappearance of an older Australia while they dismantled its foundations. They wanted to remake the nation and they denounced the prime minister for breaking with the past.

Writing in the *IPA Review*, Patrick Morgan observed that 'People feel that Old Australia is going down the drain'. The country needed unifying symbols but Mabo and the republic divided them. Keating deployed cultural nationalism as a political weapon with his anti-British speeches on Gallipoli, Kokoda and Churchill's diversion of troops from the defence of Australia, but he did so at the expense of national cohesion. Morgan likened Keating to a surgeon making incisions where there was no wound.

Gerard Henderson, who had left Howard's office to establish the Sydney Institute, widened the charge. 'Australians are variously portrayed as racist, sexist, materialist and with very little culture. This is alienated history at its worst.' Henderson also returned the blame to the history profession, since 'so much of our history is taught by the alienated and discontented'. It was at this low-point in the fortunes of Australian conservatism that Henderson issued his rallying cry: 'It is time to junk guilt and alienation. Down with the falsification of Australian history.'

The lesson of the 1993 election seemed clear. The electorate was weary of constant upheaval, sceptical of economic rationalism, craving respite from the dictates of the market. Many were uncomfortable with Keating's vituperative style but at least he spoke to their doubts and uncertainties with a Big Picture of Australia and its place in the world. That Big Picture was far from impregnable. Many felt uncomfortable with its breadth and associated its colourful hyperbole with the antique clocks and Zegna suits of its creator. Many longed for a more homely, less challenging national story. The task of the conservatives was to provide it.

Shortly after the 1993 election Geoffrey Blainey delivered the John Latham Memorial Lecture, which again commemorated a former conservative leader. Blainey's purpose was to draw up a balance sheet of 'our history', to determine 'what has been good and what has been bad in the history of Australia' and suggest an appropriate reckoning. His generation had been raised on what he called 'the Three Cheers view of history', a patriotic version that celebrated Australian history as a resounding success. Since then a rival version had arisen which he now called 'the Black Armband view'. It had been apparent in the Bicentenary, and his 'friend and undergraduate teacher, Manning Clark, who was almost the official historian in 1988', had done much to propagate the gloomy view of Australia with his Old Testament phrases. Multiculturalists had spread the message that until they arrived much of Australian history was a disgrace.

Blainey's balance sheet had four entries. The first was economic performance and here the great achievement was Australian production of food, fibres and minerals for world market, which yielded a remarkably high standard of living. The second was ecology: the economic success had inflicted considerable damage on the natural environment. The third was democracy: Australia had a remarkable record of democratic achievement, though intellectual circles disregarded it when they introduced affirmative action and the High Court threatened it by usurping the legislature in its Mabo decision. 'We became a rights-mad society in the 1970s and 1980s' and this threatened democracy.

Finally, there was the treatment of Aboriginals, which many Australians saw as 'the blot on Australian history'. Blainey was more tentative. His view was that the contempt of the colonists for Aboriginal culture, the removal of their freedoms, the breaking of their links with the land and the killing of them—he thought the death toll might have reached 20 000 —was 'lamentable'. On the other hand, he saw the supplanting of the earlier society by the new one as inevitable. No treaty was possible because the Aboriginals had no organisation to make one. Their way of life supported a high standard of living but it was fragmented, violent and wasteful of resources. The recent recognition of their native title 'almost tries to restore this archaic and untenable way of life'. Furthermore, the vilification of Aboriginals by nineteenth-century Europeans was now 'almost matched by the vilification of those same Europeans at the hand of present day moralists'.

In summary, Blainey saw some episodes in the past that were regrettable, some flaws and failures, but concluded that Australia 'stands out as one of the world's success stories'. He found it 'ironical' that many of the nation's political and intellectual leaders were so eager to denounce earlier generations and discount their hard-won success.

The address exhibited many of Blainey's characteristic devices. It employed the qualifying phrases, 'some', 'perhaps', 'in part', 'at times', 'to some extent', and emphasised that he was offering a personal view. It juxtaposed just two alternatives, the good and the bad, as debits and credits in a balance sheet. Blainey suggested that the Black Armband view might represent 'the swing of a pendulum from a view that had been too favourable, too self-congratulatory' to an opposite extreme that 'is even more unreal and decidedly jaundiced'. He placed himself, as he does so often, somewhere in the middle, between the extremes.

The speech, however, made strong criticism of the Labor government and the intelligentsia associated with it. Blainey noted at the outset that the issues he treated 'are central in Australian politics'. Throughout his address he chipped away at the record of the Hawke and Keating governments. It had interfered with the Bicentenary, its economic record was poor (this was a persistent theme of his commentary), and it had eroded democracy. Similarly, his adverse reference to Manning Clark was a novel element, for while the two old friends held sharply different views neither had joined in condemnation of the other during Clark's lifetime.

Much of the effect of Blainey's criticism was gained by its oblique nature. In contrast to Patrick Morgan, Gerard Henderson and other polemicists, he was not responding directly to Keating's version of Australian history; nor was he impugning Clark's integrity. Rather, he was incorporating their positions into a larger framework of his own to suggest they were partial and unbalanced.

He also relied heavily on a determinist view of history. The largest debit on his balance sheet was the destruction of Aboriginal society, but it was inescapable. 'In 1788 the world was becoming one world' and 'Aboriginal Australia was a world almost as remote, as different as outer space' and could not survive the impact of the colonisers. How should we respond to this fatal impact? Blainey proffered two alternatives, 'deep shame or wide regret', and his preference for the latter was determined by his conviction of its inevitability. The outcome was final and absolute: after their initial subjugation, Aboriginal people disappear from Blainey's historical consideration until they reappear in the late twentieth century as a discordant interest group claiming special rights.

Historical determinism is a harsh doctrine. The poet W. H. Auden was under its spell when he wrote that 'History to the defeated/May say Alas but cannot help or pardon'; but it was this very fatalism of Blainey's historical accountancy that troubled many. How can the benefits of one group be totted up and discounted against the losses of another, asked the historian Graeme Davison? 'We cannot put tears in one pan of the balance and laughter in the other.'

Blainey's most striking metaphor was the Black Armband. It had been prefigured by earlier commentators, such as John Hirst who in 1988 rejected 'the blackening of our past', and it was implicit in the earlier theme of guilt, but Blainey had once again coined a phrase that gained universal currency. Some thought it referred to skin colour—hence the rejoinder that he belonged to the 'white blindfold' school of history—and condemned its insensitivity.

Furthermore, the Black Armband had strong associations with Aboriginal protest and mourning. The members of the Aboriginal Progressive Association had worn them when they met in Sydney on Australia Day 1938 to remember the deaths that had followed the arrival of the Europeans. Black armbands were worn again in 1970 on the two hundredth anniversary of Cook's landing at Botany Bay, and again during the Aboriginal protest march in 1988. This new usage appropriated their symbol.

Blainey explained afterwards that he had at the back of his mind the custom of Australian Rules football teams to wear a black armband when a club worthy has died. But that analogy is surely strained. The football players who wear a black armband exhibit no signs of guilt or rancour: on the contrary, they play with pride and determination. The metaphor seems as unlikely as the immigration scoreboard and its secret room.

Be that as it may, it was taken up. Politics relies on stock phrases, for political debate is conducted in the staccato of the mass media and a few words have to conjure up a wealth of meaning. Politicians, moreover, do not have the luxury of digression: they have to be on message, and drive home the message by constant repetition. Blainey has recalled that his Latham lecture aroused interest, but no strong reactions until John Howard used the phrase 'Black Armband history' in a speech three years later and it then 'took off like a rocket'.

That understates the immediate impact of his intervention, which recast the History Wars in terms far more favourable to the conservatives, and it ignores Howard's adoption of the phrase just a few weeks after Blainey minted it. While still a shadow minister, he attached the Black Armband to 'Paul Keating's convoluted and usually erroneous excursions into Australia's past'. But the fiercest argument over the Black Armband broke when Howard gave it his prime ministerial imprimatur.

Several months after Blainey gave the Latham lecture, John Howard delivered an address to the Samuel Griffith Society. 'The Prime Minister', he said, 'is engaged in a major exercise of re-writing Australian history'. He was principally concerned with Keating's denigration of his own party and what he would call the Liberal/conservative contribution to Australian history. Hence, in a subsequent address to the Sydney Institute, he warned that 'very few Liberals understand just how committed Paul Keating and many in the Labor Party are to the quite ruthless use of history'. They used it as a political weapon 'to marginalise the Liberal/conservative side of Australian politics'.

In these and other statements Howard was reclaiming the ground that Hewson had surrendered. He was not alone in

this, for other Liberals were reviving the symbols and traditions of their party. They sought a broader, more moderate
image. Howard could see that the narrow economic program
of *Fightback!* was not enough, but he remained a devotee of
the market and concentrated instead on rehabilitating the
Menzies era to affirm the capacity of the Liberals to act in the
national interest. No-one did this better than he and he won
back the leadership at the beginning of 1995.

Could he take the next step? It was obvious that Keating
would portray him as yesterday's man and rake up the immigration controversy that had brought him undone in 1988.
Labor's attempt to do so provoked a lengthy historical debate
as Howard claimed that it was the Holt government that had
ended the White Australia Policy in 1966, while Labor ministers insisted the achievement belonged to Gough Whitlam
and Al Grassby. The debate ended inconclusively and represented a tactical victory for the Coalition, as it had negated
Labor's advantage.

Howard had learned from his earlier discomfiture back in
1988 and was assisted by a new speechwriter, Christopher
Pearson, as he avoided entanglement in the issues that had
tripped him up in the past: immigration, multiculturalism,
Aboriginal affairs and the republic. He worked on the theme
of inclusiveness. The Coalition would govern 'For All Of Us',
in contrast to 'the noisy, self-interested clamour of powerful
vested interests with scant regard for the national interest'. He
made few commitments, for he was determined to present as
small a target as possible. Whenever Keating tried to draw him
into a clinch, he countered with a charge of political correctness and broke free.

The tyranny of political correctness was a popular topic in the
lead-up to the 1996 election. The weekend magazine of the
Australian had carried an article on it in the previous year,
entitled 'Careful, Someone Might Hear You'. It presented

sixteen martyrs, among them Geoffrey Blainey, Christopher Pearson and the irrepressible president of the Victorian branch of the RSL, Bruce Ruxton. The talk-back hosts John Laws and Alan Jones warned against the virus, as did leading conservatives such as John Stone and Hugh Morgan. A content analysis of three leading Australian papers revealed that political correctness crept into the political vocabulary in the early 1990s and reached peak usage in 1996.

It came from the United States as a new term of abuse for the 'academic thought-police' of the new class. The neo-conservatives turned their attention to the universities during the Reagan era. They alleged that the campuses were dominated by former sixties radicals who taught their students that western civilisation was irredeemably racist, patriarchal, homophobic and exploitative. In a series of books funded by right-wing foundations—Allan Bloom's *The Closing of the American Mind* (1987), Roger Kimball's *Tenured Radicals* (1990) and Dinesh D'Souza's *Illiberal Education* (1991)—this charge of political correctness was expounded. The tenured radicals imposed a tyranny of political correctness that replaced merit with affirmative action, enforced restrictive speech codes, victimised dissident colleagues, rooted out all elements of the Western Canon, denied truth and beauty, and poisoned young minds with obscure and nihilistic theory.

The *Australian* newspaper introduced political correctness to this country in 1991 with a series of syndicated articles. It had an exotic feel, for there was already a local colloquialism. The Australian left had previously used the phrase 'ideologically sound', but it carried ironical overtones—if you said that someone was 'ideologically sound', you implied that he or she was excessively zealous. Political correctness allowed no such hints of idiosyncrasy. When Robert Manne expounded the term in *Quadrant*, he suggested that it indicated membership of an 'intellectual pack' marked by smugness, severity, intolerance, even 'self-totalitarianism'. Among its local manifestations he noted the refusal to allow discussion of the genetic component of intelligence, the effects of day-care on babies and the ethnic composition of the migrant intake.

Political correctness shifted the terms of the History Wars. Previously it had been conducted in the language of guilt. John Carroll had accused the new class of projecting its own guilt onto society, and summoning ordinary Australians to repent for the circumstances of every group it provided with an oppressed historical identity. Writing in *Quadrant* in 1988, the British political philosopher Kenneth Minogue created the figure of 'the one-legged Black Lesbian' to ridicule this grievance industry. He wanted to liberate conservatives from the burden of guilt. The new allegation of political correctness turned the issue into one of freedom of thought and expression.

The Coalition victory in 1996 brought no relaxation of the protests against the tyranny of political correctness. The columnist Les Carlyon called the politically correct 'a boring lot who murder the language and pretend to be liberal'. P. P. McGuinness claimed that the 'PC movement' suppressed serious discussion.

Relief was at hand. The new prime minister put paid to the injury of gender-inclusive language when he reimposed the term 'chairman' on those who sat in the chair of government bodies. He also reduced the authority of the Office for the Status of Women, and for good measure scrapped the Bureau on Immigration, Multiculturalism and Population Studies as well as the Office of Multicultural Affairs in his own department. James Jupp had contracts with these two agencies to prepare a second edition of his reference work on *The Australian People*. The contracts were cancelled.

With such gestures the new government established the new regime. It would put an end to political correctness because government had no business telling people what they should think. It would rein in the affirmative action agencies that told people how they should conduct their affairs, and it would curb the interest groups that battened on them. Learning from the previous election that the electorate desired security, Howard had undertaken to make the Australian people feel 'relaxed and comfortable'. Once in office, he quickly claimed to have lifted the pall of censorship that had hung over them.

But these early changes also changed the valency of political correctness. It was one thing to allow use of the term 'chairman', another to enforce it. Howard gave political correctness a strident, embattled edge by using it to justify some of his most contentious changes. When early moves against the Aboriginal and Torres Strait Islander Commission brought protest, he replied that he would not be intimidated by notions of political correctness. These and other statements had a querulous tone, aggravated by his wrinkled brow and thin voice. Howard was still growing into his new office, and still wavered between affirmation and recrimination.

The uncertainty was apparent in major speeches he delivered during 1996. The Sir Thomas Playford Memorial Lecture, presented in Adelaide on 5 July 1996, gave him an opportunity to praise the achievement of that Liberal patriarch but the comparison between then and now was disturbing. The prime minister noted uncertainties of employment, rising levels of family breakdown, excessive influence of special interests, the declining sense of community and weakened confidence in public institutions. He signalled his intentions to reduce government and public expenditure, free the labour market, and restore choice and individual responsibility. 'We are not a government beholden to political correctness', he declared, but one committed to 'broad community values' and 'practical outcomes'; not a government of economic rationalism but of economic common sense; 'not a government of ideology' but of 'ideas and ideals'.

The speech was most notable for its prosecution of the History Wars. This was the occasion on which Howard declared that 'One of the more insidious developments in Australian political life over the past decade or so has been the attempt to rewrite Australian history in the service of a partisan political cause'. It was insidious because it was partial and divisive. It sought to 'stifle voices of dissent' with 'abuse and vitriol' and 'to demean, pillory and tear down many great people of Australia's past who had no opportunity to answer back', especially Sir Robert Menzies.

Howard was still fighting the battles of the last few years. He prosecuted them in parliament and on talk-back radio. 'I profoundly reject the black armband view of Australian history', he told the House in October. To teach children 'that we're part of a sort of racist and bigoted history', he told John Laws, 'is something that Australians reject'.

It was perhaps inevitable that Howard would return to the same theme when he gave the Sir Robert Menzies Lecture on 'The Liberal Tradition' later in the year. Paul Keating had made a 'sustained, personalised and vindictive attack assault on the Menzies legacy' as part of his attempt to rewrite history. 'It failed because it aimed to establish a form of historical correctness as a particular offshoot of political correctness.' Howard went on to vindicate Menzies as a prescient, patriotic and practical leader, and made a veiled attack on Manning Clark for 'the historical portrayal of Labor as the "enlargers" of Australian life and the political opponents of Labor as mere "straighteners"'. More broadly, he rejected what he called the 'black armband view' that 'most Australian history since 1788 has been little more than a disgraceful story of imperialism, exploitation, racism, sexism and other forms of discrimination'.

It is evident in these speeches that political correctness had taken on meanings absent from its American usage. There it applied to educational practices, here it extended to public policy. When Howard used it as the antonym for practical outcomes on social issues, for example, it signified Aboriginal self-determination. The primary Australian usage retained strong historical overtones, so that Howard's Menzies lecture joined political correctness to historical correctness. He invoked the Black Armband view of history to encompass both Keating's partisan uses of history and the disgraceful story told by the historians.

Howard's response employs two arguments. The first is to allow that there are 'black marks upon our history' but that they are outweighed by the achievements. Like Blainey, he does not try to defend the Three Cheers school (in both of his lectures Howard called this the view through 'rose-tinted glasses'), and he allows some of the same faults: the mistreatment of Aboriginals, environmental damage and one of his own, sectarianism. But his balance sheet of Australian history remains 'one of heroic achievement'.

Howard's second argument is to suggest that whatever blemishes there might be in the historical record, they are not the responsibility of the present generation. The Black Armband historians, he alleged, read history backwards, imposing their own moral values on the past rather than understanding it in its own terms. This was an argument the government employed in its response to a report on the Stolen Generations of Aboriginal children in 1997. The government would not apologise because that 'could imply that present generations are in some way responsible and accountable for the actions of earlier generations, actions that were sanctioned by the laws of the time, and that were believed to be in the best interests of the children concerned'.

Howard took the same stand when he addressed the Australian Reconciliation Convention in the same year. He expressed his personal sorrow for what had happened in the past, only to insist that Australia was now 'one of the fairest, most egalitarian and tolerant societies in the world'. Some of the delegates to the convention were affronted by this uncompromising speech and stood to turn their backs on the prime minister, but their action only strengthened his insistence on practical measures rather than 'symbolic gestures'.

The prime minister's two arguments are difficult to reconcile. The first of them suggests that the nation's history is of vital importance; the second that we shouldn't hold ourselves responsible for it. The first is an affirmative view, the second defensive. Some commentators have observed that Howard is remarkably selective in his denial of responsibility for historic wrongs since he insists that some past events, Gallipoli for example, must be kept alive to command our respect.

My own view is that the first argument is particularly unpersuasive. In contrast to Blainey's evaluation of the costs and benefits of 200 years of history, Howard simply ticks off the items in his national ledger. His positive balance is reached by assertion rather than audit: it allows no complexity, gives no suggestion of familiarity with alternative views of Australian history. He cares about history, for he has the ancestral attachment of a conservative traditionalist, but his historical knowledge is thin and his attempts to articulate it—as in the speech he delivered in Melbourne's Exhibition Building in 2001 for the commemoration of the opening of the first Commonwealth parliament—are unconvincing.

Six months after he took office in 1996, Howard welcomed 'the fact that people can now talk about certain things without living in fear of being branded as a bigot or a racist'. This possibility was tested by Pauline Hanson, the Independent member for Oxley, who had recently delivered her maiden speech. Hanson stood in 1996 as an Independent after losing Liberal endorsement when she alleged that Aboriginals received privileged treatment, and her claim to be a martyr to political correctness helped her to win election. The maiden speech, offering a fish and chip shop owner's condemnation of Asian immigration, multiculturalism, assistance to Aboriginals and the 'reverse racism' of political correctness, laid the foundations for a new populist political movement.

It attracted some alarming followers. In 1997 a group of supporters produced a manifesto for her One Nation Party, *Pauline Hanson: The Truth*. Among its lurid warnings of the degenerate intelligentsia, it paid particular attention to the historians. Manning Clark was said to have been 'in bed with the radical feminists (God help him)' and he 'contributed to the situation where Australian history has become Australian anti-history, a historical revisionism of feminism, Asianism, multiculturalism and Aboriginalism'.

Having been caught out once by Hanson, Howard was not going to censure her again. He told Alan Jones after the maiden speech that 'I certainly believe in her right to say what she said. I thought some of the things she said were an accurate reflection of how people feel.' Initially he saw Hansonism as a legacy of Labor that catalysed discontent with Keating's Big Picture and helped drive a wedge between Labor's urban elite and his own battlers, thereby attracting working-class voters away from the ALP.

He was not alone in this tactic. Chris Mitchell, the editor of the *Courier-Mail*, described Hansonism as 'the bastard child of Paul Keating and Don Watson'. He added the child had been 'finally adopted by John Howard'. It was only when Hanson's mixture of prejudice and criticism of economic liberalism began to draw voters from the Coalition that Howard appreciated the threat she posed to his own side, and the National Party's decision in 1998 to give preferences to the One Nation Party in Queensland created serious political damage.

There was further fallout from Howard's attack on historical correctness. Historians contested Blainey's depiction of a Black Armband orthodoxy, but with limited effect because they did so in academic forums. If the national media noted these protests, they only confirmed the suspicion that intellectuals did indeed wear Black Armbands. This was an argument over history as a political resource and it had limited use for history as a discipline.

Blainey commended Howard's Robert Menzies lecture as an attempt to 'restore sanity' and extended his original criticism. The Black Armband view of history, he now charged, 'while pretending to be anti-racist, is intent on permanently dividing Australia on the basis of race'. It had infected the High Court, where judges pontificated 'in emotive terms on the basis of near ignorance'. There had been earlier swings in the interpretation of the past but this one had 'run wild'.

The atmosphere was strident and unforgiving, the passions so violent that they began to shake the conservative camp. Robert Manne, the editor of *Quadrant*, found himself unable to rejoice in the overthrow of historical correctness. He and several of his colleagues were troubled by the prejudices that Howard had released. The prime minister's reckless extenuation of Pauline Hanson's prejudices disturbed them. His seeming inability to grasp the moral gravity of Indigenous issues alarmed them. Paul Keating had declared in his Redfern Park speech that white Australians had taken the land, introduced the diseases, committed the murders, taken the children. After Manne resigned its editorship in 1997, *Quadrant* would contest every one of those claims.

CHAPTER 8

FRONTIER CONFLICT

Aboriginal issues did not create deep divisions in Australian politics until the 1980s. The principal parties all endorsed the discriminatory practices that prevailed for most of the twentieth century and all embraced assimilationist policies after the Second World War. The 1967 referendum, giving the Commonwealth legislative power for Aboriginal Australians, had bipartisan support, and in 1976 Malcolm Fraser completed land rights legislation that Gough Whitlam had begun.

Insofar as Aboriginal activism impinged on Australian politics, it was through association with the left. The Communist Party championed the Aboriginal cause from the 1930s; left-wing unions gave support to the land rights movement from the 1940s, and student radicals joined with Aboriginal activists on the Freedom Ride through rural New South Wales in 1965. Such associations aroused conservative mistrust, though the stark patterns of disadvantage and exclusion tugged at the conscience of humanitarians in the Liberal Party. Hence its support for the abolition of overt discrimination and, later, acceptance of remedial measures.

From the 1980s this broad consensus began to break down. The determination of the new Labor government to extend land rights met resistance from several states. Labor's desire to allow Aboriginals a greater measure of self-determination aroused fears of separatism. Its inquiries into aspects of past and present policies—racist violence, the separation of Aboriginal children from their parents, and Aboriginal deaths in custody —confronted Australians with findings that some found hard to accept. More broadly, the growing appreciation of Aboriginal tradition, art, literature and music unsettled the conventional version of Australian history and disturbed cultural conservatives.

Business interests initially led the opposition to the extension of Aboriginal land rights, but their objections quickly went beyond an economic reckoning. In 1984 Hugh Morgan, who had been president of the Mining Industry Council, claimed biblical support for his industry and said that the restitution of Aboriginal control was 'a symbolic step back to the world of paganism, superstition, fear and darkness'. He also cited Geoffrey Blainey's *Triumph of the Nomads* to characterise the 'ancient customs' of the Aboriginals as vengeful, and rebutted talk of 'genocide' against them as 'white middle-class guilt'.

This way of dismissing Aboriginal claims found ready expression in business-funded organisations such as the Institute of Public Affairs. It soon made its way into the conservative house-journal, *Quadrant*, which had previously been sensitive to Aboriginal disadvantage. In 1985 its media commentator, Anthony McAdam, denounced 'the now fashionable charge of "genocide"' as an 'exercise in national denigration' that impugned the nation's honour.

The Hawke and Keating governments struggled over the following decade to meet the expectations they raised, but did set in train a number of initiatives that the Coalition inherited on its return to office in 1996. In response to the Mabo judgement, the Keating government had created a

National Native Title Tribunal, and the High Court would revisit the issue of native title in a further landmark judgement on a case brought by the Wik peoples of Cape York Peninsula. An inquiry by the Human Rights and Equal Opportunity Commission into the removal of Aboriginal children was due to report. And the government had established a Council for Aboriginal Reconciliation that was asked to devise some lasting accommodation.

An early indication of the Howard government's intentions came with the launch of a book by the new minister for Aboriginal affairs, John Herron. The book's author, Geoffrey Partington, was a South Australian academic and History Warrior who championed Australia's British origins. He traced the repugnant policy of Aboriginal separatism back to 'Nugget' Coombs, a singularly influential public servant and government adviser who sympathised with Aboriginal aspirations, and whom Partington blamed for departing from the assimilationist goals championed by Paul Hasluck. Hasluck, the minister responsible for Aboriginal affairs in the Northern Territory from 1951 to 1963, had defended his administration in a book of his own in 1988 (with a foreword by Geoffrey Blainey, who castigated 'the self-righteousness and ignorance of today's critics').

Partington's book came with encomia from right-wing pundits. Frank Devine, a columnist in the *Australian*, said it was 'set to cause pain to the simple minded'; R. J. Stove, a *Quadrant* regular, claimed it 'resoundingly tells against the cramped anxieties of today's "politically correct" censorship of the past'. There was also a foreword from Peter Howson, a former Liberal politician, who wrote that the 'tragic state of contemporary Aboriginal society is in large measure due to the abandonment of Hasluckian policies of unforced assimilation'. Echoing Stove, John Howard dismissed the outcry against his minister for launching the book as the work of 'thought police'.

The unforced nature of assimilation was called into question in the following year by the report into the separation of
Aboriginal children from their parents. The government's
failure to accept its recommendations, conservative commentators' denial of its veracity and their ostentatious insensitivity
to the grief it recorded caused a split within *Quadrant*. While
Robert Manne had fallen out with Les Murray over his refusal
to publish the canard that Manning Clark was an anti-Semite,
it was his own writing on Aboriginal issues that most disturbed
Murray and the old guard.

Manne and his friend Raymond Gaita, a philosopher,
found the report and the Howard government's response
deeply disturbing. For some years they had been wrestling
with the moral implications of the project of reconciliation.
Their growing appreciation that settlers had usurped the
rights of Indigenous Australians persuaded them of the need
for an appropriate acknowledgement—not guilt, for no individual could bear responsibility for the crimes of others, but
shame, because Australians were implicated in their country's
past and shared a legacy of historical shame.

The report on the stolen children produced a stronger
response; Manne described it as 'one of the most shameful, if
not *the* most shameful episode in twentieth-century Australian
history'. For seventy years state governments had removed
children of mixed descent from their Aboriginal parents to
merge them into European society. In its most sinister, inter-
war phase, when the administrators still expected the 'tribal
natives' to die out, it constituted what Manne described as a
'eugenics program of constructive miscegenation' to breed out
the colour of the mixed-descent population and solve what
was then regarded as 'the Aboriginal problem'. To the Howard
government's response that these administrators thought they
were acting in the best interests of the children, Manne rejoined
that the Nazis had also claimed good intentions. Gaita argued
that genocide encompassed other ways of eliminating a people

than killing them, and Manne canvassed the possibility that this particular phase of Australian policy might have been genocidal in intention if not in effect.

These were the writings that caused Les Murray to allege that Robert Manne had taken up the 'received leftist line on Aborigines', and the meeting of the *Quadrant* board at which he resigned the editorship at the end of 1997 was dominated by argument over the Aboriginal question. The new editor, P. P. McGuinness, announced at the outset that the journal would discard the 'mawkish sentimentality' that had overtaken its discussion of the subject in recent years.

Thereafter, as the Howard government hardened its stand against apology or reparation for the Stolen Generations, placed further restriction on native title, stood aloof from the Council for Aboriginal Reconciliation and boycotted its public ceremonies, *Quadrant* urged it on. The magazine was by no means alone in strenuous denial. McGuinness popularised it in his column in the *Sydney Morning Herald*, as did Frank Devine in the *Australian*, Christopher Pearson in the *Australian Financial Review*, Andrew Bolt in the *Herald-Sun*, Piers Ackerman and Michael Duffy in the *Daily Telegraph*, and other right-wing polemicists who seemed at times to conduct a competition in vitriol. But *Quadrant* provided a seminary for the ideas they propagated, and the prime minister praised its contribution when he opened the journal's new offices in Sydney in 2000. He also claimed a new phase in the ideological offensive. The intellectual divide was now 'not so much between so-called elite opinion and popular opinion but between political correctness and common sense'.

Quadrant organised two conferences on Aboriginal issues. The first, entitled 'Rousseau and Reality', occurred in August 1999 and the second, 'Truth and Sentimentality', in September 2000. They attracted *Quadrant* regulars, former Aboriginal administrators, professional non-apologists working for organisations such as the Institute of Public Affairs and sympathetic journalists well placed to publicise the proceedings.

The first conference, at which John Herron provided the after-dinner speech, affirmed the values of western civilisation against the romanticisation of the noble savage. It was strongly influenced by a dissident anthropologist, Roger Sandall, who would shortly publish a book on what he called *The Culture Cult*. His argument was that 'spoiled white urbanites', like Jean-Jacques Rousseau, projected their fantasies onto indigenous cultures and ignored all the evidence that contradicted their 'designer tribalism'.

The gathering was also notable for a reappearance of Peter Howson, Minister for the Environment, Aborigines and the Arts from 1971 to 1972 in the dying days of Coalition rule by divine right and the final phase of white paternalism. Howson had subsequently published a political diary in which self-regard was so ludicrously disproportionate to capacity that it turned him into a figure of ridicule. He had long brooded over his humiliation and now came forward to reclaim the high moral ground over the 'rent-seeking' apologists for the Aboriginal cause.

The second gathering celebrated the failure of a legal action brought by two victims of the removal of Aboriginal children, but went further. This was where Keith Windschuttle outlined his argument that the frontier massacres of Australian history were a myth. Windschuttle would publish three articles on this subject in subsequent issues of *Quadrant*, prefacing them with an attack on three 'white activists', 'Nugget' Coombs, Henry Reynolds and myself, whom he accused of seeking 'the reorganisation and even the eventual break-up of the Australian nation'.

McGuinness set the context for this exercise in a *Quadrant* editorial late in 2000. Australian history, he said, was dominated by a school of 1970s radicals who spread malicious claims of Aboriginal maltreatment in order to justify a separatist enclave. He named this the '*Oxford Companion* school', taking aim at the *Oxford Companion to Australian History*, which I had edited along with Graeme Davison and John Hirst, and which drew on several hundred contributors who included Geoffrey Blainey, John Carroll, Ian Hancock (the historian of the Liberal Party) and Allan Martin (Menzies' biographer). Hirst himself was a contributor to *Quadrant* and the *IPA Review*, while Davison was a man of such studied moderation that when colleagues in a coffee queue taxed him with failure to declare his position he ordered black with a dash.

There was a further feature of the scene that McGuinness set. Shortly before this Australian exercise in historical denial, the Holocaust denier David Irving had brought and lost legal proceedings in a British court against an academic critic. The spectre of the European Holocaust, the most systematic and terrible of all projects in genocide, hung over the Australians who protested that their country's hands were spotless. Manne, whose parents were survivors of the Holocaust, had already drawn attention to parallels between the German solution for the Jewish problem and the Australian solution in the 1930s for the Aboriginal problem.

Michael Duffy, one of the more reckless columnists, had warned of the 'growing links between Jewish and Aboriginal Australians'. The most generous interpretation of this extraordinary observation is that Duffy meant Jews are unduly sensitive to any suggestion of genocide, but this cannot justify his minatory tone. The figure of the Jew as rootless intellectual and revolutionary agitator is a stock-in-trade of anti-Semitism.

Other Australian deniers tried to turn the comparison with David Irving around. McGuinness likened his own company to the defendants in the action brought by Irving, resolute in their affirmation of truth despite personal abuse and false allegations 'of Irving-esque scale'. (So, also, Chris Mitchell has described Manning Clark as 'a David Irving of the Left'.) With such projection of their own tactics onto their opponents, the deniers set about rewriting Australian history.

The first item of Keating's Redfern Park declaration was that 'We took the traditional lands and smashed the original way of life'. These would seem to be indisputable statements of historical fact, for no-one denied that Aboriginal people had been deprived of the resources that supported them when pastoralists moved into the plains and valleys, farmers cleared the land for cultivation and miners consumed the forests. It was the official recognition of this dispossession that created conservative resistance. Land rights legislation and the decisions of the High Court provided avenues for Aboriginal claimants to seek restoration of their land, and did so on the basis of their prior occupancy and ownership.

The finding of the High Court in the Mabo case aroused particular indignation, as we have seen, and much of it was ill-informed. Geoffrey Blainey read the judgement of Justices Deane and Gaudron out of context to rebuke their historical ignorance, while Geoffrey Partington published a tract on *The Australian History of Henry Reynolds* to show that it had misled the court. Other critics condemned judicial activism as an undemocratic usurpation of the role of parliament. Tim Fischer spoke of the need to ensure the appointment of 'capital C Conservatives' to the bench, seemingly oblivious of the unconservative character of this assault on the court's independence.

The effect of the Wik decision in 1996 was to renew an alarmist campaign that pastoral leaseholders would be turned off the land they had made productive. 'We must have certainty', insisted organisations representing farmers who wrestled each year with the vagaries of nature and had recently thrown over their regulatory protection for the uncertainty of a free market. The Howard government was able to persuade independent members of the Senate to accept enough of its 1998 Native Title Amendment Act to circumscribe the court's decisions.

The earlier land rights legislation of the Commonwealth placed a particular emphasis on traditional occupancy. It required claimants to be members of a 'local descent group' with a 'common spiritual affiliation to a site on the land' who could demonstrate that they had maintained their links to it. This definition restricted its application to areas where the impact of European occupation was light, and precluded those urban Aboriginals whose original way of life, as Keating put it, had been smashed. In practice, claims relied heavily on anthropologists and linguists who could help establish customary ownership.

Henry Reynolds claimed that after Mabo a different sort of expertise was needed. 'The post-Mabo world', he wrote, 'requires historians who can establish if, when and how preexisting native title had been extinguished'. He drew attention to the operation of the Waitangi Tribunal in New Zealand, which required a similar knowledge of the past and was the largest single employer of historians in that country.

His confidence was misplaced. The National Native Title Tribunal operates as a court of law, in which all parties have legal representation. The tribunal is certainly interested in establishing the historical circumstances of native title since it requires applicants to show the continuity of traditional law and custom. In practice this means searching out passages recording Aboriginal land use in reports, diaries, newspapers and other historical sources. It is work that any competent researcher can undertake. Historians trained to look for the contextual and conditional character of historical knowledge are of little use to the tribunal.

The opponents of native title had their own legal expertise, but they also enlisted publicists to undermine the legitimacy of Aboriginal rights. Ron Brunton was an anthropologist (his doctoral research was on the ritual use of kava in the Pacific) who had previously worked for the Liberal Party. The Institute of Public Affairs employed him from the early 1990s. He worked at first as director of its Environmental Policy Unit, and in 1993 wrote a critical response to the report of the Royal Commission into Aboriginal Deaths in Custody for perpetuating the false impression 'that people are disadvantaged simply because of their Aboriginal identity'. Subsequently, as director of the Institute's Indigenous Affairs Unit, he wrote regularly in its *Review*, *Quadrant* and the national press. These are the grounds cited by Senator Alston for his recent appointment to the board of the ABC.

Brunton became aware of a dispute in South Australia between Aboriginals and a developer. The developer wished to build a bridge from the town of Goolwa to Hindmarsh Island in the mouth of the Murray, to provide access to a proposed marina. A group of Ngarrindjeri women claimed in 1993 that the island had sacred significance and urged the federal minister to use his powers under the Aboriginal and Torres Strait Islander Heritage Protection Act of 1984 to preserve the area. The minister obtained a report in 1994 from Professor Cheryl Saunders that corroborated the women's claims, as did an Adelaide anthropologist in another report to the Aboriginal Legal Rights organisation. He placed a twenty-five year ban on the development.

The Federal Court quashed the minister's order on the procedural grounds that he had not personally read confidential statements made by the Ngarrindjeri women, in accordance with their belief that the contents should not be shown to men. That restriction did not bother their representative in the Commonwealth parliament, Ian McLachlan, who had risen through the National Farmers Federation and the H. R. Nicholls Society to close in on the Liberal leadership. He produced copies of their statements. The House of Representatives censured him and he subsequently resigned from the shadow cabinet. By this time the Hindmarsh Island affair had become a touchstone of fears and resentment.

Chris Kenny, an Adelaide journalist, found a number of Ngarrindjeri women who denied that the island had ever been a site of women's secret tradition. Two appeared with him on television in May 1995 and said that the whole claim had been fabricated. Kenny was a columnist for Christopher

Pearson's *Adelaide Review* and Pearson helped to edit his book on the controversy, which in turn was published by Michael Duffy. At its Canberra launch, three of the dissident women dined with 'their faithful and trusted friend Ron Brunton', and John Howard commended them for withstanding 'the Labor tide of political correctness'.

Soon after, Brunton made a lengthy submission to a royal commission appointed by the Liberal government of South Australia to inquire into the Hindmarsh Island bridge; for good measure he had another right-wing think-tank, the Tasman Institute, publish it. Brunton argued that it was extremely unlikely that this 'secret women's business' could have escaped notice by earlier anthropologists. Rather, he attributed its appearance to naïve legislation from governments that wished to show sympathy for Aboriginal tradition, to an Aboriginal cultural revival that created such tradition, and to an anthropological profession 'committed more to a role of advocacy than to independent scholarship'.

The royal commission found late in 1995 that the secret women's business had been fabricated. The Commonwealth, meanwhile, initiated a new heritage report, which again turned out to be invalid on procedural grounds but found no evidence of a customary interest that would justify continuing the heritage ban. By this time the Howard government was in office. It tabled the report and implemented its recommendation by legislating in 1997 to remove the Hindmarsh bridge area from the Heritage Protection Act.

Brunton assisted and welcomed this outcome in *Quadrant* and in his newspaper column. He also had the principal Ngarrindjeri dissident contribute an article to the *IPA Review*, deprecating the weight of the tradition that she felt able to enunciate. The importance of the affair, Brunton proclaimed, lay in the fact that for the first time a group of Aboriginals 'stood up to defend the integrity of their past against fraudulent, politically-motivated claims'. Roger Sandall used Hindmarsh Island as a primary example of the Culture Cult. A

subsequent lengthy reassessment of the Hindmarsh Island
affair by the anthropologist Diane Bell did not shift Brunton:
'Hindmarsh Island and the hoaxing of Australian Anthropology' was the title of his response.

Another investigator, Margaret Simons, has recently
returned to the Hindmarsh Island affair. She argues that the
Ngarrindjeri women were not lying and that 'the white men
who steered the case against them gave birth to a kind of anti-
political correctness at least as silly, dangerous and ideologically blind to the evidence as what it sought to replace'.

The affair caused damage to most of the participants,
including the original Ngarrindjeri women and those with
whom they were already at loggerheads before the claim of
secret women's knowledge was made and denied. Both groups
enlisted outside support and both in turn were used for purposes other than their own. Brunton's defence of independent
scholarship against advocacy was belied by his own service of
interests opposed to Aboriginal rights; his claims of political
motivation were made in the prosecution of a political campaign designed to discredit and roll back those rights. Even so,
the media coverage of the episode raised new doubts about
the reliability of testimony and the credibility of those who
interpreted it.

'We took the children from their mothers', was another of
Keating's declarations. This legacy of the past was particularly
painful to its victims, yet scarcely recognised by non-Aboriginal
Australians until a young historian, Peter Read, began working in the records of the Aborigines Protection Board of New
South Wales in the late 1970s and found thousands of files
documenting the practice. He helped to establish Link-Up, an
agency that sought to reunite Aboriginal families, and its
director asked him to write a paper setting out the background of separation. The paper circulated in duplicated

format until the state government published it in 1982. Read wanted to call the work 'The Lost Generations', but his partner, Jay Arthur, thought that a little euphemistic and suggested *The Stolen Generations*.

As increasing numbers of Aboriginal people told their stories of removal, the Stolen Generations weighed on the public conscience. At the end of 1994 the minister for Aboriginal affairs announced that he would ask the Human Rights and Equal Opportunity Commission to investigate the phenomenon. The subsequent inquiry was conducted by Sir Ronald Wilson, the president of the commission and a former High Court judge, and Mick Dodson, its Aboriginal and Torres Strait Islander social justice commissioner. They took written and oral evidence from 535 Aboriginal witnesses and completed their report, *Bringing Them Home*, early in 1997. It provided a history of the removal practices of state and Commonwealth governments and estimated that, from 1910 to 1970, between one in ten and one in three Aboriginal children had been separated from their families by force, duress or undue pressure. The authors found that this fell within the United Nations Convention on the Prevention and Punishment of the Crime of Genocide, since it was a course of action calculated to destroy a people.

Their report quoted extensively from the testimony of the victims. It revealed heart-rending stories of dislocation, loss, loneliness and abuse, of pain that continued to torment both parents and children. Kim Beazley, the leader of the Opposition, wept when the report was tabled in the Commonwealth parliament. State parliaments, churches, trade unions, schools and various other organisations issued formal apologies and expressed their profound sorrow. The prime minister, however, would not agree to an apology by the Commonwealth.

Bringing Them Home called for reparation to the victims of child removal by monetary compensation and other means. Above all, it sought apologies from the governments, churches and other agencies that had created the Stolen Generations.

'For victims of gross human rights violations', the authors explained, 'establishing the truth about the past is a critically important measure of reparation'. To have that truth recognised and acknowledged, an apology was needed. Mick Dodson explained that it was not a matter of individual guilt but, rather, an acceptance of 'collective responsibility'. Speaking at the Reconciliation Conference in Melbourne in May 1997, his brother Patrick emphasised the need for a reciprocal process to reunite the nation, 'one part of which apologises for the wrongs of the past' and the other part of which 'accepts that apology and forgives'. The nation would be at peace with itself only when it had the courage to 'own the truth of its past, and therefore free itself from the chains of the past'.

These appeals fell on deaf ears. Both John Howard and John Herron offered their own personal apologies for the pain and suffering of the Stolen Generations but would not let the parliament apologise. They argued that such a step would be to admit liability and open the way to financial claims, and they were not prepared to offer compensation. They argued that no government could be expected to apologise for the actions of a predecessor. And Senator Herron argued that, in any case, these past actions had been lawful and in many cases taken with benevolent intentions of doing the best for the children concerned.

His cavil began as an argument of extenuation and gradually expanded into outright denial. By 2000, when the Senate was conducting an inquiry into the issue of compensation for the Stolen Generations, the government reached that conclusion. It disputed the methodology and findings of the inquiry to argue that at most 10 per cent of Aboriginal children had been separated from their parents under a program that was 'essentially lawful and benign in intent', and concluded that 'there was never a "generation" of "stolen" children'.

The government's final rejection of *Bringing Them Home* was prepared by a concerted right-wing campaign to discredit it. Early in 1998 the Institute of Public Affairs published Ron

Brunton's hostile evaluation of the report, so hostile that he accused its authors of *Betraying the Victims*. Brunton made a mixture of serious and trivial charges. First, the report failed to make clear the distinction between Aboriginal children of mixed descent, who were removed, and those of full descent, who were not (for its authors were constrained by the sensitivity many Aboriginal people feel for such distinctions), and it had also failed to distinguish between the eugenic phase of racial engineering and the subsequent phase when welfare motives overlaid racial ones. Second, the report had not tested the claims made by witnesses against the historical record (this also was a valid criticism, though the government refused the commission the resources needed to do so).

Brunton disputed the report's claim of genocide, which he said had been 'greeted by those people in the universities, churches and other usually suspect institutions who know in the depths of their bowels that Australia is bad'. His own suggestion that a program of birth control would also fall within the United Nations definition of genocide trivialised the issue. He criticised the authors for quoting only 143 of their 535 witnesses and suggested (without any foundation) that this was a biased selection and might even have represented a deliberate suppression of contrary evidence. He raised the possibility of false memories (again, without justification), and he attacked Sir Ronald Wilson on the grounds that he was an elder of the Presbyterian church and on the board of a home for separated Aboriginal children in Perth (even though the report gave the lie to Brunton's charge of a cover-up of that connection).

After Brunton came Peter Howson, who somehow managed to link the story of an Aboriginal baby abandoned by his mother in a rabbit burrow with an episode in the Cold War when an American spy had allegedly hidden documents in a pumpkin gourd. Brunton and Howson were present at the subsequent *Quadrant* gatherings, along with a former patrol officer and an administrator who protested against the calumnies of the Stolen Generations.

These arguments prepared the way for the government's submission to the Senate inquiry in April 2000, and for a sustained campaign in the press by the right-wing commentators. 'The Howard Government', said Frank Devine in the *Australian*, 'has done a sensible and admirable thing in taking a stand against the sloganeering use of stolen generations to club it and the nation into submission to the demands of Aboriginal activists'. Piers Ackerman wrote in the *Daily Telegraph* that *Bringing Them Home* relied on 'untried, untested, unsworn and unsupported statements presented by tragically, emotionally disturbed individuals to a willing audience of social engineers bent on attracting a new welfare market'. Michael Duffy claimed that no-one knew how many children had really been stolen—the number could be 'as low as several thousand'—but the 'enthusiastic embrace of falsehood' served the political and career interests, and the self-esteem and moral vanity, of well-educated, powerful white Australians. 'In truth it is actually just the latest form of racism.'

The prime minister insisted that his government's submission was 'a factual analysis of the issues and should not be subject to exaggerated responses', but the exaggerated responses came from those who supported his denial and they were directed at those who sought to come to terms with the past. Sir Ronald Wilson was subjected to sustained denigration. Michael Duffy derided him as 'Sir Ronald the Evangelist', while Piers Ackerman dubbed Sir William Deane, a former High Court colleague and now the governor-general, 'Holy Billy', for his apology to the Stolen Generations. They were part of what another columnist called the 'moral mafia' and Michael Duffy referred to as 'white maggots'. Most Australians, he added, would support reconciliation if only the Aboriginals and their supporters would agree to 'stop talking about the past'.

Talking about the past was the whole basis of reconciliation. Talking about the injuries of the past, listening to the
victims, acknowledging what had happened, offering contrition and receiving its acceptance were how such injuries were
to be healed. In Africa, South America and the former communist countries of Eastern Europe, this process was followed
in the closing years of the twentieth century to settle its traumatic legacy. As Henry Reynolds has observed, the process has
usually involved some official body that compiles a record of
the past wrongs, incorporating the testimony of those who
suffered them, both as an act of reparative justice and as a
process of reconciliation.

The two purposes are not easy to reconcile. In the former
communist countries, the process is sometimes described as
one of lustration, an act of moral purification. Elsewhere the
body that performs the activity usually takes the title of a
Truth Commission, for historical truth is crucial to those who
come before them. A legal scholar notes that they are part of
a social movement for factual recovery because people want to
know the facts. 'The banners they proclaim through the streets
might just as well carry the motto of the nineteenth-century
German historian, Leopold von Ranke: to discover the past
"as it really was".' This demand for historical truth cannot
be served by legal procedures (since the application of legal
standards of evidence to the testimony of the victims would
impair the process of reconciliation) and it sits uneasily with
many historians who are accustomed to searching out alternative meanings.

The process also requires the co-operation of those who
are called on to accept responsibility for what has happened.
Without such acceptance, the moral force of the past is lost
and reconciliation gives way to rancour. It might have been
possible to give the *Bringing Them Home* report a stronger historical foundation: it could have provided a more authoritative
account of separation policies, and if allowed to do so it could
have used the records to test, corroborate and amplify the

testimony of its witnesses. But that would not satisfy the deniers who were determined to discredit the report by any means. The opportunity to settle the past was lost.

Keating also stated at Redfern Park that 'We brought the diseases'. This proposition had been canvassed when Noel Butlin, an economic historian at the Australian National University, turned in the 1980s to Aboriginal history. He had previously worked on the European history of Australia, using the statistical series that were part of the European toolkit to create quantitative studies of economic development. He then decided to look at the process whereby resource use passed from the original inhabitants to the newcomers, and in order to do so needed to establish the Aboriginal population in 1788 and afterwards. The result was a book, *Our Original Aggression*, which suggested there had been a massive depopulation of Aboriginals.

The generally accepted estimate of the Aboriginal population in 1788 was 300 000. Butlin argued that it might have been five times that figure. Among the factors that caused a rapid decline after the arrival of the Europeans was disease, for Aboriginals had not been exposed to many of the most lethal diseases and lacked resistance. Smallpox epidemics in 1789 and again around 1828 were particularly lethal. Butlin speculated that the first of these epidemics might well have been spread deliberately from bottles of smallpox virus the colonists brought with them on the First Fleet to provide immunity from the disease.

Other historians contested Butlin's explanation of the source of the smallpox epidemic. They argued it had come from Macassan fishermen, who mixed with Aboriginals on the northern coast of Australia, and this disagreement was pursued in academic journals after Butlin's book appeared. The most recent work on the subject, by Judy Campbell, draws on medical research that indicates the bottles of small-pox virus probably would not have remained active after the long voyage.

Hugh Morgan, the mining executive, was not interested in such niceties. He accused Butlin of mounting a campaign to denigrate 'our ancestors' and of alleging that Governor Phillip was guilty of genocide. Charles Wilson, an economic historian from Cambridge, offered *Quadrant* a critical review of Butlin's 'imaginary history' and for good measure chastised him for questioning Geoffrey Blainey's argument that internecine violence was one of the factors that had kept the Aboriginal population low.

Butlin saw off both these critics. He sympathised with Hugh Morgan as a 'very active public speaker' who was prob-ably preoccupied with Aboriginal land claims. He gently corrected Morgan's misapprehension that he had an animus against Governor Phillip and remarked that this advocate of the new right evidently 'felt the only good bureaucrat is a dead one'. He chastised the Englishman's ignorance of Aus-tralian history, anthropology and geography, and suggested that 'it is time the Australians (and the British) grew up'.

While medical historians and demographers continue to explore the impact of disease on Aboriginals during the white occupation of Australia, the issue finds little place in public debate. It is a surprising omission since the deniers frequently invoke the effects of disease as an alternative to white violence in order to explain the rapid decline of Aboriginal numbers. They treat death by illness as an exoneration of responsibility, a consequence that the newcomers could not have prevented. It figures heavily in the apologetics of Keith Windschuttle.

'We committed the murders.' This was the most chilling of Keating's admissions, and there was surprising agreement that it was so. We have already seen how Geoffrey Blainey acknow-

ledged in his 1993 Latham lecture on the Black Armband that
the settlers had killed many Aboriginals, perhaps as many as
20 000. Earlier, in his history of nineteenth-century Australia,
Blainey had included a chapter on 'War on the Grasslands'. He
noted that in Tasmania guerrilla war gave way to military
operations, and this 'warfare and private violence' was 'devastating'. He described other theatres in New South Wales,
Victoria and Western Australia.

The number of 20 000 Aboriginal casualties had been estimated in 1981 by Henry Reynolds. He drew on a number of
regional studies to calculate that between 2000 and 2500
Europeans were killed in frontier clashes; but the records were
far less forthcoming on casualties on the other side of the
frontier, and he fell back on ratios of black-to-white casualties.
In Tasmania he suggested a ratio of 4 to 1; in Queensland,
where the settlers had the advantages of horses, breech-loading
rifles and revolvers, he suggested 10 to 1. Hence his 'informed
guess' of a death toll of 20 000. Another historian, Richard
Broome, independently reached the same figure with a similar
methodology.

Yet in 2000, when the *Quadrant* group held its conference
on 'Truth and Sentimentality', this figure was described as 'a
wild overestimate based on pure speculation'. In the next three
issues of *Quadrant*, Keith Windschuttle set out his arguments
about 'The Myths of Frontier Massacres in Australian History'.
The first of them considered four particular incidents of conflict between Europeans and Aboriginals, two in the 1830s
and two in the 1920s, to argue that only the last of them, at
Coniston station in the Northern Territory, could properly be
described as a massacre. The second instalment disputed the
reckoning of 20 000 Aboriginal deaths at the hands of Europeans, and the third attacked the motives of those Europeans
—beginning with the Christian missionaries in the early
nineteenth century—who had 'invented' the massacres.

Windschuttle was not the first to dispute the accepted version of particular massacres. He has said that a book published

in the previous year by a Western Australian journalist, Rod Moran, arguing that an alleged massacre at Forrest Creek in Western Australia in 1926 was a *Massacre Myth*, had drawn the subject to his attention. He was, however, the first to extend the argument on a national scale and to claim there had been a persistent and systematic misrepresentation of frontier conflict. He was the first to challenge the veracity of the historians who had written on the subject.

Windschuttle had graduated with an honours degree in history from the University of Sydney in the late 1960s and then taught social policy, sociology and media studies in a number of universities before taking early retirement. A former student radical, he remained active on the left and published trenchant criticisms of the Australian media and unemployment. His 1994 polemic on *The Killing of History* signalled a change of direction with its combative assault on historians such as Greg Dening and Inga Clendinnen whom he accused of turning their backs on an objective, knowable past—though there were left-wing historians (notably Eric Hobsbawm) who shared his aversion to cultural relativism. This was not a charge that applied to the principal historians who studied Aboriginal history and in 1994 Windschuttle singled out Henry Reynolds for praise. Now he was accusing Reynolds of creating myths of genocide.

His claims found wide coverage. He engaged in a debate with Reynolds at Bob Gould's bookshop in Sydney, on the ABC's Lateline Program and at the Press Club in Canberra. The National Museum, which he criticised for promoting the myths of frontier massacres, convened a forum at which he extended his criticism to its building, for he interpreted the zigzag structure of its design as a lightning bolt, taken from the Jewish Museum in Berlin and signifying that the Aboriginals had also suffered a holocaust. The other participants in the forum examined a range of particular incidents, discussed the sources that allowed the reconstruction of what had happened, reflected on the patterns of frontier contact. None of this deflected Windschuttle from his quarry: 'the fictions and fabrications of our academic historians'.

Following his initial foray, Windschuttle embarked on a project of examining the evidence for the whole of Australian frontier history to test what he now took to be the historical orthodoxy—the 'genocide thesis'. This was a mammoth undertaking and he has so far published the results for one colony, Tasmania, during the first half of the nineteenth century, in 471 pages—the fact that he is his own publisher allows an amplitude that few commercial presses permit.

It is the first volume of a series entitled *The Fabrication of Aboriginal History*, and has again been taken up enthusiastically by the publicists who had previously denied the Stolen Generations. Janet Albrechtsen, an opinionated columnist for the *Australian* who had shown no previous interest in the subject, pronounced that Windschuttle 'uncovers the truth'. Geoffrey Blainey hailed the work as 'one of the most important and devastating written on Australian history in recent years'.

He might not write to length but he is a publisher's dream. Windschuttle never declines an invitation to promote his book. When I went up to the Blue Mountains town of Blackheath earlier this year to debate with him (he has since conducted debates with Patricia Grimshaw, Lyndall Ryan and Henry Reynolds), he began by giving the audience the address of his website where transcripts of previous arguments sit alongside his various publications. He is drawn to argument and confrontation though not always comfortable with the audience reaction: it is as if he needs to provoke hostility to reassure himself that his polemics are striking home.

His book has two purposes: to examine the reliability of the historians who had written about race relations in colonial Van Diemen's Land, and to propose a counter-history. It works by a loose reading of the work of those historians and a close reading of their treatment of massacres. Windschuttle treats the historians who have worked over the past twenty-five years on Aboriginal history as all implicated in the genocide thesis. He calls them 'the orthodox school' and he claims that they maintain the orthodoxy by covering up each other's mistakes and suppressing any contrary interpretation. He alleges that they were formed in the radicalism of the sixties and accuses them of a deliberate politicisation of history.

This school comprises prominent historians such as Henry Reynolds, Lyndall Ryan and the late Lloyd Robson, archaeologists such as John Mulvaney and the late Rhys Jones, local historians such as the late Brian Plomley and younger researchers such as Sharon Morgan. The ages of these scholars range over several decades; they vary widely in views and sympathies. The idea that they colluded in a political project is as absurd as his allegation that they victimise dissidents is offensive. I know only one of the two historians he cites as victims of suppression, for she completed her doctoral thesis in my history department: I read it, praised it and encouraged publication.

He misreads those whom he castigates. He repeatedly alleges that Reynolds and Ryan sought to depict the frontier as a place of indiscriminate white killing. Yet Reynolds was principally interested in the Aboriginal response to the newcomer, and consistently argued that it took a variety of forms, from co-operation and partnership to resistance and warfare. Ryan was concerned to relate the story of the dispossession and survival of Tasmanian Aboriginals, and frontier violence was only one part of her story. So far from their creating an 'orthodox school', other historians had long since challenged the emphasis on frontier violence and queried the idea of a frontier with Europeans on one side and Aboriginals on the other.

The greater part of Windschuttle's book is given over to a minute examination of the massacres. He scrutinises the historians' treatment of these events, tracks their references back to the archives and compares their versions against the original source. This is by far the most damaging of his criticisms, as he finds some of the sources do not support what the historians reported, while others do not even exist; I shall return to this aspect. He pays careful attention to chronology and topography, consistency and plausibility—when and where did the incident occur? who was there and can we trust their version of what happened?—to reduce the number of casualties. He imposes stringent standards of evidence—from reputable eyewitnesses and preferably corroborated—to rule out higher numbers.

He applies these forensic techniques to prosecute the historians, but he also acts as the counsel for the defence for the colonial authorities. They were engaged in the peaceful settlement of a new colony, and encountered 'senseless violence' from its primitive inhabitants, yet they endeavoured to preserve the rule of law to protect both peoples. They were, in any case, 'Christians to whom the killing of the innocent would have been abhorrent'. So far from practising genocide, they ensured that this 'was the least violent of all Europe's encounters with the New World'.

So how had the allegations of massacres arisen and lodged so firmly in the early histories of Henry Melville, John West and James Bonwick that were discussed in Chapter 3? Windschuttle attributes the allegations to liberal critics of the administration who employed the charge of imperial brutality as a rhetorical tactic, and to Evangelical Christians who wanted to justify their own missionary activities. That these Christians were appalled by the actions of their murderous compatriots and co-religionists is a contradiction that escapes him.

The 'orthodox' school of early Tasmanian history told a story of sporadic conflict in the early years of colonial settlement, usually over food resources and the abduction of Aboriginal women and children as sexual partners and servants, escalating in the 1820s with the spread of pastoralism. The governor declared martial law in the settled districts in 1828 and by 1834 a few hundred survivors were confined to settlements. Both Ryan and Reynolds dwelt on the strength of the resistance during this 'Black War' and the challenge that these outnumbered defenders with their guerrilla tactics posed to the invaders.

Windschuttle's counter-history portrays the Aboriginals as incapable of fighting a war since they had no government and no notion of territory or even land; incapable of guerrilla war since they did not know the word. A warrior named Musquito was not a freedom fighter because he had been sent from Sydney and later accompanied his master on a voyage to Mauritius; he was nothing more than a violent criminal.

This is not so much a counter-history of the Aboriginal response as an exercise in incomprehension. If the Aboriginals had no government, then how did they regulate their affairs? If they had no notion of territory, why did they object to whites hunting their game? If guerrilla war has to be named to be practised, then the story of Robin Hood has to be discarded. At the Blackheath debate a woman in the audience asked Windschuttle how he knew of Musquito's voyage to Mauritius. He replied that it was in the original records. But his own reference is to a report in the *Hobart Town Gazette*, and he accompanies it with a note that Lyndall Ryan misdated the voyage. The Blackheath questioner revealed that the ship's manifest does not list Musquito as a passenger. After Windschuttle's evidential strictures, this was a damaging slip.

To drive home his denial of massacres, Windschuttle made a count of all inter-racial homicide in the first thirty years of settlement. He used a book by Brian Plomley that listed clashes from 1803 to 1831, added some of his own, took out others, and then estimated the number of Aboriginal casualties (allowing just one in most cases and giving ten as the highest toll from any clash) to come up with a total of 118. Since the European death toll for the 'Black War' of 1824 to 1831 came to 187, he concluded there was 'nothing that resembled genocide or any attempt at it'. As a method it is extremely flimsy (the figures he allocates to each incident are no more reliable than those used earlier by Reynolds and Broome for a national estimate, which he had dismissed as guesswork). In any case it rested on a misconception: Plomley made no count of Aboriginal deaths since he was recording only those incidents that the settlers reported.

Even so, Windschuttle's finding that the 'orthodox school' had grossly exaggerated the number of Aboriginals killed placed considerable pressure on his own 'counter-history'. How could an island of Aboriginals have plummeted with the advent of the Europeans to the point that after thirty years there were only a few hundred survivors? Windschuttle fell back on several sketchy arguments.

First, he revised downwards the size of the Aboriginal population prior to European settlement to as few as 2000; this again was a guesstimate that made no reference to the work of demographic historians. Second, he used a particularly tendentious American anthropologist to claim that the Tasmanian Aboriginals were primitive, dysfunctional and on the verge of collapse, principally because the brutal treatment of women threatened their reproduction. Hence, he argued, with the introduction of disease and the attachment of Aboriginal women to European men, the numbers fell rapidly. In a final insult he suggests that the Tasmanian Aboriginals owed their survival up to that time 'more to good fortune than good management'.

The Fabrication of Aboriginal History is a shocking book, shocking in its allegation of fabrication and also in its refusal of the interpretive framework that earlier historians employed. Its most challenging argument is that the colonisation of Australia was carried out under the rule of law, with restraint and a minimum of bloodshed. Yet Windschuttle is so intent on reducing the body count that he fails to register the tragedy of this fatal encounter. Taxed with his lack of compassion, he replied: 'You can't really be serious about feeling sympathy for someone who died 200 years ago'.

Windschuttle professed to be astonished by the hostile reception of his book. Robert Manne made an early and cogent criticism of its method, and also drew attention to the plagiarism of the American anthropologist, Robert Edgerton. Windschuttle rejected the charge angrily. 'I won't cop that', he was reported as saying, 'I'll sue the bastard'. He also claimed 'it is a measure of how desperate my critics are that they have to resort to character assassination'. But that was precisely what he had done in his own depiction of the 'orthodox school' and subsequent reference to 'university teachers with overt left-wing commitments'.

His strongest ground was the allegation that historians had misrepresented the evidence for massacres—and if his book had simply stuck to that claim and not ventured into a farrago of innuendo and meretricious reinterpretation it would have been far more effective. The charge of falsifying the sources is a serious and a damaging one; serious because honesty in reporting evidence is a basic requirement of any scholarly enterprise, damaging because while many follow the arguments in the History Wars with varying degrees of confidence, they do at least expect historians to tell the truth.

The questions Windschuttle raised about previous accounts of Tasmanian massacres could not be evaded. Suggestions from some historians that these were no more than 'a clutch of regrettable mistakes' or 'half a dozen alleged gaffes' or 'a few minor errors' were unhelpful. They came across as special pleading and only increased the suspicion that something was seriously amiss with the standards, if not the integrity, of the profession.

First-year undergraduates are instructed in the rules of evidence: go back to the original source, report it accurately, document it fully. The same principles apply in advanced research, where the higher degree candidate is expected to provide exhaustive documentation and always verify it. It used to be academic folklore that a thesis examiner could be expected to check at least one footnote in every ten, and if any proved to be inaccurate, then the search would be extended. I suspect the practice has declined in these days of heavy university workloads, and possibly also its salutary effect on the preparation of theses.

It is easy enough to understand how errors can creep in. Lyndall Ryan, who is the chief object of Windschuttle's charges, began research for the thesis on which her book is based in 1970. Many of the archival sources she used had not been arranged and given their present reference numbers. She was working in a pre-computer era, taking notes in pencil and retyping successive drafts. As she gathered her notes on a particular incident, it was all too easy to conflate one note on the official report with another that recorded a newspaper item and yet another from a subsequent commentator who had estimated the number of casualties. Her thesis, which she submitted in 1975, provided 1351 separate references in almost 1000 footnotes. Her book, which appeared in 1981, reduced these to 857 references in a little over 500 footnotes.

It is harder to explain why all the errors are in one direction. Windschuttle charges her with 'at least 17 cases where she either invented atrocities and other incidents or provided false footnotes'. Some of these alleged inventions arise from a difference of reinterpretation and some raise the issue of her accuracy in reporting the evidence. She has replied with a consideration of two of her footnotes. In one she allows that she referred to the wrong newspaper but that the remaining references are correct. In the other, to which Windschuttle devoted four pages, she cited seven references and now claims that one of them named the wrong newspaper, one referred to the wrong official report and that there were three missing references that supported her interpretation. This is something less than a case of fabrication, and many might hope that a similar magnifying glass is not held up to their work.

That is what Windschuttle proposes to do in further volumes dealing with mainland Australia. This particular phase of the History Wars is likely to be with us some time, and we can expect further recalculation of Aboriginal deaths and more claims that the massacres are a myth. Some might conclude that there is no alternative to the campaign of denial but to compile as full an inventory as possible of the casualties of the frontier wars. It would be a lengthy, grisly and always imprecise business as the records are neither comprehensive nor unambiguous.

At the closing session of the forum at the National Museum in 2001, Tim Rowse noted the limitation of arguing over precisely how many Aboriginals died at the hands of European settlers. He said that even if it could be shown that not one person was killed in the act of conquest, we would still be left with the fact that ownership and sovereignty of this country passed from the original owners and sovereigns, without their consent, to uninvited newcomers. Such a transformation would remain a traumatic story. It is the absence of any sense of this tragedy, the complete lack of compassion for its victims, that is the most disturbing quality of Windschuttle's rewriting of Aboriginal history.

CHAPTER 9

WHAT DO THEY TEACH
OUR CHILDREN?

In a letter to the *Age* in 2001, a dismayed Howard Hutchins from Wonga Park complained that his granddaughter had been the latest victim of educational untruths about our past: 'Surely Australian heritage-destroying political correctness has gone too far? Our children—thus all our futures—are suffering from the non-teaching of our very recent history, and distortion of our early history.'

To be sure, Geoffrey Blainey had warned in his Latham lecture eight years earlier that the 'Black Armband' view of history was moving beyond the confines of the academy. 'Now schoolchildren are often the target for these views', he cautioned. The educationalist Kevin Donnelly has also argued against what he described as a growing political bias within history teaching. A national document on history curriculum, he maintained, 'describes early European settlement as an "invasion" and belittles Australia's Anglo-Celtic history and traditions'. Keith Windschuttle's claims that frontier conflict has been 'fabricated' by an academic orthodoxy intent on politicising Australian history sounds the latest alarm over historical interpretation; and how to teach students this contested past intensifies the growing anxiety over Australian history.

The History Wars have been fought in universities, museums and newspaper opinion pages. The classroom has become another battlefront. While new commentators with particular educational interests or expertise make an appearance in this chapter, many familiar figures re-emerge as the History War crusaders fight on a new front. Polarised historical interpretations, most vivid in the black-and-white battlefield metaphors, resonate in discussions of history syllabuses and school texts. The divided readings of the past have been repeated in history teaching, where contrasting historical descriptions of colonisation such as 'invasion' and 'settlement' provide the ammunition.

Anxiety over what school children should know is no recent phenomenon. The school History Wars are simply the latest manifestation of a perennial concern about historical knowledge and national identity. Nevertheless, the expansion of the Wars into schools has added a new and vital dimension to the contemporary historical debate: it is through the image of the child, a symbol of the future, that the struggle over the past is increasingly conducted. The heated contest over 'our history' has intensified because of a collective anxiety over what 'our children' should be taught.

Alarm over students' knowledge of the national heritage has been expressed alongside concern over current educational standards more broadly as well as approaches to history teaching in particular. They come together in the allegation that the country's future is being let down by its past. This has been largely a conservative polemic, where critical readings of Australian history in syllabuses are dismissed as historically bleak, politically biased and educationally lax.

Increasingly, however, historians, teachers and commentators of varying political persuasions have employed the child as a symbol of the future. This isn't simply a debate over contrasting historical approaches, or contested historical terms. It is also a struggle over common ground. Education is a national concern—it is everyone's business. Pedagogical as well as political beliefs about what students should know frame the debate over school history. In this way, the discourse of standards, of educational rigour and historical core knowledge has become the salient language of history education. And it is this rhetoric—of the future of the past, the child projected onto the nation—that has given the educational arena of the History Wars such urgency.

First appearing in New South Wales schools around 1830, history education initially supplemented religion and the classics. Emphasising the transmission of facts and morals, early texts explained the dominance of 'civilised' English-speaking countries, stressing loyalty to the empire and civic duty. Courses were dominated by 'great men, great deeds and great events'. After the First World War, and the 'birth' of national identity that many took from Gallipoli, more Australian perspectives made it into history texts and syllabuses—although well into the mid-twentieth century, themes were still bound by ideas of history-as-progress and the advance of civilisation through the British Empire.

In the 1960s and 1970s, critical approaches to Australian history questioned established interpretations of settlement and progress. Historians pursued voices frequently absent from the national narrative. Social histories of feminist, migrant and Aboriginal perspectives challenged the exclusiveness of traditional historical approaches. Corresponding with this shift towards more critical, inclusive readings of Australia's past was a reconceptualisation of the content and methodology of history taught in schools.

The 1957 New South Wales *Syllabus in History* had described 'the aim of the course' as 'the appreciation of man's main accomplishments, set in their order of general development', and suggested a study of Aboriginal people as an appropriate study of 'stone age man' at the 'threshold of history'. A teaching exercise in *Agora,* the journal of the History Teachers' Association of Victoria, from 1969 suggested that students imagine themselves as a squatter in the 1840s:

> By the 1840s squatters had taken up the greater part of the best grazing land in Eastern Australia. Because these men laid the foundations on which rests our staple industry, you are going to examine some aspects of the lives of these important pioneers.

The dispossession and dispersal 'these pioneers' inflicted upon the Indigenous population was not mentioned.

In subsequent teaching documents, however, there was recognition of the need for a reappraisal of Australian history, and syllabuses began to reflect the changing concerns of historians. Teachers and curriculum designers increasingly emphasised the importance of relating the experiences of minority groups to students. The growing influence of such ideas was also present in education policy. In 1980 the Queensland Aboriginal and Torres Strait Islander Education Consultative Committee was established to oversee education policy and curriculum documents in that state. Two years later, policy mandating Aboriginal perspectives in education was legislated in New South Wales.

In methodology, also, approaches to history teaching became more progressive. By 1972 the New South Wales History Syllabus differed radically from the one it replaced, which had continued almost unchanged since 1957. In Australia and abroad, history was increasingly imbued with an educational philosophy of student equity and the need for educational relevance. The traditional discipline came under increasing criticism from curriculum reformers for being old, stale and simply unrelated to students' needs. 'Relevance' became an educational ethos. Discrete disciplines were replaced with integrated courses of study geared towards promoting social awareness and equity. Ideas of personal development and learning objectives such as critical thinking replaced prescriptions of content as the central tenets of syllabus development.

These changes came under fire from those who feared that the abandonment of content would damage the education system irreparably. Writing for the *Sydney Morning Herald* in 1975, the professor of English at the University of Sydney, Leonie Kramer, argued that theories of 'knowledge acquired in active process' were too vague, and would lower standards in a system 'already afflicted with growing problems of literacy'.

In 1976 the *Bulletin* ran the cover story, 'Australia's Educational Scandal: We're Turning Out Millions of Dunces'. Inside, it lamented that while spending for education had increased, 'the output of real education has declined'. The education historian Alan Barcan has also read this change in teaching methods critically. Ideals of increasing equality between teachers' and students' knowledge were accompanied by what he has described as a decline in traditional academic standards. The 'age of relativism' emphasised personal rather than wider social concerns.

The shift away from a more chronological syllabus structure was central to such concerns over history teaching. An emphasis on themes such as gender or class rather than facts, critics felt, would loosen the rigour of an objective study of the past. In the lead-up to the Bicentenary, historical debate centred on issues of race. Patrick O'Farrell, a professor of history at the University of New South Wales, contributed a critical article on the state of the subject to *Teaching History*, the journal of the History Teachers' Association of New South Wales. While the study of Aboriginal people 'should not be forgotten', he conceded, 'it must not be allowed to become a liability, a millstone on the present'.

The educationalist Geoffrey Partington warned that teaching an overly negative history endangered 'our children'. The 'crude politicization of Australian education,' he wrote, the 'unscholarly dismissals of the mainline experience of the

Australian people during the last two centuries, and the ruthless indoctrination of Australia's children in the name of neo-Marxist versions of social justice, dominate discussion about history teaching as Australia approaches its bicentenary'.

Contrasting historical interpretations were conspicuous if only for the tension they provoked during the Bicentennial celebrations and Survival Day protests. Concern over history teaching during the Bicentenary was part of the vexatious issue of whether Australian history should be celebrated at all. Conservative journals such as *Quadrant* and the *IPA Review* consistently argued against what they saw as a public denigration of Australia's colonial heritage. Ken Baker had criticised the negative momentum associated with the Bicentenary, insisting that its 'function should be to remind us of the achievements of the past 200 years, of our debt to our forebears, and our obligations to future generations'. The 'New History', he later warned, was replacing Australia's collective myths by the systematic exposure of their dark side.

Leonie Kramer contributed a hostile review of a new Australian history school text. Sue Fabian's *The Changing Australians —A Social History* was simply wrong, she argued, for ignoring Australia's proud pioneering settlement, and for its cynical rejection of British imperialism. In a similar attack on allegedly biased teaching approaches, Geoffrey Partington maintained that 'it is entirely irresponsible, as well as historically false' for teachers and curriculum designers 'to adopt the one-sided view of white wickedness, which is the new orthodoxy in teaching about race relations in Australia since 1788'.

By 1988 governments were developing policy initiatives in an attempt to quell the unease over how Australian history should be taught. In response to pressing demands from state education departments and Aboriginal groups, the federal government called a meeting of state and federal education ministers to rewrite school curricula and encompass Aboriginal perspectives. The acting federal minister for education, and former minister for Aboriginal affairs, Clyde Holding, said contemporary racial tension was rooted in a popular ignorance of the historical treatment of Aboriginal people.

The curriculum meeting was organised amidst growing public concern over possible Indigenous and non-Indigenous protest during the 'Celebration of a Nation'. Teacher unions had threatened to ban school Bicentennial programs that did not encompass Aboriginal perspectives. Defending the threat, Barbara Fitzgerald, the multicultural coordinator of the New South Wales Teachers' Federation, said that students 'can go through school and university now and can come across virtually nothing to do with Australia before 1788. Apart from being offensive, it's non-historical.' In response, the New South Wales Education Department permitted Aboriginal teachers and students to boycott some Bicentennial activities.

Such actions aroused considerable complaint. The federal Opposition leader, John Howard, said that Aboriginal people had a right to lawful and peaceful dissent, but hoped they would exercise this right prudently. He said present-day white Australians were not responsible for the oppression of Aboriginals in the past and accused the federal government of downgrading the Bicentenary. Contrasting readings of the past had clearly converged—and how to represent that past in schools became a source of considerable tension and anxiety. In time, the Bicentenary would become a critical symbol of the polarisation that we now term the 'History Wars'.

After the Bicentenary, new history syllabuses attracted increasing criticism from commentators who rejected much of their content for misrepresenting 'our' history. According to the Sydney journalist P. P. McGuinness, the 1991 Australian history strand of the New South Wales syllabus had been full of 'buzzwords' that were 'politically correct', such as 'invasion', 'genocide', 'assimilation', 'integration', 'resistance', 'culture conflict', 'dispossession', 'racism', 'discrimination', 'Aboriginality', 'paternalism', 'terra nullius', 'civil rights', 'land degradation' and 'self-determination'.

'This is not about understanding the past in order not to repeat it', McGuinness insisted, 'but about controlling the future through indoctrinating our children'. 'The notion that Australian history should be taught', he added later, 'to little children and in schools and colleges, as the history of an invasion is the product of a political propagandistic version of history. Our history does not belong to an undistinguished syllabus committee of pedants but to the community as a whole.'

McGuinness's insistence that 'invasion' had been introduced with politically partisan motives to sully Australian history characterised the conservative attack on the overly gloomy, politically progressive views they saw dominating history syllabuses in Australia. Many campaigned against 'politically correct' history teaching on the grounds it was reckless and damaging. Argument raged across a number of states during the 1990s, as anxiety over 'our children' heightened.

In 1994 the Brisbane *Courier-Mail* investigated a new Queensland Year Five Social Studies sourcebook for suggesting that 'explorer', 'pioneer' and 'discover' were value-laden terms. The sourcebook had been introduced to replace an earlier text, removed in 1992 because the education department deemed it racist and discriminatory. An information sheet in the sourcebook, which was sent to all schools, outlined the views presented by the department's draft support material:

> Terms such as **discovery**, **pioneers** or **exploration** should be used in their historical context. With approximately 40 000 years of **occupation** of Australia, **Indigenous** people had already discovered, explored and named all parts of the continent. Various parts were re-named by **European explorers** . . .

Many **Aborigines** and **Torres Strait Islanders** interpret the **arrival** of the First Fleet and the subsequent spread of **European settlements** as an **invasion**. Many **non-Indigenous people**, including a considerable number of historians, agree with the application of the term 'invasion' to some of the events which have taken place since the **transportation** of **convicts** and the establishment of the **penal colony** in 1788. Others argue that the terms **colonisation, non-Indigenous occupation** or **settlement** accurately describe the same events and actions.

The state Opposition leader, Rob Borbidge, said the book was a disgrace. 'This is just the tip of the iceberg of the effort that's underway to make our entire education system politically correct and many stupidities will have to be weeded out.' Bob Quinn, the shadow minister for education, agreed: 'White people came out here and settled and that is it'.

Responses from Labor Premier Wayne Goss contradicted his own education department. He rejected the department's attempts to remove the offending representations of Indigenous people from the previous sourcebook, and argued that terms like 'invasion' went too far. There was a need to present Australian history honestly and fairly, he said, but 'this does not mean that we need to reinvent the language'. 'I think that just about all Australians would not regard what happened in 1788 as an invasion', he asserted. 'There is a world of difference between the arrival of the First Fleet and what most people understand as an invasion.'

Goss was under political and popular pressure to distance himself from the revision his own government had commissioned. Editorials complaining of government attempts to 'rewrite history' ensured that the debate became a heated and controversial focus of public discussion. Meanwhile, the bulk of correspondence to the *Courier-Mail* displayed disbelief and anger that European colonisation could be construed as anything but 'settlement'; 'invasion' was simply an unhelpful term of political correctness.

Geoff Temby from Hamilton complained of double standards: 'what about the British people who were forcibly transported here in chains, and their descendents? Are they invaders? And what about the Europeans and Asians who have been encouraged and financially sponsored by governments to migrate here? Are they invaders?' Another correspondent, Barry G. Shield, felt that the reluctance to use terms from a proud pioneering history was misplaced and ill-founded. 'That Mitchell, Leichhardt, Stuart, Oxley etc. were going where countless other feet had trod does not detract from the fact that, as far as the Europeans were concerned, they were exploring new territory, and were thus "pioneers".'

Goss maintained that his intervention was designed to ensure that schools would teach 'the facts' so that students could 'make up their own mind as to whether they regard the events of 1788 as an invasion or settlement'. Yet his explanation ignored the premise of the new Queensland text, which included an attempt to provide contrasting historical perspectives of European colonisation ('invasion' *and* 'settlement'). Moreover, the debate overlooked the fact that the previous sourcebook, in spite of its significant shortcomings, itself had used the word 'invasion' to describe the establishment of the Australian colonies.

Goss had astutely identified how politically damaging the furore could become. By accepting the *Courier-Mail*'s populist attack on the sourcebook, he attempted to defuse the charges of prejudice and political correctness levelled by the paper. In doing so, he effectively legitimated its tabloid scare tactics.

There were similar arguments in other states. At the 1994 state conference of the National Party, the New South Wales Liberal minister for education, Virginia Chadwick, was condemned for allowing the word 'invasion' to be included in the new primary social studies syllabus in place of 'settlement'. The delegate who initiated the motion of censure insisted on promoting the pioneering heritage of Australian history: 'The wording as is—settlement instead of invasion—portrays the idea [that] white man came into Australia and settled without the idea of invading the country'.

The draft was consequently toned down. 'Invasion' was removed from some sections of the syllabus and replaced by more 'neutral' terms, such as 'arrival of British people' and 'before 1788'. In response, the New South Wales Teachers' Federation threatened to ban the syllabus. John Howard, then in Opposition, accused the federation of attempting to distort the past to make a 'contemporary political point'. Its members were guilty of 'ideologically driven intellectual thuggery'. 'The description "invasion"', he later maintained, 'should never have been in the syllabus in the first place'. Aligning himself with the conservative campaign against 'invasion', Howard capitalised astutely on public anxiety over teaching an unduly negative or Black Armband Australian story.

Speaking with the Sydney talk-back radio host John Laws after his election in 1996, Prime Minister Howard denounced the history curriculum: 'To tell children whose parents were not part of that maltreatment', he suggested, 'to tell children who themselves have been no part of it, that we're all part of it, that we're part of a sort of racist and bigoted history is something that Australians reject.' Howard refused to acknowledge the historical continuity of race relations on the one hand, while commemorating the unbroken legacy of the Anzac legend on the other.

In Victoria, too, political ideologies influenced shifts in syllabus design. In the unit of Koori history in the 1991 senior *History Study Design*, for example, the syllabus stated that 'In order to retain control of their unique cultural identity, Koori people have responded in a variety of ways to continuous pressures to disperse and assimilate since the European invasion'. By 1996, the text was the same but for the last two words: 'In order to retain control of their unique cultural identity, Koori people have responded in a variety of ways to continuous pressures to disperse and assimilate since the British settlement'.

Overhaul of the syllabus began directly after a state election and change of government. The curriculum developed under the former Labor government had come under increasing conservative criticism that its emphasis on concepts such as 'power', 'race', 'gender', 'class' and 'ideology' was politically biased. The former *History Study Design* was summarily rewritten in line with the priorities of the new administration led by Liberal Premier Jeff Kennett.

Yet divisions along party lines are not always so overt. Indeed, the positions taken up by Goss and Chadwick run counter to the black–white, left–right dichotomy implied by terms such as 'History Wars'. Each incursion by politicians into the curriculum, however, reveals the political valency of history education: governments motivated by popular concerns have quickly intervened in educational battles for the past. And the school History Wars have been very public battles, intensified by media coverage and public opinion. No politician can afford to be seen promoting critical history to 'our children'. More than simply an ideological struggle, contest over school history is also a political strategy.

The syllabus, with its power to define the nation's past, is seen to define the nation itself. It presents public figures wishing to make their mark on 'our history' with an irresistible temptation. The image of 'our' youth as a collective empty vessel waiting to be taught 'the Australian story' is inherent in this compulsion. In fact, it is the child—this vulnerable image of the future—that has underpinned the conflict over the past in schools. As the debate has become more heated, and moved seemingly beyond explicit political divisions, the child has become even more vital as a site of contention.

The extension of the History Wars into schools has not been confined to Australia. Disputes over history textbooks and syllabuses generate concern around the world and demonstrate a great investment in the past. The development of national histories in countries such as Israel, where the past is so contested, has been fraught with difficulty. Likewise, history teaching in nations that have undergone reconstruction, such as post-war Germany or Japan, has aroused considerable anxiety and unease. In Japan there has been continuing tension regarding the recognition in schools of the nation's military imperialism in the 1930s and 1940s. Attempts to acknowledge the brutal invasion and occupation of China, for instance, or the treatment of 'comfort women' by the Japanese army, have been rejected by many Japanese nationalists as unpatriotic.

For thirty-five years, the Japanese Ministry of Education was embroiled in a battle to censor a history text by a professor and former high school history teacher, Ienaga Saburo. He had written in his 1962 edition that 'many of the Japanese officers and soldiers violated Chinese women' during their occupation. The ministry ordered that the passage be deleted. 'The violation of women', it stated, 'is something that happened on every battlefield in every era of human history. This is not an issue that needs to be taken up with respect to the Japanese Army in particular.'

Ienaga finally won a legal appeal in 1997. Yet only four years later a new Japanese textbook presenting this history more benignly was released. According to Nobukatsu Fujioka, professor of education at Tokyo University and founder of the Japanese Society for Textbook Reform, 'Japanese children are only taught their country has done bad things. They are not taught anything they can be proud of. The current textbooks only teach them how to apologise.'

The Second World War evokes particularly heated debate. In 2002 the German ambassador accused the British syllabus of fuelling xenophobia by concentrating on the Nazi era of his country's history. 'I think it is very important that people know as much as possible about the Nazi period and the Holocaust', Thomas Matussek acknowledged. 'But what is equally important is the history of Germany in the past 45 years and the success story of modern German democracy.'

Only three days later, it was England's turn to lay blame for apparent political bias and historical inaccuracy. History teaching in Scotland was accused of propounding excessively nationalist sentiments. According to the *Daily Mail*, the so-called 'Braveheart' approach of the Scottish history curriculum was fuelling 'anti-English bigotry'. This unease over national representations revived memories of the debate over the English curriculum more than ten years earlier.

Anxious that the development and teaching of history curricula had become too diffuse and progressive, Margaret Thatcher's Tory government attempted to return curriculum design to a national set of core knowledge. The schools minister, Baroness Margaret Blatch, attacked the 'silly sixties-based approach' of contemporary teaching methods. The government asked the National Curriculum Council in 1990 to ensure that the learning of facts came before vague, so-called 'skills' in its review of how history should be taught. It was 'absolutely right', added Prime Minister Thatcher, for the new history curriculum to concentrate on monarchs, insisting that 'children should know the great landmarks of British history'.

It was not national curriculum, but national standards, that formed the focus of America's history teaching Wars. Unlike syllabuses, which direct learning approaches, standards outline learning targets. As such, this debate was a contest over expectations of student attainment, rather than simply contrasting approaches to the past.

While the 'invasion–settlement' debate was raging in Australia, the development of the National History Standards in the United States generated overwhelming public interest and discussion. Initiated with a view to national testing, the National History Standards were funded by President George Bush's National Committee of Excellence in Education in 1989, and continued under the subsequent Clinton administration. Yet by their release in 1994, the standards aroused considerable discontent and criticism from academics, educationalists and commentators across the country.

Lynne Cheney, the director of the National Endowment for the Humanities, which had helped finance their development, spoke out angrily against the new standards. 'The general drift of the document becomes apparent when one realises that not a single one of the 31 standards mentions the Constitution.' She continued: 'The authors tend to save their unqualified admiration for people, places and events that are politically correct ... We are a better people than the National Standards indicate, and our children deserve better'. The educationalist Diane Ravitch insisted that 'the implicit theme' in the standards document 'seems to be the ongoing (and usually unsuccessful) struggle by the oppressed to wrest rights and power from selfish white male Protestants'.

A conservative columnist, Charles Krauthammer, dismissed the standards in the *Washington Post*, for being 'hijacked by the educational establishment and turned into a classic of political correctness'. The rhetoric of the conservative attack mirrored the school History Wars in Australia: 'our children' were in danger from politically correct national apologies for colonial greed. Moreover, the 'hijacking' of history curricula by moderates threatened educational standards.

In January 1995 the US Senate considered a resolution against the standards. It moved also to cut funding to the National Centre for History in the Schools at UCLA, which had overseen the development of the standards. The resolutions were passed 99 to 1. Senator Slade Gorton, who introduced them, called for standards that showed 'a decent respect for the contributions of western civilisation, and US history, ideas, and institutions, to the increase of freedom and prosperity around the world'. In response, Gary Nash, a historian and a key member of the writing team, argued that the detractors had confused the role of standards with that of a textbook. The standards, he contended, were designed to reduce the emphasis on overly dry school texts and the memorisation of names, dates and places.

In his later analysis of the episode, Nash defended the standards against charges of political and historical partiality. Critical historians were not unpatriotic, he insisted, but believed in reforming America to make it a better place. His attempt to define progressive history as following the democratic trajectory of America itself failed to dampen the conservative critique. While eventually upheld by two independent committees, the attack on the standards had tapped into a deeply politicised anxiety over American nationality and identity which was inseparable from understandings of its past.

The equation of educational standards with national understanding has also powerfully influenced recent debates in Australia. In 2000, the *Courier-Mail* again exposed Queensland's new Studies of Society and Environment (SOSE) syllabus for apparent political bias and educational inadequacy. 'Captain Cook and Sir Robert Menzies do not feature in a new Queensland schools syllabus booklet', wrote Martin Thomas, 'but Eddie Mabo and Ho Chi Minh do'. Claims of political one-sidedness prompted the media campaign. Opposition to the new syllabus, continued Thomas, objected to the way it advocated 'environmental zealotry and communist heroes while dismissing white settlement as an invasion'.

Ted Wilson remonstrated that the syllabus was gravely misrepresentative of 'our history'. 'To omit people such as Captain Cook, Robert Menzies and many others from the teaching of history is ludicrous', he considered. 'We are trying to instil national pride and feelings of self-worth in our youth but are denying them the most important part of their heritage.'

As the debate wore on, argument over educational standards came to the fore. In 1989 the states and territories agreed to the creation of a new national curriculum framework that would be defined by common standards in key learning areas. History, along with geography, literature, politics and other subjects in the humanities and social sciences, was subsumed into a single key learning area called Studies of Society and Environment. While these standards could be taught through traditional disciplines such as history, schools increasingly dropped such subjects in favour of integrated approaches called SOSE.

The incorporation of history into SOSE by all states except New South Wales during the 1990s was criticised by a number of history educators and teacher associations for weakening the discipline. Enrolments in Senior History had declined in most states, history was often being taught by teachers with no background in the discipline, and many teachers felt the subject was being squeezed out of increasingly crowded SOSE syllabuses by the inclusion of units such as drug education.

The Queensland debate was framed by a growing professional concern over the state of history within SOSE, and the *Courier-Mail* used this educational anxiety to maintain political pressure against the Queensland School Curriculum Council. John Lidstone, an associate professor of education at the Queensland University of Technology, criticised SOSE for its tendency to deteriorate into studies of 'good causes', for having no internationally agreed standards of rigour, and therefore little potential for seeding a lifelong love of learning.

The Melbourne journalist Andrew Bolt contended that the 'education experts' of the Beattie Labor government in Queensland had 'launched the most radical attempt in Australia to indoctrinate children in key Left-wing values'. The renaming, he added, had allowed 'education ideologues to drop content-based teaching of traditional subjects and switch to [the] teaching of mere opinions without alerting parents to what they are up to'.

Similar concerns about the educational standards of the syllabus were expressed in letters and editorials. Writing to the *Courier-Mail*, John Meredith advised that those 'who devised the new curriculum are more concerned with promoting their own opinions than teaching the facts that must be known if students are to have a good education'. In a similar tone, an editorial advocated that the syllabus 'ought to be dumped for something less ideological and more in tune with what students need'. Rather than reproducing 'the values' of the syllabus writers, another insisted, 'Our children need knowledge that ensures they are as smart—or smarter than—children from the US, Singapore or Japan'.

Responding to criticism of its grave deficiencies, a number of teachers and syllabus designers argued that on the contrary the SOSE syllabus was of a high educational standard—although the *Courier-Mail* chose not to print a number of these rejoinders. State school principals maintained that the syllabus 'will ensure young Queenslanders learn to become active and informed citizens in an increasingly complex and ever-changing world'.

An unpublished letter from the Queensland School Curriculum Council insisted that the 'new syllabus is serious about developing children's knowledge of Australia's past. It specifies what students should know and be able to do by identifying a comprehensive set of core learning outcomes and associated key concepts.' The History Wars had apparently moved from a debate over the values of the syllabus to its relevance for 'Queensland children'. Educational standards, rather than explicit political divisions, increasingly framed the campaign against the syllabus.

Despite this rhetorical shift, the campaign remained highly political. First, the defence by the *Courier-Mail* that its coverage of the debate was balanced and objective reflected the way it had taken up the controversy of history teaching as a public issue. The pretence of 'balance' was made despite editorialising and investigative journalism that was continually dismissive of the new syllabus. Capitalising on widespread anxiety about history, even shifting its line to encompass emerging discussions about historical standards in education, the paper's criticism of the SOSE syllabus for being narrow and polemical ignored the fact that it was itself advocating an approach to the past that prescribed historical knowledge.

Second, educational standards make political sense. Politicians keen to emphasise their commitment to teaching and learning have increasingly adopted more rigid systems of testing and educational accountability. History is no exception. In New South Wales, Labor Premier Bob Carr made headlines by strengthening the mandatory Australian History syllabus, prescribing increased teaching time and a compulsory exam at the end of Year 10. Even before his election, Carr campaigned with the promise that a Labor government would overhaul the curriculum in New South Wales. 'There is a core of knowledge that each citizen should have as a result of his or her schooling', he asserted.

At the federal level, too, there has been strong support for programs and initiatives designed to overcome the apparent lack of national historical knowledge of 'our children'. Between 1997 and 2001, the federal government contributed $29 million to the civics education program, Discovering Democracy. Launching the report of the National Inquiry into the State of History in Schools in 2000, Education Minister David Kemp said that he had commissioned the inquiry because he 'was concerned that, as we approach the Centenary of Federation, the study of history was declining in our schools'.

Being 'strong on history' is good politics. On Constitution Day 2002, only a few days after the first anniversary of September 11, President George W. Bush announced massive increases in funding for national history teaching. (In February 2003 the 'Teaching of Traditional American History' initiative was budgeted at US$100 million.) It was 'Especially important in a time of war', he said, 'that our children understand the context of why we fight'. 'History is important for our children to understand', he added, 'to give them a better sense of how to understand what we do and a sense of what it means to be an American'. 'When children are given the real history of America', Bush maintained, 'they will also learn to love America. Our Founders believed the study of history and citizenship should be at the core of every American's education. Yet today, our children have large and disturbing gaps in their knowledge of history.'

'Our children' have become the defining image of the school History Wars. At once 'all our futures', as Howard Hutchins insisted, they are also an imaginary conduit for the past. The increasing alignment of the Wars with educational debates over standards and expected student attainment reflects the political struggle to locate a figure which unifies rather than polarises. Politicians and educators of various leanings have attempted to define the terms of historical debates with a more collective image, which 'the child' provides. Yet far from ending the contest over the past, debate has intensified with the insertion of this symbol of the future into the History Wars.

CHAPTER 10

WORKING THROUGH THE MUSEUM'S LABELS

In October 2000 a member of the Council of the National Museum of Australia wrote to the chair of the council to express his concern with the exhibitions it was shortly to display. The council had been briefed on the selection of the themes and objects that had been prepared for the opening of the museum in the following year. It had debated at length the way the exhibits would be displayed and this council member was given the opportunity to examine the explanatory labels that would accompany them. There were thousands of them and when he wrote to the chair of the council he said that 'I am still working my way through these labels but I have read enough of them to be able to predict that we are heading for trouble'.

The council member was David Barnett, who with his wife Pru Goward had written a biography of his friend John Howard two years earlier. The council chair was Tony Staley, a former minister in the Fraser government and the federal president of the Liberal Party from 1993 to 1999.

Barnett's objections ranged widely. He objected to the text that accompanied an exhibit on the disappearance of Harold Holt because it referred to a claim that the prime minister had been a spy and was picked up off the coast of Portsea by a Chinese submarine. He objected to the inclusion of the trade union activist and Labor senator, Bill Morrow, who had been awarded the Lenin Peace Prize, and the anti-nuclear protester Benny Zable. 'Why Benny Zable, and not Hugh Morgan, who created wealth for Australia and jobs for Australians?' He objected to the inclusion of popular entertainers such as The Wiggles. He objected to an exhibit on the Stolen Generations as 'a victim episode'. And he objected to the glamorisation of a bushranger, Captain Moonlite.

These and other objections covered considerable ground. Barnett's sensitivity to the treatment of the death of Harold Holt (the label had in fact quoted a newspaper report of the Chinese spy claim, and described it as 'the most bizarre hypo-thesis') carried an implication that Liberal politicians were singled out for irreverence: 'if we think death is so funny, why don't we have Ben Chifley as well as Harold Holt?' The pro-posal to replace protesters with businessmen was polemical: Barnett suggested that Chris Corrigan, a union buster and self-confessed liar, should balance the 'Marxist rubbish' he found in the exhibits. The objection to the treatment of In-digenous issues was provocative: claiming that he had never seen a reference to Faith Bandler 'that was not positive', Barnett somehow concluded that 'the tenor of the labels is racism'.

Barnett expected a different sort of exhibition, a different sort of museum. In a memo he wrote to the acting director earlier in the year, he said that the role of a museum was to 'present history, not to debate it'. In his letter to Tony Staley he said that a national museum could be expected to provide 'interesting exhibits dealing with the founding fathers and telling us who past prime ministers have been and something about them, without being egregious'. He argued that the National Museum should not advocate causes, should not be a 'gateway for political activism' and 'should not be a contributor to the reworking of Australian history into political correctness'. He warned of trouble from the public, the parliament and the media—and he was well placed to arrange it.

Tony Staley had a problem. The museum was due to open in less than six months, and the opening was fixed in the calendar for the Centenary of Federation. It would not be possible to start anew and assemble a wholly new exhibition. Even if Barnett's views had been shared by other members of the council, there were limits to its capacity to ride roughshod over a statutory agency of the Commonwealth. Staley therefore decided to seek an expert review of David Barnett's concerns and he asked Geoffrey Blainey who should undertake it. Blainey recommended Graeme Davison, a professor of history at Monash University with a longstanding interest in public history.

Davison examined Barnett's allegations in detail, checked them against the relevant historical sources, and concluded that the criticisms were ill-founded. The overwhelming majority of the labels were correct and based on sound scholarship. This did not mean that every label of every individual exhibit had to be acceptable to every visitor, he advised, for that would make for 'a very bland museum'. Davison argued that a museum could be 'simultaneously provocative and scholarly', and that it would necessarily 'register strongly partisan viewpoints'. The role of the council was to ensure there was a sufficient variety of these viewpoints, and beyond that should not interfere. He referred back to the blueprint of the museum contained in a report written twenty-five years earlier, to which Geoffrey Blainey had contributed: it insisted that a national museum should encourage debate and not shy away from controversy.

There was a sting in his own report. He detected an underlying theme in David Barnett's letter that the labels expressed 'a kind of systematic bias in the interpretation of Australian history', the bias of political correctness. He said that Barnett 'gives the impression—which I am sure he does not really hold—that the museum should follow the historical views of the government of the day'. Davison hoped that this was not the view of Tony Staley and his council, who would surely appreciate that the historical interpretations presented in the museum must 'survive changes of government and councils'.

This was a shrewd thrust. One of the spoils of our system of government is the appointment of lay members to a vast range of public boards, councils and advisory bodies. These appointments carry modest remuneration but confer status and influence. The morning airflights to Canberra are swollen with passengers carrying their agenda and papers, bringing their expertise, expectations and interests—others will have flown in the evening before to beat the fog and claim their travel allowance.

The escalation of the History Wars and the background battle of ideas give particular significance to cultural agencies such as the ABC, the Australia Council, the National Gallery, the National Library, the National Archives and now the National Museum. The members of their governing bodies are appointed for fixed terms by the minister or the Executive Council. There used to be an expectation that those appointed would bring a range of useful qualities drawn from a spread of states: hence, for example, the National Library would hope to have some scholars, some librarians, some well-connected business executives, someone from Perth and Brisbane as well as Sydney and Melbourne.

Over the past two decades such expectations have yielded to the brute dictates of *realpolitik*. While I was a member of the Council of the National Library in the late 1980s and early 1990s, the membership narrowed to true believers from New South Wales and we found ourselves with not one representative of News Corporation but two. The Howard government has followed the same pattern. When the term of Michael Kroger on the board of the ABC expired, the government appointed the former Liberal staff-member and researcher for the Institute of Public Affairs, Ron Brunton. Not content with the prime minister's biographer on the Council of the National Museum, it added his former speechwriter—perhaps we should be grateful that John Howard prefers power-walking to equestrian exercise or his regard for history might have tempted him to follow the emperor Caligula and make his horse a consul.

These political appointees are outspoken in their allegations of bias, highly interventionist in their demands. They have taken an unprecedented interest in the way cultural institutions deal with the past. Any suggestion of the Black Armband incurs their displeasure. Richard Alston, the minister for communications, information technology and the arts, and Rod Kemp, the junior minister for the arts, also take a keen interest, so keen that some of these bodies have succumbed to self-censorship. Dr Brian Kennedy, the director-general of the National Gallery, went so far as to seek Senator Alston's approval of a proposed exhibition. A senior curator, John McDonald, who prepared an essay to accompany a display by the gallery on the theme of federation, was told that it paid too much attention to reconciliation and the republic.

Those who resist such pressures are punished. When the original term of Dawn Casey as director of the National Museum expired in 2002, the government granted her just one further year.

Tony Staley accepted the advice of Graeme Davison and the museum opened in March 2001 with its exhibition intact. It presented an irresistible target in the History Wars. 'Museum offers tangled vision of Australia', 'National pride and prejudices', 'Making an exhibition of ourselves' and 'A nation trivialised—White history a "bad joke"' were among the headlines used by the newspaper columnists who specialised in such rhetoric.

Miranda Devine, a tabloid columnist, claimed that the museum had 'adopted the left-wing position on every conceivable issue' and that its 'underlying message' was one of 'sneering ridicule for white Australia'. Piers Ackerman spoke for most of the tabloid intellectuals when he said the museum suffered from political correctness, but others complained of its absence. Pru Goward, who was the head of the Office for the Status of Women, alleged that the museum trivialised the contribution of women.

Barnett's earlier criticisms became public in June when the *Sydney Morning Herald* obtained his letter to Tony Staley as well as Davison's subsequent report. In September Keith Windschuttle took up the campaign in a long article in *Quadrant*. He too directed his primary criticism at the presentation of non-Indigenous history, which he saw as 'a repository of nothing more that the intellectual poverty of the tertiary-educated middle class of the post-Vietnam era'.

By December Windschuttle was emphasising his dissatisfaction with the museum's presentation of frontier conflict, and also his complaint that the very design of the museum shaped its building as a lightning bolt, a symbol taken from the Jewish Museum that signified Aboriginals suffered the equivalent of a Holocaust. Windschuttle repeated this claim a year later in his book on *The Fabrication of Australian History*, and more recently still in his submission to a review of the museum.

Windschuttle contributed to the public campaign against the National Museum but the decisive campaign was conducted in its council. David Barnett was a persistent but clumsy antagonist. Christopher Pearson was a more skilful operator, using his contacts in the prime minister's office to put pressure on the council, its chair and even its minister. Some council members resisted. A review of the museum seemed to offer some resolution of the debilitating disputes that racked its council.

There was then a further argument over its composition and terms of reference. Rod Kemp, the minister, chose John Carroll to chair it, and we have already seen their association during the Bicentennial phase of the History Wars. Christopher Pearson added Philip Jones, the senior curator of anthropology at the South Australian Museum and an important ally during the Hindmarsh Island affair. Cathy Santamaria, formerly a deputy secretary of the department and a supporter of Dawn Casey, nominated Richard Longes, a Sydney businessman with Aboriginal interests.

Andrew Reeves, a former museum director, noted the absence from the review of a historian, a woman or an Indigenous representative. Various historians were canvassed but none were found acceptable. Geoffrey Blainey declined. John Hirst was vetoed as a republican, Graeme Davison's connection with the *Oxford Companion to Australian History* disqualified him. In the end, Patricia Vickers-Rich, a palaeobiologist from Monash University, was added.

It is a political maxim that you should not establish an inquiry unless you know at the outset what you wish it to find. In this case, the trail from the government to the Council is so clearly marked, the connection between the History Wars and the review so clearly articulated, as to leave no-one in doubt of the timing and purpose. Against the weight of expectations, John Carroll and his three colleagues affirmed the approach taken by the National Museum and accepted that it should treat controversial issues. Their report, delivered in July 2003, 'came to the conclusion that political or cultural bias is not a systemic problem at the NMA'.

The battle over the National Museum marks a new phase in the History Wars. Previously waged over the popular depiction and political uses of Australian history, it had concentrated its attack on academic historians. The allegation that these historians besmirched the national reputation fed claims that they were impotent and frustrated university radicals. The accusation that they falsified the past challenged the authority of their lamentations. The purpose was to weaken the influence of Black Armband history by discrediting its proponents.

The attack on the museum went further. Here the object was to impose control on a public institution, to override the professional judgement of its staff and to root out exhibitions that challenged the critics' preferred version of history. This was no longer a campaign against political correctness, it was an imposition of affirmative orthodoxy.

The public museum is a particular kind of national institution that serves the need for preservation and display, commemoration and instruction, research and entertainment. The nineteenth-century museum combined its scientific role of collecting natural history, fauna, flora and human artefacts with the civic role of educating and enlightening its citizens. The twentieth-century museum took on the responsibility of representing the nation's values and identity. Hence Dawn Casey, the director of the National Museum of Australia, spoke after it opened of the responsibility to help visitors 'to understand Australian history and nationhood better'.

The National Museum also took on an expectation of inclusiveness. When Senator Alston announced its construction in 1996, he said it would be a place 'where all the stories of our nation are told and our unique cultural mix is explored'. This in turn altered the museum from a storehouse of exotic objects to a presenter of 'diverse stories', as the director of the National Museum put it; the visitor was no longer instructed but invited to enter into a conversation. The museum became a meeting place where the various groups that made up the nation could meet—or, as Dawn Casey put it, the new museum provided a 'a forum, a place for dialogue, a social agent' for healing and reconciliation.

Cases of scientific specimens gave way to objects drawn from everyday life—in the case of the National Museum, an inverted Hills hoist and a Victa lawn-mower attracted particular attention—that would serve as cues to memory. The modern museum was no longer a repository and a place of solemn hush. It was expected to draw large numbers of visitors, to count them and to respond to their expectations. It became a place of entertainment, with shops and restaurants, a background buzz of commentary and interactive exhibits.

With these transformations the museum gave up its claim to omniscience. The long-delayed National Museum had received its charter from a Committee of Inquiry into Museums and National Collections established by the Whitlam government in 1974. Two members of that committee were John Mulvaney and Geoffrey Blainey. Mulvaney was the archaeologist who gave the Aboriginal occupation of this country a new depth and complexity, while Blainey was at the time completing his history of Aboriginal Australia, *Triumph of the Nomads*.

Sharing the excitement of intellectual discovery, they could see that an Australian national museum would have to challenge its visitors. If the human history of Australia was marked by a twelve-hour clock-face, they declared, 'the era of the white man would run for only the last three or four minutes'. The National Museum would therefore need to confront Australians with a deep history of human endeavour that would shrink its familiar landmarks and unsettle the familiar version of Australian history.

Mulvaney and Blainey said that the museum should comprise three main themes: Aborigines in Australia, Europeans in Australia, and human interaction with the Australian environment. It should draw on 'recent history' to show how knowledge of Australia's natural history and human history was 'unfolding in exciting ways', and Aboriginal people should help determine how their story was told. The two men anticipated controversy and advised that the museum should not shy from it: 'In our view, too many museums concentrate on certainty and dogma, thereby forsaking the function of stimulating legitimate doubt and thoughtful discussion'.

These themes and the principles behind them were affirmed in 1980 when the Fraser government enacted legislation to establish the National Museum, and again in 1996 when the Howard government undertook to build it. The director of the museum at that time placed such emphasis on its role as a 'social history museum . . . telling the wonderful story of Australia' that Mulvaney worried that it might become a Disneyland tourist facility. He also rejected the proposition that the museum should tell the story of Australia: 'The idea we had is that there was no such single story.'

When Dawn Casey became director, she asked four scholars—Geoffrey Bolton, John Mulvaney, Kay Saunders and Graeme Davison—to serve as the museum's advisers. They prepared guidelines that upheld the original generous vision. Not all council members agreed. David Barnett wanted to include a statement that the National Museum would 'celebrate the creation of a proud nation in a scant 200 years' and 'strengthen our national pride'. The advisers managed to persuade the council that the scant 200 years omitted most of Australian history.

Barnett also objected to the advisers' statement that the museum should 'challenge' the visitor to reflect on our past. A meeting between Christopher Pearson and Graeme Davison (who had drafted the guidelines) failed to overcome this difference. Davison was backed by Bolton and Mulvaney (Kay Saunders had bowed out) in a threat to make their views public and the council bowed to their advice.

The guidelines adopted by the museum committed it to 'promote informed debate on historical and scientific issues of national importance'. The same guidelines recognised that visitors would expect to find something more than a seminar on Australian history and science. They would expect 'an uplifting and exciting vision of the national past' and the museum should 'strengthen their sense of national pride and belonging'.

The advisers managed to avoid reference to national identity, which is to be found in the mission statements of so many other national museums. Graeme Davison was conscious of its popularity and wary of the expectations it set in motion. He has pointed out that national identity is a comparatively new idea. Nations once appealed to race or blood as the basis of their nationhood; subsequent generations of Australians spoke of the national character or way of life. Identity came later, from psychoanalysis, and suggests that the nation acquires or even discovers an identity in a process that continues throughout its life-course. This concern for national identity, moreover, arose at the very point when the identity politics of sex, race and ethnicity were fracturing the older, essentialist versions of nationhood. National identity, if you like, is a search occasioned by its absence.

For that very reason it is a term the History Warriors discourage. In his Sir Robert Menzies Lecture oration in 1996, the prime minister condemned the 'endless and agonised navel-gazing about who we are or, as seems to have happened over recent years, as part of a "perpetual seminar" for elite opinion about our national identity'. David Barnett found signs of such indulgence when he read the National Museum's labels and he reminded Tony Staley that 'the prime minister was adamant that the Museum was not to define an Australian identity'.

While the advisers had not written a pursuit of the national identity into the guidelines, Graeme Davison found it hard to believe that the curators of a national museum could abstain from the subject—and equally hard to believe 'that the PM should have ordered them to do so, or that the Museum should take any notice if he did'. His incredulity is understandable, for such an instruction would be a grossly improper interference as well as an exercise in political correctness. Davison's own view was that an exhibit dealing with national identity should recognise its pluralist character and be respectful of the differences it would necessarily find.

The new museology, with its emphasis on selection, interpretation and display, serves this attempt to recognise diversity and create a conversation that its component communities can share. But the museum is also a custodian of heritage, and a national museum is expected to safeguard the legacy of the past. Many look to the museum as a place of permanence in a changing world, and are uneasy with innovatory practices of the museum profession.

These expectations operated with particular force on our first national museum, the Australian War Memorial. Opened in the darkest days of the Second World War and prominently situated on Anzac Parade, in alignment with Capital Hill, it provided a permanent display of the relics of the Great War along with documentary records and exhibitions of the principal engagements.

The War Memorial was shaped by C. E. W. Bean, the official war correspondent and later the official war historian, who as early as 1917 wrote an article entitled 'Australian Records Preserved as Sacred Things'. It was Bean who selected the site and laid down the principles that informed its display galleries: the items should be carefully selected and precisely labelled; they should not celebrate individual heroes or glorify war. Their purpose was to preserve the memory of those who gave their lives, and the memorial's central cloisters record the names of every Australian fatality, without military ranks or decorations.

The War Memorial decayed as Bean's founding principles were neglected or abandoned, and other traditions were superimposed on them. He was the acknowledged leader of the memorial and its contact point with government until his resignation from the governing body in 1963, but the post subsequently fell into the hands of retired senior officers. He had called for professional curatorial staff as he realised that his generation, with its intimate knowledge of the Great War, would pass away, but the memorial was staffed by public servants chosen for their record of service in the Second World War.

Bean's idea of the memorial was truly democratic. He strenuously opposed the display of military honours because he believed that the awards for valour were far from comprehensive and that every man who served in the trenches showed bravery. His successor insisted on the creation of 'VC Corner' and the War Memorial subsequently spent large sums on acquiring Victoria Crosses. Bean wanted the exhibitions to be renewed so that they would engage younger generations but later custodians resisted tampering with the original dioramas. He pushed for extensions so that the memorial could provide adequate space for the Second World War but they were not made until 1971 and meanwhile the memorial disposed of many items.

In the 1970s the War Memorial embarked on a belated program of renewal. Curators and conservators were recruited. A History, Publications and Library branch was created. Handbooks and guides were prepared, education programs introduced, grants provided to support historical research on the collections and an annual conference organised. War history, which had scarcely existed outside the military college, was introduced into the school and university curriculum and became a lively branch of the historical discipline. Michael McKernan, an accomplished historian from the University of New South Wales, joined the War Memorial in 1981 and guided these endeavours as deputy director.

Yet this very success brought suspicion from traditionalists who doubted that younger scholars, with no combat experience, could improve on the official histories and looked askance on their new forms of interpretation. There was similar resistance within the memorial to the alteration of familiar displays. A former president of the volunteer guides wondered if all the innovation was not 'change for change's sake' and added that 'I don't think Dr Bean would approve of what is happening here'. Wielding his new broom, the director proposed in 1977 to rename the institution the Australian

War Memorial Museum, a proposal scuttled by ex-service organisations. One historian on the staff observed the wariness of his colleagues. They feared that the president of the RSL regarded the War Memorial as a shrine. 'It's a memorial', he claimed, 'because it is a museum, an archive, a gallery and a centre of research'.

A major dispute broke out in 1983 over further extensions to the War Memorial and escalated into an argument between the professional staff and the military custodians. Sir William Keys, the president of the RSL, gained an early success when he had the government transfer the memorial from the Arts portfolio to the Department of Veterans' Affairs. But the chair of the War Memorial Council, a former admiral, walked the plank after he lost the support of his wardroom, and the director, an ex-air vice-marshal, followed soon after grumbling against the radicals who had undermined him. One of his parliamentary supporters alleged that 'a small dishonest cadre of dishonest academics' was conspiring to turn the memorial into a peace museum.

The new chair of the council was Dame Beryl Beaurepaire, who had served in the Women's Auxiliary Australian Air Force but was unacceptable to Keys on at least two grounds: her sex and her lack of military seniority. He responded by forming a memorial 'watch-dog' committee at the seventieth congress of the RSL in 1985 and increased his criticism of the memorial's 'trendy attitudes'. But Beaurepaire, an able and determined woman, saw him off and rode out the storm. No History Warrior, William Keys was able to examine his position and became a great supporter of Beryl Beaurepaire.

This controversy, then, ended in an affirmation of the independence of the War Memorial, the place of the nation's most potent stories, from those who sought to police its activities. The outcome invites comparison with the episode a decade later when the Smithsonian Museum mounted its exhibition of war history. As related in Chapter 1, the attempt to present a critical account of the story of the *Enola Gay* and the dropping of the atomic bomb on Hiroshima and Nagasaki brought a barrage of condemnation from right-wing commentators. A crucial player in that controversy was the veterans' organisations, which had been invited onto the museum's advisory committee but broke ranks when the hostilities began to condemn the insult to national honour. The director resigned, and the exhibition was revised to meet the veterans' wishes.

Why did their Australian counterparts fail in a similar campaign against the Australian War Memorial? Part of the explanation lies in the role played by council members. Beryl Beaurepaire, a stout defender of the memorial, had been the vice-president of the Victorian division of the Liberal Party. Yvonne McComb, a former president of the Queensland division of the Liberal Party, was another well-informed and supportive council member. These two women, with their extensive connections, ensured that the controversy did not form on party lines. The Labor government's appointment of Beaurepaire to chair the War Memorial Council was a welcome instance of respect for its non-partisan character.

More than this, however, the argument over the War Memorial occurred before the terms of the History Wars were established, before the idea of political correctness had taken root and the denunciation of Black Armband history had created such suspicion of any tampering with the past. It was the Enola Gay dispute that gave rise to the term 'History Wars', and the publicity generated around it alerted Australian publicists to its potential. Back in the 1980s it was still possible to call for a more inclusive commemoration of war without attracting accusations of betrayal. In 1984 the Council of the War Memorial agreed to include a chapter on frontier conflict, entitled 'The Struggle for Australia', in its book for the Bicentenary on 200 years of Australian warfare. It excited no controversy.

Indeed, when the memorial was exploring the extensions to the building that sparked the upsurge of criticism, its design consultant asked Geoffrey Blainey for suggestions about how the displays could be improved. Blainey recommended a more interpretive approach. He also proposed that the memorial should broaden its coverage to include a section on warfare between Europeans and Aboriginals. Such a proposal today would invite accusations of falsehood and moral vanity. It passed unnoticed at the time.

Equally, Beryl Beaurepaire lent great dignity to the Entombment of the Unknown Australian Soldier in the War Memorial on Remembrance Day 1993. The occasion was devised as a way of marking the seventy-fifth anniversary of Armistice Day, 1918. The burial within the memorial of a representative of the war dead had been proposed often, but foundered on the objection that the unknown soldier in Westminster Abbey represented all who had fallen during the Great War in the service of the British Empire. That imperial tradition had faded, and it was now thought appropriate to bring back the remains of an Australian soldier before the last surviving veterans passed away. So an unknown soldier was disinterred from Villers-Bretonneux, sealed in a coffin, flown to Canberra, exhibited in Kings Hall of Old Parliament House and finally reinterred in the War Memorial.

Beryl Beaurepaire's biographer remarks on the symbolism of a civilian and a mother presiding over a military funeral: 'War, her presence told the nation, is an evil and a blight, but it has given Australians great reason for pride in their country and its people'. This was the occasion of a speech by Paul Keating: 'We do not know this Australian's name and we never will', but 'he is one of us'. He died in the Great War, 'a mad, brutal, awful struggle' and 'by his deeds proved that real nobility and grandeur belongs not to empires and nations but to the people'. The oration has a poignancy that would now be unthinkable.

The new circumstances of the History Wars were revealed in New Zealand during a protracted argument over its national museum, Te Papa. Unlike Australia, where the states formed the principal collections, New Zealand had a Colonial Museum in the nineteenth century, which became the Dominion Museum in 1907 and the National Museum in 1973. It was a museum of natural history and anthropology, and moved into social history with a major exhibition, 'Te Maori', in the mid-1980s.

That exhibition served the official policy of biculturalism that was adopted in the 1970s with the revival of the Treaty of Waitangi and the government began planning a new museum with a new name, the Museum of New Zealand Te Papa Tongerewa (meaning a repository of precious things); subsequently the name was abbreviated to Te Papa (our place). As with other national museums, the object was to express 'the total culture of New Zealand', and in this case it would 'express the bicultural nature of the country, recognising the mana and significance of the two mainstreams of tradition' and 'providing the means for each to contribute effectively to a statement of the nation's identity'.

It was recognised from the beginning that 'traditionally held views of New Zealand are being scrutinised' and that many New Zealanders found the reappraisal disturbing; but it was 'an essential part of the nation's growth towards maturity'. The disturbing consequences were apparent when the museum opened a preliminary exhibition in 1993, designed by a curatorial team of four men and four women, four of them Maori and four Pakeha. There were angry complaints about the bicultural balance. Among the entries in the visitors' book was the charge: 'filled with Maori junk, it's a kiss and make up to the natives'.

These reactions boded ill for the new Te Papa museum that was planned to open in a new building on the Wellington waterfront, and Jock Phillips, the head of the government's Historical Branch, was asked to help design its Pakeha exhibits. He came up with a similar approach to that adopted by the National Museum of Australia. There would be no gallery of heroes, as that would 'lay down narrow definitions of the New

Zealand type'. Rather, the intention was that 'visitors would emerge from the history exhibitions with some new ways of thinking about national identity and with some interesting material to think about'. Hence there would be an exhibition of the non-Maori settlement of New Zealand to accompany its Maori settlement, and there would be an exhibition on the interaction with the environment.

The debate surrounding Te Papa was more intense than that over its Australian counterpart. The critics had more time to question its design and programs since Te Papa did not open until 1998. Much of the criticism was directed at its architecture, which gestured biculturally with two sections: the Maori one, more traditional and facing over the water; and the European one, turned inwards and distinctly unprepossessing. There was also criticism of the high-tech gimmickry and the theme-park atmosphere. Te Papa showed depressing enthusiasm for corporate-speak with a 'vision statement' proclaiming that it was a 'competitive, commercially responsive customer focused organisation that occupies a leading role in the national and global recreation and leisure market place'.

When Te Papa opened in 1998 there was particular criticism of the way that it jumbled objects together, juxtaposing household items, industrial design, signs and videos with paintings and sculpture. John McDonald, then still a curator at the National Gallery of Australia, saw the failure to attribute cultural and historical values as a fundamental problem. Others took a contemporary artwork, 'Virgin in a Condom', as representative of the denigration of sacred values. The leader of the Christian Heritage Party claimed that 'it's increasingly clear that any faith or belief is acceptable in New Zealand, except for the Christian faith'.

In 2000 Prime Minister Helen Clark agreed that the museum treated art 'like an old fridge' and she commissioned a review. The review was undertaken by two New Zealanders and an Australian museum director. It advised that Te Papa should respect the integrity of all the objects it displayed, but found it had achieved its purpose of providing a 'forum for the nation'.

Te Papa continues to divide opinion. The original arguments arose when non-Maori traditionalists took exception to the reinterpretation of their past once it was placed in a bicultural context. Some expressed contempt for the presentation of Maori culture as a living presence; more objected to the apparent devaluation of Pakeha culture, and this in turn fed claims of political correctness. Among the responses to the 1993 exhibition of social history were 'bring back the interesting exhibitions, there's more to life than the Maoris' and 'where has New Zealand's museum gone, it's now the Maori museum'.

Their preference for an older version of the past—when they were still New Zealanders, not Pakeha—was fuelled by the failure of Te Papa's designers to provide them with their heroes and familiar landmarks. Te Papa confounded their expectations. Its jumbling together of popular and high culture, its refusal to provide guidance or make judgements, its apparent insult of traditional values, turned attention back to the historians and curators who had hijacked New Zealand history.

These concerns emerged late in the preparation of the National Museum of Australia. Here the argument was not on the museum's treatment of history but the failure to build it. The need for a national museum in the national capital had been urged long before the 1974 Committee of Inquiry recommended it be established. The Fraser government enacted the Museum of Australia in 1980 and appointed an Interim Council. A director was appointed in 1984, and curators began collecting material. The name was changed to the National Museum of Australia in 1985 and a visitors' centre was established at Yarramundi Reach, on the shore of Lake Burley Griffin.

Both as treasurer and prime minister, Paul Keating was not persuaded 'that another huge and hugely expensive building on the banks of Burley Griffin ranked high among the things we need for a better life'. He was more interested in art than artefacts, taking a keen interest in the National Gallery as well as the smaller National Portrait Gallery established in Old Parliament House. In the full flush of enthusiasm for his high-tech *Creative Nation*, he thought that the National Museum might do better to arrange travelling exhibitions backed by multi-media electronic materials than build 'yet another massive mausoleum'.

The Labor government therefore decided to build just the Gallery of Aboriginal Australia, along with new premises for the Institute of Aboriginal and Torres Strait Islander Studies, and to put them both closer to the parliamentary triangle on land occupied by the former Canberra Hospital on Acton peninsula. The Coalition went to the 1996 election with a commitment to build the full museum at Yarramundi Reach, then switched it and the institute to the Acton site with a construction budget of $135 million.

The chief minister of the ACT encouraged Canberrans to view the demolition of the old hospital building by explosion in 1997, and pieces of it showered spectators, killing a young girl. Even though the local Ngunnawal people performed a smoking ceremony to cleanse a place that had been associated with sickness and death, misfortune continued to dog it. The new building was an undistinguished pastiche of several other designs, and there was insufficient consultation with the museum staff who were arranging the exhibition. The presence on the museum's council of vigilant inspectors of political correctness made their task more difficult.

Particular attention was paid to the labels that would accompany each object and build up the story-line of each thematic exhibit. As those involved have observed, historians and journalists often approach museums as if they were illustrated history books—or in Jock Phillips' phrase, they read the museum as 'a book upon a wall'. But an exhibition is an emotional experience. It uses other senses in a visual display that combines space, movement and sound. The arrangement of the objects, the use of lighting and other visual cues make up an ambience that the label can only supplement. One of the difficulties for the National Museum was that its collection was so recent: the iconic objects of Australian history had already been acquired by other institutions, and partly for this reason its exhibition would lean heavily on the new techniques of display that make little use of text.

Even so, the curators who wrote the labels operated under close supervision. After they were drafted, the labels went to the head of the team for that particular gallery, and then to the head of the program, and then to the editorial staff. After that the expert advisers saw them, as did the director and—as the result of David Barnett's intervention—some members of the council. The whole process was complicated by the difficulty of designing displays for galleries that were still under construction, against a tight timetable and staff turnover. A further difficulty was that only some of the readers were able to see images of the objects the labels accompanied, and sometimes they saw the image without the full text.

Constantly rewriting their labels for such a diverse range of readers, the curators did their best. A common method was to tell the personal story of some participant in the events under display. This allowed the visitor to respond without overt direction, and was a useful technique in the treatment of controversial subjects. Several quotations could be used to suggest different sides to an argument.

The team working on the Horizons gallery incorporated a section dealing with refugees, a subject that was controversial because it was so topical. They played safe with a text that explained that Australia had long provided a haven for refugees, and took the example of Germans who found shelter in South Australia in the 1840s. Alongside this exhibit was an oversized poster with 'SINK THEM' in large letters, while the computerised interactive gave testimony from refugees from the Holocaust, Vietnam, Africa and other places of racial, religious and political persecution. The texts of interactives did not undergo the same stringent examination as those of labels on the wall. Thus the staff employed both self-censorship and ingenuity to overcome their constraints.

David Barnett's criticism was directed at the choice of exhibits and the wording of their labels. He was offended by the museum's consideration of contentious issues and the failure to affirm an authoritative record of public achievement that he expected of a national institution. As Tony Staley put it, 'David has the very classic, traditional view of museums'. Of his thirty-five specific complaints, only two were concerned with Aboriginal exhibits.

When Keith Windschuttle took up the attack on the National Museum, he was not at first exercised by its treatment of Aboriginal history: he described the gallery on First Australians as 'a great success'. Rather, he followed the line taken in New Zealand and contrasted the respect and reverence accorded to Indigenous culture with the 'mockery and irony' meted out to white culture. From 1788 onwards, he claimed, the European presence was 'largely portrayed as a series of disasters'.

He attributed this denigration of European Australia to the new museology, which falsified the museum to make it serve political purposes. Hence, he claimed, the new museologists misrepresented the history of the institution to depict the first museums as places of aristocratic taste and imperial trophies, followed in the nineteenth century by national museums that glorified the nation-state. The intellectuals who proclaimed the fashionable new museology therefore sought to remake the museum into a display of postcolonial, multicultural egalitarianism that would confront the dark side of the national past with a display of 'victimised interest groups'. The result was a meretricious, disjointed and boring exhibition of 'the traditional Melbourne view of Australian history', which was driving university students from the subject.

Windschuttle accused Graeme Davison of foisting this view on the National Museum. He claimed that Davison drafted its guidelines and wrote a paper that codified the new museology. He stated that this paper served as the museum's postmodernist blueprint; the council, he added, was 'completely taken in' by Davison's arguments. Davison's paper, 'National Museums in a Global Age', was in fact delivered in July 1999, when the museum was well advanced on its opening exhibition. So far from prescribing the new museology, it made a number of critical observations on it. Windschuttle's misreading of Davison's views is as dishonest as any of the charges of intellectual dishonesty he makes against the historical profession.

Davison joined with Geoffrey Bolton and John Mulvaney to draft guidelines that were rewritten with council members and finally adopted at the end of 2000. Windschuttle never quotes them, for they would reveal that his allegation of a Melbourne view of history is a furphy. His claim that 'student numbers have plummeted' in university courses in Australian history is unsupported by any evidence. If he had looked at the enrolment figures, the lie would have been apparent.

His growing condemnation of the National Museum's depiction of Aboriginal history revealed a similar kind of simplifying dogmatism. While praising the 'invaluable ethnographic collection', he deprecated the 'cultural propaganda' that accompanied it. He took particular exception with the section dealing with 'Contested Frontiers'. Lights on the floor of this exhibition space spelt out placenames—such as 'Slaughterhouse Creek', 'Massacre Bay', 'Attack Spring'—as reminders of the lethal encounters that marked the European occupation of Australia. Windschuttle alleged that these names were 'drawn not from real names but invented for this display'. In fact, as Davison has pointed out, there are six

Slaughterhouse Creeks on the national database; there is a Massacre Bay on the Victorian coast, and Attack Spring is near Moree in New South Wales.

Windschuttle objected to a label stating that Aboriginals caught killing cattle in the Kimberley district of Western Australia were transported to Rottnest Island or executed, on the grounds that cattle killing was not a capital crime and the 'vast majority' of Aboriginals imprisoned on Rottnest were convicted of serious felonies. Cathie Clement, a Western Australian researcher, has pointed to more than thirty examples of Aboriginal people sentenced to lengthy imprisonment for crimes involving Kimberley cattle. She also quotes passages from police journals that describe the shooting of Aboriginals suspected of killing cattle. The only point of contention in this label is the word 'execution'.

He also objected to a display of Bells Falls Gorge as part of the Contested Frontier exhibit. There is a local tradition that a group of Aboriginal people had been shot or forced to jump to their death at the top of the falls in the 1820s. The story had been examined by David Roberts in the course of his doctoral research at the University of Newcastle, and he noted that there was no documentary evidence to support it. Windschuttle cited Roberts' investigation and accused the National Museum of producing an 'elaborate display' of a story that was a 'complete fabrication'. But Roberts had not said the story was a complete fabrication and his published research lends no support to Windschuttle's claim that the local legend 'can't possibly be accurate'.

The difficulty arises when the viewer tries to make sense of the discordant images and text. Nowhere in the display is it stated that Aboriginal people were massacred at Bells Falls in the 1820s. Instead the exhibit has a photo of Bells Falls, with labels that refer to violent conflict at the time in the Bathurst region, give some quotations from the period (that make no reference to Bells Falls) and present the statement of a present-day Wiradjuri elder that 'This is a place of great sadness'.

Given the lack of evidence that a massacre occurred at Bells Falls Gorge, it would have been better to have chosen another incident from New South Wales in the early colonial period that could be properly documented. The representation of an oral tradition was an ambitious enterprise, calling for greater care than the curators achieved. Windschuttle's treatment of the exhibit, however, is scarcely careful. He distorts what Roberts had to say about the tradition and he distorts the museum's treatment of it. He says the museum recorded that Bells Falls was 'a place of great sadness'; the label makes clear that this is a present-day Aboriginal statement.

So far from the National Museum falsifying history, it is Windschuttle who falsifies the museum's presentation of frontier conflict and the historical research on which it is based. That such sloppy and tendentious arguments can lay the ground for the present review is an indictment of those responsible for its welfare. Windschuttle was a peripheral player in the events that led to the review. He contributed to the public campaign of criticism and connected the arguments over curatorial practice to the History Wars. The damage was done from within as an exercise in political interference with a public institution. Under the pretence of combating political correctness, the National Museum has been subjected to a shameful exercise in ideological rectification.

CONCLUSION

This account of the History Wars began with the prime minister's attack on 'the attempt to rewrite Australian history in the service of a partisan political cause'. It suggested why the first part of his warning betrays a misunderstanding of the nature of historical knowledge. History is not revealed to us in tablets of stone, it has to be created from the remains of the past. It is not fixed and final but a form of knowledge that is constantly being supplemented and reworked. Research and rewriting is an essential aspect of any academic discipline. No-one takes exception to the discovery of a gene. Few would object to a rewriting of tectonic plates.

The accusation that this rewriting of history serves a partisan political purpose raises the stakes. It suggests that historians have betrayed their duty to objectivity. Keith Windschuttle accuses the present generation of historians of politicising history. He says that they write from 'an overtly partisan position' to 'select evidence that supports their cause and either omit, suppress or falsify the rest'. He notes their role as advocates and activists in support of Aboriginal causes. He charges them with vanity, self-indulgence and corruption of their profession by abandoning its commitment to truth and objectivity.

Windschuttle quotes the declaration made by Henry Reynolds in 1981 when he announced that *The Other Side of the Frontier* 'was not conceived, researched or written in a mood of detached scholarship. It is inescapably political, dealing as it must with issues that have aroused deep passions since 1788 and will continue to do so into the foreseeable future.' Windschuttle regards this statement as a smoking gun in his case against the recent politicisation of history.

What would he make of the statement of Sir John Seeley, the professor of modern history at Cambridge from 1869 to 1895, that 'our University must be a great seminary of politicians'? What would he make of John Elkington, the professor of history at Melbourne who explained in 1903 that he had 'always endeavoured to create a school of statesmanship'? What would he make of Arnold Wood, the first professor of history at Sydney, who was threatened with dismissal in 1902 for his agitation against the South African War, or Ernest Scott at Melbourne who championed the Great War?

The second and third chapters of this book provided a brief sketch of what historians do and what they have said about Australian history. I explained that the writing of history began as a way of knowing the past, making it memorable and using it for guidance about the conduct of human affairs. The study of history developed as a form of inquiry into the past as it actually occurred, that formulation signalling history's standing as an academic discipline with rules that governed its practice.

Those rules still obtain but they do not exhaust the ways that history is practised. Historians interrogate the sources and assemble their findings into coherent patterns. They present their interpretations in writing and endow them with persuasive devices that literature allows. They search for novelty and they respond to new concerns and altered sensibilities, for they are engaged in a dialogue between past and present. They also bring their own sympathies to the vocation, for why would they become historians if they were not so engaged? Previous generations of Australian historians applied these techniques to uphold colonial progress, imperial duty, radical nationalism and other causes.

It is hardly surprising that Australian history should have been so political since it deals with events whose consequences are still with us. It offers alternative readings of the national story, the path we have trod and the future directions in which it leads. Historians cannot avoid argument and controversy, but they are expected to conduct their work under the scrutiny of a collegial inspection that maintains the standards of academic honesty and intellectual fair dealing. If there were no rules of evidence and interpretation, if historians were free to simply make it up, then their accounts of Australian history would have no warrant and little import. They would be just another form of invention and the heated arguments over the historical profession would not have arisen.

Fabrication of history is the very charge that Keith Windschuttle levels against them, but this is a recent accusation. In the History Wars that built out of arguments over Manning Clark and Geoffrey Blainey, the Bicentenary and Black Armband history, the chief point of dispute was the politics of history. Manning Clark was condemned as a class traitor who disparaged his country's past. Geoffrey Blainey served as an academic victim of political correctness. The battle over the Bicentenary was fought between those who wanted to celebrate Australian achievement and those whom they accused of imposing a hairshirt. The Black Armband denoted the excessive gloom that enveloped the national achievement. From this series of allegations of a radical distemper in the history profession came John Howard's attack on 'the attempt to rewrite Australian history in the service of a partisan political cause'.

If the History Wars arose out of concern over the politicisation of history, then it is noteworthy that the prosecutors were themselves advocates of a partisan political cause. We have seen how the Australian Association for Cultural Freedom took up the early running as a Cold War exercise, and its journal *Quadrant* has since maintained a close interest in the misdeeds of historians. The Institute of Public Affairs, an organisation created and funded by the corporate sector, led the Bicentennial history campaign. More recent conservative initiatives such as the Samuel Griffith Society and the H. R. Nicholls Society have engaged in the History Wars with the explicit intention of rewriting Australian history.

How did we reach this state of affairs? Its origins go back to the upsurge of interest in Australia's history. The ties of imperial sentiment were weakening when Britain turned in the early 1960s to Europe. The American alliance came under strain with growing opposition to the Vietnam War. A protest movement emerged in the universities, which had grown rapidly in the post-war decades, and it spread into a more general challenge to the conservative values of the Menzies era. As part of this transformation there was an upsurge of interest in Australian literature, theatre and film, recovering national traditions and exploring new possibilities.

Gough Whitlam fostered this interest with the creation of an Australian Film and Television School, a Public Lending Right, the Heritage Commission, the Australia Council. His cultural patronage is sometimes seen as a grandiloquent indulgence, along with his recondite historical allusions. Whitlam was not the first prime minister to have received a university education in history but he was the first since Alfred Deakin to treat Australian history seriously. He saw it as vital to a fully independent and confident nationhood.

His successors have also appreciated its significance—hence Fraser's initiation of such an ambitious Bicentenary and Hawke's Aboriginal initiatives. The legacy of the past is in any case impossible to ignore. Whether it involves the Stolen Generations or the head of state, native forests or the family, immigration or diplomacy, arguments over public policy keep returning to the legacy of the past. Australian history is now part of the political vocabulary.

The new uses of Australian history, as a source of guidance, criticism and debate, unsettled the older conservatism. The Anglophile orientation of the Menzies generation, who saw Australia deriving its culture and values from Britain, offered little guidance. The Cold War mentality, which bound Australia to the western alliance and western values, was inattentive to national concerns. Those who resisted the historians' questioning of the past were on the defensive.

They took the offensive by adopting tactics that had been worked out in the United States. First, in the early 1980s, they took up the American neoconservatives' charge of new class guilt. This cast the historians along with other intellectuals as privileged and disaffected radicals intent on blackening the past and making Australians feel ashamed. Second, in the early 1990s, they followed the American discovery of political correctness. This allowed them to accuse a malevolent intelligentsia of imposing its views on the rest of the country and preventing any disagreement.

Finally, in 1994, they noted the fate of the Smithsonian Museum when it raised questions about the United States Air Force's use of the atomic bomb in the war against Japan. The incident provided like-minded Australians with a lesson in how they could prevail over their opponents here. From this final precedent also came the compelling figure of the History Wars, to characterise their crusade.

It is surely remarkable that the Australians who seek to defend the national honour should be such slavish imitators in their methods and arguments. Yet the working out of these arguments has also drawn on local lessons. The chief of them was the disaster that befell John Howard in 1988 when he embarked on the backward-looking *Future Directions* with the white picket fence and was drawn into criticism of multiculturalism and Asian immigration. Here he followed Geoffrey

Blainey, who in 1984 had tied his own criticism to a defence
of an older Australia.

Howard learned his lesson. The second time around he
gave no hostages to fortune. He undertook in 1996 to govern
'For All Of Us', and fended off awkward questions about how
that might affect particular segments of the national community with an insistence that he was not beholden to political correctness. Once in office, he took up the prosecution of
the History Wars with a vengeance, helped this time by
Geoffrey Blainey's Black Armband epithet. By 1999 the prime
minister even proposed a new preamble to the Constitution
that proclaimed 'Australians are free to be proud of their
country and heritage'.

As in the United States, the Australian History Wars were
conducted by ukase. They were prepared in house journals
such as *Quadrant* and the *IPA Review*, privileged forums such as
the parliament, and closed ones such as the news conference or
media briefing. They were proclaimed in the popular press by
columnists who had space reserved for their pronouncements,
who admitted no right of reply and yet portrayed themselves
as audacious champions of the underdog. These fundamental-
ists handed down arbitrary edicts against any form of Australian
history that was deemed to impugn the national honour.

The offenders were held up to ridicule and abuse. Their
evidence and argument were not examined, the issues they
raised were not assessed, and the possibility that such views
were possible was not entertained. The quality of the scholarship was not a consideration. The standard of judgement was
insistently political, judging the transgressor against an idealised
national history. Perhaps the most significant recent development has been the involvement of Keith Windschuttle, a
polemicist of similar ferocity but the first of the History
Warriors to engage with the substance of history.

The first casualty when war comes is truth. The History
Wars respect few of the conventions that govern historical

debate. History, like other professional disciplines, is characterised by lively argument as new interpretations challenge old orthodoxies: you are expected to be familiar with alternative interpretations and give a fair account of them; to demonstrate the consonance of your interpretation with the available evidence and persuade your peers of its plausibility; to present your own argument as persuasively as possible but not by resorting to personal abuse of those with whom you disagree; to allow others a right of reply.

Not so the History Warriors. They obey only Rafferty's rules. They caricature their opponents and impugn their motives. They appeal to loyalty, hope, fear and prejudice. In their intimidation of the history profession, they act as bullies. In submitting history to a loyalty test, they debase it. Australians deserve more from their history than the History Wars.

SOURCES

1 HISTORY UNDER FIRE

'One of the more insidious developments': John Howard, Sir Thomas Playford Memorial Lecture, 5 July 1996.

Paul Keating had been the chief tormenter: Keating's jibe is recalled by Don Watson in 'Crowning a Nation', *The Australian's Review of Books*, July 1999, pp. 10–13; his principal speeches are gathered together by Mark Ryan in *Advancing Australia: The Speeches of Paul Keating, Prime Minister*, Cremorne, NSW: Big Picture Publications, 1995.

'I do not take the black armband view': Howard in *Commonwealth Parliamentary Debates*, House of Representatives, 29 October 1996, p. 5976.

The Black Armband epithet: Geoffrey Blainey, Sir John Latham Memorial Lecture, April 1993, appeared as 'Drawing Up a Balance Sheet of Our History', *Quadrant*, vol. 37, nos 7–8, July–August 1993, pp. 10–15.

'the balance sheet . . . is a very generous and benign one':
Howard in *Commonwealth Parliamentary Debates*, House of
Representatives, 30 October 1996, p. 6158.

'endless and agonised navel-gazing': Sir Robert Menzies
Lecture, 18 November 1996.

'the chattering class': See P. P. McGuinness at random.

'whingeing intellectuals': John Carroll, 'C. E. W. Bean and 1988',
Quadrant, vol. 29, no. 6, June 1985, p. 47.

a 'guilt industry': Hugh Morgan, 'The Guilt Industry', *IPA Review*,
vol. 42, no. 1, May–July 1988, p. 18.

**'Much of our history is taught by the alienated and
discontented'**: Gerard Henderson, 'Rewriting Our History',
Bulletin, 19 January – 2 February 1993, pp. 26–7.

The history departments: Keith Windschuttle, *The Fabrication of
Aboriginal History. Volume One: Van Diemen's Land, 1803–1847*,
Sydney: Macleay Press, 2002, pp. 6, 400–4.

'I am sure that you will readily appreciate': Charles Spry to
Robert Menzies, 9 April 1952, National Archives of Australia: CRS
A6119/64 item 43, quoted in David McKnight, *Australia's Spies and
Their Secrets*, St Leonards, NSW: Allen & Unwin, 1994, p. 147.

These dossiers were compiled: Ward's security file, CRS
A6119/278, is in the National Archives. Russel Ward, *A Radical Life*,
South Melbourne: Macmillan, 1988, p. 237.

Ward . . . was advised to go quietly: Correspondence between
Ward and R. M. Crawford, 8, 13, 28 February 1956, in Crawford
Papers, University of Melbourne Archives.

Menzies stated: *Commonwealth Parliamentary Debates*, House of
Representatives, vol. 29, p. 3675, 7 December 1960.

In fact, the director-general of ASIO's minute: The minute in
Ward's file is dated 5 December 1960.

Thatcher set out to restore pride: Robert Phillips, *History Teaching, Nationhood and the State: A Study in Educational Politics*, London: Cassell, 1998.

Rush Limbaugh: Gary B. Nash, Charlotte Crabtree and Ross E. Dunn, *History on Trial: Culture Wars and the Teaching of the Past*, New York: Alfred A. Knopf, 1998, pp. 5, 22.

the Smithsonian Museum prepared an exhibition: Edward T. Linenthal and Tom Engelhardt (eds), *History Wars: The Enola Gay and Other Battles for the American Past*, New York: Metropolitan Books, 1996, pp. 180, 186.

Canadian historian: J. L. Granatstein, *Who Killed Canadian History?*, Toronto: HarperCollins, 1998.

strident polemic: Keith Windschuttle, *The Killing of History: How Literary Critics and Social Theorists Are Murdering Our Past*, Sydney: Macleay Press, 1994.

'For the next two hundred odd pages': Humphrey McQueen, *A New Britannia: An Argument concerning the Social Origins of Australian Radicalism and Nationalism*, Ringwood, Vic.: Penguin Books, 1970, p. 12.

2 WHAT DO HISTORIANS DO?

'We have ruled a line': Ian Collins, the new president of the Carlton Football Club, was quoted in the *Age*, 20 February 2003.

J. H. Plumb: *The Death of the Past*, London: Macmillan, 1969.

An influential textbook: Ch. V. Langlois and Ch. Seignobos, *Introduction to the Study of History*, trans. G. G. Berry, London: Duckworth, 1898, pp. 3, 17, 211, 303, 312, 314.

***The Australian Legend* sold 40 000 copies:** *Historical Studies*, vol. 18, no. 71, October 1978, [p. ii].

Some 350 academics are retained: A census of academic historians, in *Australian Historical Association Bulletin*, no. 86, June 1998, pp. 5–9, enumerated 350 full-time members of staff in 32 of the country's 37 universities.

Some will form a sense of this country's past: Further details of the non-academic uses of the past can be found in entries for commissioned history, genealogy, historical film, historical societies, historical television, history painting, local history, monuments, novels, pioneer settlements, public history, school history and war memorials in Graeme Davison, John Hirst and Stuart Macintyre (eds), *The Oxford Companion to Australian History*, Melbourne: Oxford University Press, rev. edn, 2001.

A recent American study: Roy Rosenzweig and David Thelen, *The Presence of the Past: Popular Uses of History in American Life*, New York: Columbia University Press, 1998, and the quotation is from p. 104.

a research group at the University of Technology Sydney: Paul Ashton and Paula Hamilton, 'At Home with the Past: Initial Findings from the Survey', *Australian Cultural History* (forthcoming).

a fastidious professor of history: J. A. La Nauze, 'The Study of Australian History, 1929–1959', *Historical Studies Australia and New Zealand*, vol. 9, no. 33, November 1959, p. 3.

The academic history profession: Stuart Macintyre and Julian Thomas (eds), *The Discovery of Australian History 1890–1939*, Melbourne: Melbourne University Press, 1995.

History shared in this new bounty: Stuart Macintyre, 'History', in *Knowing Ourselves and Others: The Humanities in Australia into the 21st Century*, Canberra: Australian Research Council and National Board of Employment, Education and Training, 1998, vol. 2, pp. 139–50.

a survey of staffing in the quarter-century to 1995: Norman Etherington, 'The Historical Profession in Our Universities: Trends and Prospects', *Australian Historical Association Bulletin*, no. 83, December 1996, pp. 29–42.

Commenting . . . on the anniversary of Gallipoli: Howard's Gallipoli speech was reported as 'PM's Timely History Lesson', *Australian*, 28 April 2000.

The discipline defines the standards: I take all but the last of the characteristics of historical understanding from David Lowenthal, 'Dilemmas and Delights of Learning History', in Peter N. Stearns, Peter Seixas and Sam Wineburg (eds), *Knowing, Teaching and Learning History: National and International Perspectives*, New York: New York University Press, 2000, pp. 63–82.

3 WHAT DO THEY SAY?

The first Australian histories: Stuart Macintyre, 'The Writing of Australian History', in D. H. Borchardt and Victor Crittenden (eds), *Australians: A Guide to Sources*, Sydney: Fairfax, Syme & Weldon Associates, 1987, pp. 1–28.

'The actors in what has been called': Quoted in Macintyre, 'The Writing of Australian History', p. 14.

The wily premier of New South Wales . . . The weekly *Bulletin* **magazine:** Graeme Davison, J. W. McCarty and Ailsa McLeary (eds), *Australians: 1888*, Sydney: Fairfax, Syme & Weldon Associates, 1987, pp. 3, 15.

'to foster love of home, country and race': Quoted in A. R. Trethewy, 'The Teaching of History in State-Supported Elementary Schools', MEd. thesis, University of Melbourne, 1965, p. 51.

The first academics: Stuart Macintyre and Julian Thomas (eds), *The Discovery of Australian History 1890–1939*, Melbourne: Melbourne University Press, 1995.

'probably be used all over the world': Quoted in Stuart Macintyre, *A History for a Nation: Ernest Scott and the Making of Australian History*, Melbourne: Melbourne University Press, 1994, p. 161.

'The history of both Dominions': *Cambridge History of the British Empire*, vol. 7, Part 1, Cambridge: Cambridge University Press, 1933, p. v.

The Australian contributors: Quoted in Macintyre, *A History for a Nation*, p. 162.

Independent Australian Briton: J. A. La Nauze, *Alfred Deakin: A Biography*, Melbourne: Melbourne University Press, 1965, vol. 2, p. 483; Hancock used the phrase as a chapter title in *Australia*.

Keith Hancock incorporated: W. K. Hancock, *Australia*, London: Ernest Benn, 1930, pp. 37, 65, 66, 72, 269.

'a Melbourne coterie exclusively': Quoted in Macintyre, *A History for a Nation*, pp. 163–4.

'The origins of the people are not in the library': *Meanjin*, vol. 14, no. 3, Spring 1955, pp. 350–61.

'I have taken the view': Brian Fitzpatrick, *A Short History of the Australian Labor Movement*, Melbourne: Rawson's Bookshop, 2nd edn, 1944, p. 11.

'The Australian people made heroes of none': Brian Fitzpatrick, *The Australian Commonwealth*, Melbourne: F. W. Cheshire, 1956, p. 209.

Russel Ward showed: Russel Ward, *The Australian Legend*, Melbourne: Oxford University Press, 1958.

Other historians traced its extension into politics: R. A. Gollan, *Radical and Working Class Politics: A Study of Eastern Australia, 1850–1910*, Melbourne: Melbourne University Press, 1960; Ian Turner, *Industrial Labour and Politics: The Dynamics of the Labour Movement in Eastern Australia, 1900–1921*, Canberra: Australian National University Press, 1965.

'the great Australian illusion': Clark's lecture on 'Re-writing Australian History' appeared in T. A. G. Hungerford (ed.), *Australian Signposts: An Anthology*, Melbourne: Cheshire, 1956, p. 138.

Yet it was Manning Clark: Ken Inglis, 'Introduction' to *Geoffrey Serle: In Tribute*, Canberra: National Library of Australia, 1994, p. iii.

'the agency and creativity of women': Patricia Grimshaw, Marilyn Lake, Ann McGrath and Marian Quartly, *Creating a Nation*, Melbourne: McPhee Gribble, 1994, p. 1.

a traditional male historian: John Hirst, 'Women and History', *Quadrant*, vol. 39, no. 3, March 1995, p. 8.

'hapless children of nature': Ernest Scott, *A Short History of Australia*, London: Oxford University Press, 1916, pp. 159, 169, 185.

'a melancholy anthropological footnote': J. A. La Nauze, 'The Study of Australian History, 1929–1959', *Historical Studies Australia and New Zealand*, vol. 9, no. 33, November 1959, p. 11.

'Civilisation did not begin in Australia': C. M. H. Clark, *A History of Australia*, vol. 1, Melbourne: Melbourne University Press, 1962, p. 3.

a **'great Australian silence'**: W. E. H. Stanner, *The 1968 Boyer Lectures: After the Dreaming*, Sydney: ABC, 1968, p. 25.

'reasonable to suppose that at least 20,000 Aborigines were killed': Henry Reynolds, *The Other Side of the Frontier: An Interpretation of the Aboriginal Response to the Invasion and Settlement of Australia*, Townsville: History Department, James Cook University, 1981, pp. 98–9.

'the break-up of Australia': Keith Windschuttle, 'The Break-Up of Australia', *Quadrant*, vol. 44, no. 9, September 2000, pp. 8–16.

'Aboriginal oral history . . . is completely unreliable': Keith Windschuttle, 'Doctored Evidence and Invented Incidents', in Bain Attwood and S. G. Foster (eds), *Frontier Conflict: The Australian Experience*, Canberra: National Museum of Australia, 2003, p. 106.

an invitation to morning tea with the governor: The historian was S. J. Butlin and the incident was recalled by Malcolm McRae, 'The Tasmanian State Archives: A Note on Their Prehistory', *Archives and Manuscripts*, vol. 6, no. 1, November 1974, pp. 24–5.

the perils of such uses of the past: Eric Hobsbawm's address, 'Outside and Inside History', is in *On History*, London: Abacus edition, 1998, pp. 6, 10.

4 THE HISTORIAN UNDER FIRE: MANNING CLARK

Rising in the House of Representatives: *Commonwealth Parliamentary Debates*, House of Representatives, 28 May 1991; the speeches were reprinted as *A Tribute to the Memory of Emeritus Professor Manning Clark, AC*, Canberra: The Parliament, 1991.

'a less than rapturous view of the Manning Clark view':
Howard quoted in Brisbane *Courier-Mail*, 31 August 1996.

'partly a mountebank': Peter Ryan, 'Manning Clark', *Quadrant*,
vol. 37, no. 9, September 1993, p. 17.

This was hardly the pedigree: Manning Clark, *The Quest for
Grace*, Ringwood, Vic.: Penguin Books, 1990, pp. 26, 64.

shaped his tragic view of history: Humphrey McQueen, *Suspect
History: Manning Clark and the Future of Australia's Past*, Kent Town,
SA: Wakefield Press, 1997, pp. 4–5.

he rejected the conventional forms of academic history:
'Re-writing Australian History', in T. A. G. Hungerford (ed.),
Australian Signposts: An Anthology, Melbourne: Cheshire, 1956,
reprinted in Manning Clark, *Occasional Writings and Speeches*,
Melbourne: Fontana Books, 1980, pp. 14, 18–19.

'pink professors and puce pedagogues': Fay Anderson and
Stuart Macintyre, 'Crawford as Controversialist', in Stuart Macintyre
and Peter McPhee (eds), *Max Crawford's School of History*, Melbourne:
History Department, University of Melbourne, 2000, pp. 89–112.

Clark appeared on a radio program: Stephen Holt, *A Short
History of Manning Clark*, St Leonards, NSW: Allen & Unwin, 1999,
pp. 75–6, 80, 117.

'believed to be a communist sympathiser': Clark's ASIO file,
CRS A6119/56, item 424, and Holt, *A Short History of Manning
Clark*, p. 117.

a 'fence sitter': Judah Waten quoted in McQueen, *Suspect History*,
p. 74.

a favourable view of the Soviet achievement: McQueen, *Suspect
History*, pp. 83–5.

'Christ-like, at least in his compassion': Manning Clark, *Meeting
Soviet Man*, Sydney: Angus & Robertson, 1960, p. 12.

angered both right and left: McQueen, *Suspect History*, pp. 82–4;
Holt, *A Short History of Manning Clark*, pp. 122–3.

'Counter-Revolution in Australian History': Peter Coleman,
introduction to Coleman (ed.), *Australian Civilization: A Symposium*,
Melbourne: Cheshire, 1962, pp. 1–11.

Clark had been working on his *History*: Manning Clark,
'Themes in "A History of Australia"' (1978), in *Occasional Writings
and Speeches*, p. 81.

'a state of moral hypertension': Oskar Spate in the *Australian
Journal of Politics and History*, vol. 9, no. 2, November 1963, p. 269;
other reviews are discussed in Stuart Macintyre, 'Manning Clark's
Critics', *Meanjin*, vol. 41, no. 4, December 1982, pp. 442–52.

'History without Facts': Ellis's review appeared in the *Bulletin* on
22 September 1962, and his grievances are discussed by Andrew
Moore, '"History without Facts": M. H. Ellis, Manning Clark and
the Origins of the *Australian Dictionary of Biography*', *Journal of the
Royal Australian Historical Society*, vol. 85, no. 2, December 1999,
pp. 71–84.

**a seminar under the auspices of the Association for Cultural
Freedom:** The written record of the seminar, 'New Interpretations
of Australian History', is in the Mitchell Library and I have also
drawn on the recollections of a participant, Bob Gollan, as well as the
lengthy account given by Stephen Holt, *Manning Clark and Australian
History 1915–1963*, St Lucia: University of Queensland Press, 1982,
pp. 186–90.

'I now think there is something in Ellis's phrase': Peter
Coleman, 'Manning Clark's Misfits', *Bulletin*, 30 March 1968.

**kept up his membership of the Association for Cultural
Freedom:** Stephen Holt, 'Not the Lenin Medal', *Eureka Street*,
vol. 10, no. 6, July–August 2000, p. 37.

'wonderfully and passionately written': Barry Humphries is
quoted by Holt, *A Short History of Manning Clark*, p. 146.

Patrick White hailed Clark: John Rickard, 'Manning Clark and
Patrick White: A Reflection', *Australian Historical Studies*, vol. 25,
no. 98, April 1992, pp. 116–22.

literary editors of leading newspapers: *Sydney Morning Herald*, 21 December 1968; *Australian*, 28 December 1968.

'the years of unleavened bread': *Meanjin*, vol. 32, no. 3, September 1973; the essay is reprinted in *Occasional Writings and Speeches*, pp. 197, 202.

'history will probably be kinder than the people': *Australian*, 7 January 1976; the article is reprinted in *Occasional Writings and Speeches*, pp. 204, 208.

apocalyptic predictions: Holt, *A Short History of Manning Clark*, pp. 174, 179; *Australian*, 7 January 1976.

'Are We a Nation of Bastards?': *Meanjin*, vol. 35, no. 2, June 1976; the article is reprinted in *Occasional Writings and Speeches*, pp. 209–14; McQueen notes its misinterpretation in *Suspect History*, pp. 132–3.

'Can a guarantee be given?': *Commonwealth Parliamentary Debates*, Senate, vol. 69, p. 808, 22 September 1976, was followed by further debate in the lower house; *Commonwealth Parliamentary Debates*, House of Representatives, vol. 100, pp. 1439–44, 23 September 1976, and vol. 101, pp. 1518–19, 5 October 1976.

The Boyer lectures: Manning Clark, *A Discovery of Australia*, Sydney: Australian Broadcasting Commission, 1976, pp. 7, 12.

'I was weak on backdrop': R. M. Crawford, Manning Clark and Geoffrey Blainey, *Making History*, Fitzroy, Vic.: McPhee Gribble, 1985, p. 65, quoted by Susan Pfisterer-Smith, 'Women in a "Man's World"', in Carl Bridge (ed.), *Manning Clark: Essays on His Place in History*, Melbourne: Melbourne University Press, 1994, p. 79.

Colin Roderick: *Townsville Bulletin*, 10, 17 May 1978; this criticism is discussed along with reviews of volumes four and five of the *History* in Macintyre, 'Manning Clark's Critics'.

a new round of hostilities: Edward Kynaston in the *Australian* on 24–25 October 1981; John Carroll, letter to *Age Monthly Review*, February 1982.

'a labour of hatred and distress': Tim Hewat, 'Manning Clark's monumental labour of loathing', *Australian*, 13–14 February 1982.

'the closed shop of professional historians': Edward Kynaston, *Australian*, 24–25 October 1981.

Claudo Veliz: 'Bad History', *Quadrant*, vol. 26, no. 5, May 1982, pp. 21–6.

a pace or two apart at the Canberra cemetery: Clark, 'The Years of Unleavened Bread', pp. 198–9.

we are reliant on Ryan's retrospective testimony: Peter Ryan, 'Manning Clark', *Quadrant*, vol. 37, no. 9, September 1993, pp. 9–22; subsequent quotations are taken from this article.

Quadrant's editor relates: Robert Manne, 'Manning Clark, Peter Ryan and Us', *Quadrant*, vol. 37, no. 10, October 1993, pp. 2–3.

a predictable controversy: The responses of Keating, Ward, Hughes, Watson and myself are reported by Peter Craven, 'The Ryan Affair', in Carl Bridge (ed.), *Manning Clark*, pp. 178–9; Craven discusses the relationship between private and public life on pp. 169–71.

Robert Manne claimed subsequently: 'The Puzzles of Manning Clark', *Quadrant*, vol. 38, no. 11, November 1994; Peter Ryan in 'A Reply to My Critics', *Quadrant*, vol. 37, no. 10, October 1993, pp. 11–14.

a recent assessment of Clark's work by John Hirst: 'Australian History and European Civilisation', *Quadrant*, vol. 37, no. 5, May 1993, pp. 28–38; the first part of this article is reprinted in Bridge (ed.), *Manning Clark*, pp. 117–21.

In his reply to his critics: Ryan, 'A Reply to My Critics', p. 11.

The subsequent investigation: Sian Powell, 'Manning Clark: A Drama Unfolds', *Australian*, 31 August 1996; McQueen, *Suspect History*, pp. 11–21.

The *Courier-Mail* broke the story: *Courier-Mail*, 24 August 1996; the quotation from Alexander Downer appears in the same edition.

the *Courier-Mail* offered the story to other newspapers: The Melbourne *Herald-Sun*'s front-cover story, 'Red Agent?', appeared

also on 24 August 1996 and included pieces by Peter Kelly and
Wayne Smith; the quotation is from the editorial on 27 August 1996.

Howard adopted a similar stance: *Courier-Mail*, 31 August 1996.

**The case presented by the *Courier-Mail* quickly began to
collapse:** Retraction of report of Anne Fairbairn, *Courier-Mail* on
28 August 1996; David Marr reported Murray's prevarications along
with Dymphna Clark's statement in the *Sydney Morning Herald*,
27 August 1996. The alteration of the photo is discussed by John
Martinkus, 'Seeing Is Not Believing', *Desktop*, September 1998,
pp. 74–7.

'playing the man': Peter Charlton, *Courier-Mail*, 29 August 1996.

Wayne Smith would claim: 'Manning Clark and the *Courier-
Mail*', *Quadrant*, vol. 42, no. 9, September 1988, pp. 40–4.

It demanded answers: The *Courier-Mail*'s new questions appeared
on 8 November 1996 and its extracts of Clark on the Soviet Union
on 31 May 1997, along with comments from Manne and
Henderson. McQueen, *Suspect History*, pp. 66–76, deals with the
visits; Katerina Clark wrote to the *Australian*, 16 September 1997.

B. A. Santamaria: 'The Confusion of Manning Clark', *Australian*,
31 May 1997; the article prompted Dymphna Clark to write to him,
and a copy of her letter is in the family's papers.

This is apparent in Robert Manne's treatment: Manne's
reassessment is reprinted in *The Way We Live Now: The Controversies
of the Nineties*, Melbourne: Text Publishing, 1998, pp. 155–67. Hal
Colebatch's 'Manning Clark and Anti-Semitism' appeared in the
Adelaide Review, February 1997.

Christopher Mitchell pronounced Clark: *Courier-Mail*,
11 June 1997; the newspaper reported its further research on
27 June 1998.

5 THE HISTORIAN BETRAYED: GEOFFREY BLAINEY

'I have been under very heavy pressure': Melbourne *Herald*,
8 June 1984.

recorded by an alert local journalist: Blainey's address to Rotary was reported in the Warrnambool *Standard*, 19 March 1984.

he wrote the final passages: *Age*, 20 March, where the comments on an Asian takeover were made.

race riots: 'We Could Have a Birmingham in Australia in Ten or Fifteen Years', *Australian*, 3 April 1984.

the shadow minister . . . was calling: *Australian*, 6 April 1984.

'Geoffrey Blainey's doubts must carry weight': Peter Game in the Melbourne *Herald*, 24 March 1984.

'I have made a careful note': Tim Duncan, 'Blainey Sees a Threat to Free Speech', *Bulletin*, 3 July 1984.

Blainey refused to accept this logic: Melbourne *Herald*, 3 April, 10 May 1984.

'The distrust of free speech': Geoffrey Blainey, *All for Australia*, North Ryde, NSW: Methuen Haynes, 1984, p. 49.

'intense disappointment' in the actions of the colleagues: Melbourne *Herald*, 8 June 1984.

Two senior academics at the University of Melbourne: Victor Prescott and Colin Howard, 'Hazards of Frankness', *Look and Listen*, September 1984, p. 12.

Peter Ryan accused them: letter to the *Age*, 22 May 1984.

John Stone: Melbourne *Herald*, 10 April 1985.

described his former student: R. M. Crawford's reference for Blainey is in the University of Melbourne Archives, and I quote from it in 'Blainey and the Australian Historical Profession', in Deborah Gare et al. (eds), *The Fuss That Never Ended: The Life and Work of Geoffrey Blainey*, Melbourne: Melbourne University Press, 2003, p. 6.

Clark recalled: R. M. Crawford, Manning Clark and Geoffrey Blainey, *Making History*, Fitzroy, Vic.: McPhee Gribble, 1985, p. 61.

As Graeme Davison has observed: I draw heavily on Graeme Davison, 'Half a Determinist: Blainey and the Mechanics of History', in *The Fuss That Never Ended*, pp. 15–27, and also on his entry on Blainey in Graeme Davison, John Hirst and Stuart Macintyre (eds), *The Oxford Companion to Australian History*, Melbourne: Oxford University Press, rev. edn, 2001, pp. 74–6.

Blainey was drawn to such determinism: *Making History*, pp. 75–6.

Historians too often relied on stock responses: 'Antidotes for History', in John A. Moses (ed.), *Historical Disciplines and Culture in Australasia*, St Lucia: University of Queensland Press, 1979, pp. 92–4.

'I constantly search for the obvious': *Making History*, p. 73.

'the solitary prospector': Rob Pascoe, *The Manufacture of Australian History*, Melbourne: Oxford University Press, 1979, p. 132.

His academic colleagues: reviews of Blainey's work and comments on his rejoinders are discussed in 'Blainey and the Australian Historical Profession', pp. 10–11.

a journalist prepared a feature article: Stephen Downes, 'The Man Who Was Always Looking for Something', *Age*, 9 August 1980, quoted by Morag Fraser, 'The Media Game', in *The Fuss That Never Ended*, p. 155.

'When a historian lacks the orthodox assumptions': Blainey, 'Brian Fitzpatrick (1906–1965) and his works', *Business Archives and History*, vol. 6, no. 1, February 1966, pp. 77–81, quoted by Graeme Davison, 'Half a Determinist', p. 25; Blainey makes similar observations in his foreword to a reprint of Fitzpatrick's *The British Empire in Australia*, Melbourne: Macmillan, 1969, pp. vii–x.

'Well, I wish I hadn't said that': *Making History*, p. 70.

'I believe I've occupied the middle ground': Blainey, *Bulletin*, 5 July 1984.

polarisation of opinion: Hawke criticised him in the *Age*, 13 July, and Bill Hayden's parliamentary attack was reported in the *Age* on 24 August after the same newspaper had reported his discussions with the leader of the National Party on 14 August. The resignation from the Council of the National Museum was reported in the *Age* on 24 July.

surrendering Australia: ' "Surrender Australia" Is New Line: Blainey', *Age*, 3 April 1984. He criticised multiculturalism in a letter to the *Age*, 21 September 1984.

'at war in this controversy': Geoffrey Blainey, *All for Australia*, North Ryde, NSW: Methuen Haynes, 1984, p. vii.

'The Front Line is the Neighbourhood': *All for Australia*, p. 120.

'residents in the invaded suburbs': *All for Australia*, p. 123.

'pavements now spotted with phlegm': *All for Australia*, p. 132.

rash charges: *All for Australia*, p. 90, uses the cricket metaphor and p. 101 introduces the secret room.

'he had all the documents': *Age*, 4 October 1984.

'I might have a look at it': Jack Waterford, 'Blainey Unaware of Availability of Immigration Documents', *Canberra Times*, 8 October 1984.

'all peoples, all races, are worthy of respect': Blainey, *All for Australia*, p. 18.

'a weapon of indignation': *All for Australia*, p. 40.

Multiculturalism had ceased to be: *All for Australia*, pp. 16, 21, 31.

Peter Shergold: in Frances Milne and Peter Shergold (eds), *The Great Immigration Debate*, Sydney: Federation of Ethnic Communities Councils of Australia, 1984, chs 2 and 3.

'they were acting in a political way': *Bulletin*, 3 July 1984.

'How long do I have to live . . .?': *West Australian*, 25 September 1984.

'This land is not a rich prize': *Australian*, 3 April 1984.

Those who chanted the slogan: *All for Australia*, p. 61.

'the long phase of British Australia': *All for Australia*, p. 156.

'disowning of our past': *All for Australia*, p. 159.

university colleagues published their letter: *Age*, 19 May;
a letter of rejection by the *Sydney Morning Herald* is in the
departmental records held at the University of Melbourne Archives.

They observed that he had ready access: David Philips in
Look and Listen, November 1984, p. 27, and Andrew Markus and
Merle Ricklefs in the introduction to *Surrender Australia: Essays in
the Study and Uses of History*, Sydney: Allen & Unwin, 1985, p. 3;
they cite the poll, which appeared in the Melbourne *Herald*,
27 August 1984.

Blainey cancelled two talks: *Age*, 6 July 1984.

he wrote to . . . a member of the department: the letter to
David Philips on 25 June is in the departmental records along with
Philips' reply, 27 June. The review of *All for Australia* appeared in
Farrago, the student newspaper, in October 1984.

Another colleague: John Lack's call for Blainey to repay his salary
was reported in the *Age*, 13 July, and the assistant registrar of the
faculty's letter of 16 July is in the departmental records.

Geoffrey Blainey described the experience as 'traumatic':
Melbourne *Herald*, 8 June 1984.

the publication of a book of essays: *Surrender Australia* appeared
in April 1985, and I quote from pp. 8–9.

'those pinkies in their ivory tower': Melbourne *Herald*, 2 April
1985, where the editorial also appeared; Peter Nicholson's cartoon is
in the *Age* on the same date.

B. A. Santamaria: *Australian*, 1 September 1997.

from time to time by Peter Ryan: for example, 'Geoffrey
Blainey', *Quadrant*, vol. 39, nos 1–2, January–February 1995,
pp. 119–20; 'Apologies', *Quadrant*, vol. 44, no. 3, March 2000, p. 87;
and Ryan's review of *The Fuss That Never Ended* in the *Australian*,
15–16 March 2003.

Pauline Hanson: the maiden speech is quoted in Andrew Markus, *Race: John Howard and the Remaking of Australia*, Crows Nest, NSW: Allen & Unwin, 2001, p. 147.

6 BICENTENARY BATTLES

announced the establishment of the Australian Bicentennial Authority: Malcolm Fraser in *Commonwealth Parliamentary Debates*, House of Representatives, vol. 113, pp. 1625–6, 5 April 1979.

The Sesquicentenary: Julian Thomas, 'Heroic History and Public Spectacle: Sydney 1938', PhD thesis, Australian National University, 1991.

'to draw upon the ideas of highly imaginative and creative people': Fraser's parliamentary statement, cited above.

preliminary discussions of the great and the good: Denis O'Brien, *The Bicentennial Affair: The Inside Story of Australia's 'Birthday Bash'*, Sydney: ABC, 1991, pp. 31–3.

Critics had already alleged: *Sydney Morning Herald*, 16 October 1980.

Armstrong replied immediately: *Australian*, 17 October 1980.

'seriously and broadly educational and cultural': *Australian*, 25 August 1980, quoted by Peter Cochrane and David Goodman, 'The Great Australian Journey', in Tony Bennett et al. (eds), *Celebrating the Nation: A Critical Study of Australia's Bicentenary*, St Leonards, NSW: Allen & Unwin, 1992, p. 182.

Speaking as the ABC's Guest of Honour: Quoted in O'Brien, *The Bicentennial Affair*, p. 38, which also reports the Morgan Gallup poll, p. 45.

'inadequate, hollow and a little bit pathetic': interview with O'Brien, *The Bicentennial Affair*, p. 49.

'positive achievements and triumph': *Canberra Times*, 7 December 1981.

David Armstrong remained resistant: press interview quoted in O'Brien, *The Bicentennial Affair*, p. 53.

'a white wank': 'No White Wank', *Quadrant*, vol. 28, no. 10, October 1984, p. 6, cites an earlier use of the same phrase.

'a premature ejaculation': quoted in O'Brien, *The Bicentennial Affair*, p. 289.

Now Ken Baker . . . argued that the revised Bicentenary program: Ken Baker, 'The Bicentenary: Celebration or Apology?', *IPA Review*, vol. 38, no. 4, Summer 1985, pp. 175, 182.

The press quickly reported Baker's criticisms: The adverse headlines of the Adelaide *Advertiser*, 25 February 1985, and the Sydney *Daily Telegraph*, 25 February 1985, are quoted by O'Brien, *The Bicentennial Affair*, p. 75.

He censured contributions: The articles by Kirby and Arena appeared in the *Times on Sunday*, 7 March 1987; O'Brien, *The Bicentennial Affair*, p. 126, uses Authority records for their suppression.

'not the forum for such debate': Kirk in the *Sydney Morning Herald*, 21 March 1987, quoted by Peter Spearritt, 'Celebration of a Nation: The Triumph of Spectacle', *Australian Historical Studies*, vol. 23, no. 91, October 1988, p. 11.

the naturalist Harry Butler was omitted: *Sydney Morning Herald*, 24 November 1986.

Kirk's Authority added: O'Brien, *The Bicentennial Affair*, pp. 114, 120, 139–41.

a national television program: Meaghan Morris, 'Panorama: The Live, the Dead and the Living', in Graeme Turner (ed.), *Nation, Culture, Text*, London: Routledge, 1993, pp. 19–58.

He found encouragement from both Manning Clark and Geoffrey Blainey: Jonathan King, *The Battle for the Bicentenary*, Milsons Point, NSW: Hutchinson, 1989, pp. 21–2.

'a nation ashamed of its past': King, *The Battle for the Bicentenary*, p. 1.

'rewriting history': King, *The Battle for the Bicentenary*, p. 94.

the Authority announced it would neither support nor endorse: *Australian*, 14 November 1981.

'torpedoed by those essential twin tools': Denis O'Brien, *Bulletin*, 25 November 1981.

'a brilliant and challenging idea': 'A Battle for Sydney Harbour', *Quadrant*, vol. 25, no. 8, August 1981, p. 66.

Geoffrey Blainey counselled: King, *The Battle for the Bicentenary*, p. 70.

Tim Duncan: 'Bicentennial Blues Spoil the Party', *Bulletin*, 18 June 1985.

'tasteless and insensitive': *Sydney Morning Herald*, 5 August 1987, quoted in Bennett et al. (eds), *Celebrating the Nation*, p. 178.

'If we are going to put blank pages': Senator Kathy Martin, quoted in King, *The Battle for the Bicentenary*, pp. 122–3.

'the most moving event': Geoffrey Blainey, 'Triumph of the Quiet Majority', *Australian*, 30–31 January 1988.

During the voyage he held discussion groups: King, *The Battle for the Bicentenary*, pp. 249–51.

'I held in my hands . . . Australia's Magna Carta': King, *The Battle for the Bicentenary*, pp. 109–10, 157; his article on Phillip appeared in the *Australian*, 27 January 2003.

'where the core values of our civilization': Robert Manne (ed.), *The New Conservatism in Australia*, Melbourne: Oxford University Press, 1982, p. xi.

'a paranoid hatred of authority': John Carroll, 'Paranoid and Remissive: The Treason of the Upper Middle Class', in Manne (ed.), *The New Conservatism*, p. 3.

'producing a generation of rootless, purposeless individualism': Baker, 'The Bicentenary: Celebration or Apology?', p. 176.

'denigration of Australia's British links': John Carroll, 'The Denigration of Australia's British Links', *IPA Review*, vol. 40, no. 2, Winter 1986, pp. 27, 29.

Hugh Morgan: 'The Guilt Industry', *IPA Review*, vol. 42, no. 1, May–July 1988, pp. 17–20.

'seems more intent on rewriting history than on celebrating it': Quoted in King, *The Battle for the Bicentenary*, p. 162.

'The new totems to be worshipped': Anthony McAdam, 'Replacing Pride with Guilt', Melbourne *Herald*, 13 July 1985.

should not 'apologise in any way': John Howard, *Age*, 26 January 1986.

26 January might not be the most appropriate date: Geoffrey Blainey, 'Celebrating the Wrong Australia Day', Melbourne *Herald*, 17 January 1985; reprinted in *Blainey: Eye on Australia*, Melbourne: Schwartz Books, 1991, pp. 37–40.

Later . . . Blainey was far more polemical: 'They View Australia's History as a Saga of Shame', lecture at Mount Eliza, 4 October 1985, reprinted in *Blainey: Eye on Australia*, pp. 46–50. The lecture also appeared in the *IPA Review*, vol. 39, no. 2, Summer 1985, pp. 15–17.

Thereafter he was a constant critic: King quotes his phone conversation with Blainey in *The Battle for the Bicentenary*, p. 204, and also the Russian analogy, p. 162.

Leonie Kramer . . . objected: Peter Cochrane and David Goodman, 'The Great Australian Journey', *Australian Historical Studies*, vol. 23, no. 1, October 1988, p. 31.

the list of 'core values' that Ken Baker had published: 'The Bicentenary: Celebration or Apology?'.

specified that 'Ken Baker's ideas be taken into account': O'Brien, *The Bicentennial Affair*, p. 217.

'Guilt-ridden Canberra egg-heads': Paul Johnson, *West Australian*, 1 February 1988.

'This Australia Day marked the triumph of the people': Blainey in *Weekend Australian*, 30–31 January 1988.

'When historians look back on the Bicentenary': Robert Manne, 'Bicentennial Guilt', *Quadrant*, vol. 34, no. 3, March 1988, p. 72.

Molony took as his brief: *The Penguin Bicentennial History of Australia*, Ringwood, Vic.: Penguin, 1988, pp. ix–x.

'to write the English back into the script': James Jupp, 'Editing an Encyclopedia of the Australian People', in George Shaw (ed.), *1988 and All That: New Views of Australia's Past*, St Lucia: University of Queensland Press, 1988, p. 78.

'the clearest possible evidence': R. J. Hawke in the *Australian*, 14 September 1988, quoted by O'Brien, *The Bicentennial Affair*, p. 254.

one commentator suggested: David Carter, 'Manning Clark's Hat: Public and National Intellectuals', in Bennett et al. (eds), *Celebrating the Nation*, who cites the exhibition statement on p. 91.

Clark's leading article: 'The Beginning of Wisdom', *Time Australia*, 25 January 1988.

The production attracted venomous criticism: The articles in the *Sun* and the *Herald* are quoted by Peter Fitzpatrick, ' "History— The Musical": A Review and a Retrospect', *Australian Historical Studies*, vol. 23, no. 91, October 1988, p. 173.

'traditional Australian catechism': Alan D. Gilbert, 'Editing "Australians: A Historical Library" ', in Shaw (ed.), *1988 and All That*, pp. 98–9.

a 'hidden destiny' of probabilities and uncertainties: Alan D. Gilbert and K. S. Inglis, 'Preface' to Alan Atkinson and Marian Aveling (eds), *Australians 1838*, Sydney: Fairfax, Syme & Weldon Associates, p. xiii.

'an accumulating and brooding guilt': George Shaw introduction to *1988 and All That*, p. 6.

'critical not celebratory': Verity Burgmann and Jenny Lee set out their aims in the introduction to the four volumes of *A People's History of Australia since 1788*, Fitzroy, Vic.: McPhee Gribble, 1988, pp. ix–xiv.

to Australianise just about every form of knowledge: *Windows onto Worlds: Studying Australia at Tertiary Level*, Canberra: Australian Government Publishing Service, 1987.

'He who controls the past': Ken Baker, 'The New History', *IPA Review*, vol. 42, no. 3, December–February 1988–89, p. 50.

John Hirst: 'The Blackening of Our Past', *IPA Review*, vol. 42, no. 3, December–February 1988–89, pp. 49–54.

7 'RELAXED AND COMFORTABLE'

Geoffrey Blainey hailed the self-knighted Sir Joh: Blainey, 'Don't Write Off Sir Joh', Melbourne *Herald*, 19 February 1987, quoted in Gerard Henderson, *Menzies' Child: The Liberal Party of Australia 1944–1994*, St Leonards, NSW: Allen & Unwin, 1994, p. 292.

'professional purveyors of guilt': *Future Directions*, Canberra: Liberal Party of Australia, 1988, p. 7.

Geoffrey Blainey had recently renewed the allegation: Blainey, *Gold Coast Bulletin*, 22 April 1988, and *Sydney Morning Herald*, 18 April 1988, quoted in Paul Kelly, *The End of Certainty: The Story of the 1980s*, St Leonards, NSW: Allen & Unwin, 1992, p. 422.

'It could', he replied: Kelly, *The End of Certainty*, p. 423.

'Asian immigration has to be slowed': John Stone, Melbourne *Herald*, 9 August 1988, quoted in Kelly, *The End of Certainty*, p. 426.

'I'm being kicked': Kelly, *The End of Certainty*, p. 424.

'impossible to have a common Australian culture': Andrew Markus, *Race: John Howard and the Remaking of Australia*, Crows Nest, NSW: Allen & Unwin, 2001, p. 87.

Keating responded with a broadside: *Commonwealth Parliamentary Debates*, House of Representatives, vol. 182, p. 374, 27 February 1992, reported by Geoffrey Bolton, 'Two Pauline Versions', in Scott Prasser et al. (eds), *The Menzies Era: A Reappraisal of Government, Politics and Policy*, Sydney: Hale & Iremonger, 1995, p. 33.

'good little horatios': The H. V. Evatt Lecture, Sydney, 28 April 1993, quoted in Mark McKenna, 'Metaphors of Light and Darkness: The Politics of "Black Armband" History', *Melbourne Journal of Politics*, no. 25, 1998, pp. 74–5.

'We took the traditional lands': Mark Ryan (ed.), *Advancing Australia: The Speeches of Paul Keating, Prime Minister*, Cremorne Point, NSW: Big Picture Publications, 1995, p. 228.

The court decided: the phrase 'discriminatory denigration' was used by Justice Brennan and 'unutterable shame' by Justices Brennan and Deane, quoted by Garth Nettheim in *The Oxford Companion to the High Court of Australia*, Melbourne: Oxford University Press, 2001, pp. 446, 448.

Hugh Morgan criticised: Markus, *Race*, pp. 72–3.

Geoffrey Blainey told the Western Australian Chamber of Mines: *Age*, 13 May 1993, quoted in Markus, *Race*, p. 73.

The Monash historian, Bruce Knox: 'Fantasies and Furphies: The Australian Republican Agenda', in *Proceedings of the Samuel Griffith Society Inaugural Conference, Melbourne, July 24–26, 1992*, Melbourne: Samuel Griffith Society, 1994, p. 210, cited in Sean Brawley, '"A Comfortable and Relaxed Past": John Howard and the "Battle of History"', p. 3, electronic *Journal of Australian and New Zealand History*, 27 April 1997, <http://www.jcu.edu.au/aff/history>.

Another was H. R. Nicholls: John Stone, 'Introduction', in *Arbitration in Contempt: The Proceedings of the Inaugural Seminar of the H. R. Nicholls Society*, Melbourne: H. R. Nicholls Society, 1986, pp. 9–15; a more accurate version is that of John Rickard, *H. B. Higgins: The Rebel as Judge*, North Sydney: Allen & Unwin, 1984, pp. 185–7.

Patrick Morgan: 'Rethinking the Australian Dream', *IPA Review*, vol. 46, no. 3, 1993, pp. 37–9.

'Australians are variously portrayed': Gerard Henderson, 'Rewriting Our History', *Bulletin*, 19 January 1993.

Geoffrey Blainey delivered the John Latham Memorial Lecture: 'Drawing Up a Balance Sheet of Our History', *Quadrant*, vol. 37, nos 7–8, July–August 1993, pp. 10–15.

'History to the defeated': W. H. Auden, *A Summer Knight*.

'We cannot put tears in one pan': Graeme Davison in *Melbourne Historical Journal*, no. 26, 1998, p. 14.

the Black Armband had strong associations: McKenna, 'Metaphors of Light and Darkness', p. 71.

Blainey explained afterwards: Geoffrey Blainey, *In Our Time*, Melbourne: Information Australia, 1999, pp. v–vi.

just a few weeks after Blainey minted it: Howard used the phrase in *Australian Business Monthly*, July 1993, quoted in Markus, *Race*, p. 93.

John Howard delivered an address: 'Mr Keating's Mirage on the Hill', *Proceedings of the Third Conference of the Samuel Griffith Society, Fremantle, 5–6 November 1993*, Melbourne: Samuel Griffith Society, 1994, p. 115.

'very few Liberals understand': 'Australian Liberalism', *Sydney Papers*, vol. 6, Summer 1994, p. 37, quoted by Brawley, ' "A Comfortable and Relaxed Past" ', p. 5.

'For All Of Us': Quoted in Markus, *Race*, p. 96.

'Careful, Someone Might Hear You': Roy Eccleston, *Australian Magazine*, 29–30 July 1995, quoted in Mark Davis, *Gangland: Cultural Elites and the New Generationalism*, St Leonards, NSW: Allen & Unwin, 1997, p. 62.

reached peak usage in 1996: The content analysis was by Markus, *Race*, p. 98.

funded by right-wing foundations: James Neilson, 'The Great PC Scare', in Jeffrey Williams (ed.), *PC Wars: Politics and Theory in the Academy*, New York: Routledge, 1995, pp. 60–89.

'ideologically sound': Davis, *Gangland*, p. 47.

When Robert Manne expounded the term: 'On Political Correctness', *Quadrant*, vol. 37, nos 1–2, January–February 1993, pp. 2–3.

Kenneth Minogue: 'Not Guilty!', *Quadrant*, vol. 32, no. 12, December 1988, p. 9.

no relaxation of the protests: Les Carlyon, *Age*, 21 March 1996, and P. P. McGuinness, 'PC Movement Suppresses Serious Discussion', *Age*, 13 April 1996, are quoted by Davis, *Gangland*, pp. 48–9.

Relief was at hand: The insistence on the term 'chairman' is noted by Carol Johnson, *Governing Change: From Keating to Howard*, St Lucia: University of Queensland Press, 2000, p. 43, who on p. 41 also quotes the *Australian*, 3 April 1996, for his statement on ATSIC. James Jupp has provided details of the withdrawal of funding for *The Australian People*.

major speeches he delivered during 1996: Howard, Sir Thomas Playford Memorial Lecture, 5 July 1996.

'I profoundly reject the black armband view': *Commonwealth Parliamentary Debates*, House of Representatives, 30 October 1996, quoted in McKenna, '"Metaphors of Light and Darkness"', p. 76.

'something that Australians reject': Howard on 2UE, quoted by Judith Brett, 'Opinion', *Age*, 8 November 1996.

It was perhaps inevitable: Sir Robert Menzies Lecture, 18 November 1996.

The government would not apologise: letter to Father Frank Brennan, quoted in Robert Manne, *The Way We Live Now: The Controversies of the Nineties*, Melbourne: Text Publishing, 1998, p. 21.

'one of the fairest, most egalitarian and tolerant societies': Quoted by Markus, *Race*, p. 107.

'the fact that people can now talk': John Howard, address to the State Council of the Queensland division of the Liberal Party, 22 September 1996.

Pauline Hanson . . . had recently delivered her maiden speech: Markus, *Race*, pp. 101, 155–8, quotes from the speech and Howard's comments on it.

Among its lurid warnings: these passages from *Pauline Hanson: The Truth* Parkholme, SA: St George Publications, 1997, were reported in the *Sydney Morning Herald*, 27 June 1998.

'finally adopted by John Howard': Chris Mitchell, *Australian*, 18 June 1998.

'permanently dividing Australia on the basis of race': Geoffrey Blainey, 'Black Future', *Bulletin*, 8 April 1997.

8 FRONTIER CONFLICT

'a symbolic step back': Hugh Morgan, 'Religious Traditions, Mining and Land Rights', in Ken Baker (ed.), *The Land Rights Debate: Selected Documents*, Melbourne: Institute of Public Affairs, 1985, pp. 23, 25.

'an exercise in national denigration': Anthony McAdam, 'The Watchman Rides Again: Pilgerising Australian History', *Quadrant*, vol. 29, no. 10, October 1985, p. 68.

the launch of a book: Geoffrey Partington, *Hasluck versus Coombs: White Australia and Australia's Aborigines*, Sydney: Quakers Hill Press, 1996.

Hasluck . . . had defended his administration: *Shades of Darkness: Aboriginal Affairs, 1925–1965*, Melbourne: Melbourne University Press, 1988; the quote from Blainey's foreword is on p. v.

Partington's book came with encomia: The statements by Devine and Stove appear on the cover of *Hasluck versus Coombs*, and Peter Howson wrote the foreword.

John Howard dismissed the outcry: *Weekend Australian*, 29–30 June 1996, quoted in Mark Davis, *Gangland: Cultural Elites and the New Generationalism*, St Leonards, NSW: Allen & Unwin, 1997, p. 68.

For some years they had been wrestling: Raymond Gaita's articles on guilt and shame appeared in *Quadrant*, vol. 37, no. 9, September 1993, and no. 10, October 1993, pp. 44–8; Gaita's 'Genocide and the Stolen Generations' was republished in *A Common Humanity: Thinking about Love & Truth & Justice*, Melbourne: Text Publishing, 1999, pp. 131–55. Manne referred to it in 'The Coalition and the Aborigines', *Quadrant*, vol. 40, no. 9, September 1996, pp. 3–4.

'one of the most shameful': Robert Manne, 'The Stolen Generations', *Quadrant*, vol. 42, nos 1–2, January–February 1998, pp. 53–63; the article was republished in Manne, *The Way We Live Now: The Controversies of the Nineties*, Melbourne: Text Publishing, 1998, pp. 11–41.

These were the writings that caused: Manne recalled the split with *Quadrant* in *In Denial: The Stolen Generations and the Right*, Melbourne: Black Inc., 2001, p. 57.

'mawkish sentimentality': McGuinness in *Quadrant*, vol. 42, nos 1–2, January–February 1998, pp. 11–14.

The prime minister praised its contribution: 'The Prime Minister Opens the New *Quadrant* Office', *Quadrant*, vol. 44, no. 9, September 2000, pp. 2–3.

John Herron provided the after-dinner speech: Manne, *In Denial*, p. 81.

a dissident anthropologist: Roger Sandall, *The Culture Cult: Designer Tribalism and Other Essays*, Boulder, CO: Westview Press, 2000.

Howson . . . now came forward: Peter Howson, 'Rescued from the Rabbit Burrow', *Quadrant*, vol. 43, no. 6, June 1999, pp. 10–14.

three 'white activists': Keith Windschuttle, 'The Break-Up of Australia', *Quadrant*, vol. 44, no. 9, September 2000, pp. 8, 16.

McGuinness set the context: Editorial, *Quadrant*, vol. 44, no. 11, November 2000, pp. 2–4.

'growing links between Jewish and Aboriginal Australians': Duffy in *Daily Telegraph*, 5 January 2000.

'a David Irving of the Left': Chris Mitchell, letter to the editor, *Australian*, 11 June 1997.

Geoffrey Partington published a tract: *The Australian History of Henry Reynolds*, Holden Hill, SA: the author, 1994.

The earlier land rights legislation: The terms of the *Aboriginal Land Rights (Northern Territory) Act 1976* are discussed by Nicolas Peterson (ed.), *Aboriginal Land Rights: A Handbook*, Canberra: Institute of Aboriginal Studies, 1981.

Henry Reynolds claimed that after Mabo: 'The Public Role of History', *Dissent*, Spring 2000, p. 4; the different uses of historical evidence in Australia, Canada and New Zealand are discussed by Arthur J. Ray, 'Aboriginal Title and Treaty Rights', *New Zealand Journal of History*, vol. 37, no. 1, April 2003, pp. 5–17.

in 1993 wrote a critical response to the report of the Royal Commission: Ron Brunton, *Black Suffering, White Guilt?*, Perth: Institute of Public Affairs, 1993, p. vi.

Chris Kenny: *Women's Business*, Potts Point, NSW: Duffy and Snellgrove, 1996.

At its Canberra launch: Margaret Simons, *The Meeting of the Waters: The Hindmarsh Island Affair*, Sydney: Hodder, 2003, p. 406.

Brunton made a lengthy submission: *Blocking Business: An Anthropological Assessment of the Hindmarsh Island Dispute*, Melbourne: Tasman Institute, 1995.

He also had the principal Ngarrindjeri dissident: Dulcie Wilson, 'Telling the Truth: A Dissident Aboriginal Voice', *IPA Review*, vol. 49, no. 1, 1996, pp. 37–43.

'stood up to defend the integrity of their past': Ron Brunton, 'Unfinished Business', *Courier-Mail*, 4 April 1998.

Bell did not shift Brunton: His response to Diane Bell's *Ngarrindjeri Wurrawarrin: A World That Is, Was and Will Be*, North Melbourne: Spinifex, 1998, was in *Quadrant*, no. 43, vol. 5, May 1999, pp. 11–18.

'the white men who steered the case': Margaret Simons, 'Hindmarsh: Where Lies the Truth?', *Age*, 9 May 2003.

Read wanted to call the work: The background to *The Stolen Generations: The Removal of Aboriginal Children in New South Wales, 1883 to 1969*, Sydney: Ministry of Aboriginal Affairs, 1982, is set out in *A Rape of the Soul So Profound: The Return of the Stolen Generations*, St Leonards, NSW: Allen & Unwin, 1999, pp. 46–9.

'For victims of gross human rights violations': *Bringing Them Home: Report of the National Inquiry into the Separation of Aboriginal and Torres Strait Islander Children from Their Families*, Sydney: Human Rights and Equal Opportunity Commission, 1997, p. 277.

'collective responsibility': Mick Dodson, 'We All Bear the Cost if Apology Is Not Paid', *Age*, 18 December 1997, quoted in Bain Attwood and Andrew Markus (eds), *The Struggle for Aboriginal Rights: A Documentary History*, Crows Nest, NSW: Allen & Unwin, 1999, p. 353.

a reciprocal process to reunite the nation: Patrick Dodson in *Proceedings of the Australian Reconciliation Council*, Canberra: Reconciliation Council, 1997, p. 8, quoted by Reynolds, 'The Public Role of History', p. 5.

Senator Herron argued that in any case: letter to Father Frank Brennan, quoted in Manne, *The Way We Live Now*, p. 21.

'essentially lawful and benign in intent': The government submission to the Senate Legal and Constitutional References Committee was reported in the *Sydney Morning Herald*, 4 April 2000, and these passages are quoted by Angela Pratt, '"There Was Never a Generation of Stolen Children"', *Crossings*, vol. 5, nos 1–3, 2000, p. 22.

Ron Brunton's hostile evaluation of the report: Ron Brunton, *Betraying the Victims*, Melbourne: Institute of Public Affairs, 1998, and also Brunton's 'Genocide, the "Stolen Generations" and the "Unconvinced Generations"', *Quadrant*, vol. 42, no. 5, May 1998, pp. 19–24.

After Brunton came Peter Howson: 'Rescued from the Rabbit Burrow'.

a sustained campaign in the press: Frank Devine, 'Let Us Off the Hook with Magnanimity', *Australian*, 6 April 2000; Piers Ackerman, 'Embracing the Lie Prolongs the Pain', *Daily Telegraph*, 6 April 2000; Michael Duffy, 'The Stolen Generations', *IPA Review*, vol. 52, no. 2, July 2000, pp. 6–8.

The prime minister insisted: Michelle Grattan and Debra Jopson, 'Black Fury Explodes over Stolen Children', *Sydney Morning Herald*, 3 April 2000.

'Sir Ronald the Evangelist': Michael Duffy, *Daily Telegraph*, 12 August 2000.

'Holy Billy': Piers Ackerman, *Daily Telegraph*, 12, 29 August 2000.

'moral mafia': Andrew Bolt, *Herald-Sun*, 13 April 2000.

'white maggots': Michael Duffy, *Daily Telegraph*, 25 March 2000; these and the three epithets above are quoted by Manne, *In Denial*, pp. 71–3.

A legal scholar: Mark Osiel, *Mass Atrocity, Collective Memory and the Law*, New Brunswick, NJ: Transaction Publishers, 1997, p. vii, quoted by Reynolds, 'The Public Role of History', p. 5.

The result was a book: N. G. Butlin, *Our Original Aggression: Aboriginal Populations of South-eastern Australia 1788–1850*, North Sydney: Allen & Unwin, 1983; see also 'Macassans and Aboriginal Smallpox', *Historical Studies*, vol. 21, no. 84, April 1985, pp. 315–35, and *Economics and the Dreamtime: A Hypothetical History*, Cambridge: Cambridge University Press, 1993.

Other historians contested Butlin's explanation: Judy Campbell, 'Smallpox in Aboriginal Australia, the Early 1830s', *Historical Studies*, vol. 21, no. 84, pp. 336–58, and *Invisible Invaders: Smallpox and Other Diseases in Aboriginal Australia 1780–1880*, Melbourne: Melbourne University Press, 2002.

Hugh Morgan: *Age*, 26, 29 January 1985.

Charles Wilson: 'History, Hypothesis and Fiction: Smallpox and Aboriginal Genocide', *Quadrant*, vol. 29, no. 3, March 1985, pp. 26–33.

Butlin saw off: 'Reply to Charles Wilson and Hugh Morgan', *Quadrant*, vol. 29, no. 8, June 1985, pp. 30–3.

history of nineteenth-century Australia: Geoffrey Blainey, *A Land Half Won*, South Melbourne: Macmillan, 1980, p. 75.

The number of 20 000 Aboriginal casualties: Henry Reynolds, *The Other Side of the Frontier*, Townsville: History Department, James Cook University, pp. 98–9; Richard Broome, *Aboriginal Australians: Black Response to White Dominance*, North Sydney: Allen & Unwin, 1982, p. 51.

In the next three issues of *Quadrant*: Keith Windschuttle, 'The Myths of Frontier Massacres in Australian History', *Quadrant*, vol. 44, nos 10–12, pp. 8–21, 17–24, 6–20; he introduced the charge of invention on p. 9 of the first part.

'the fictions and fabrications of our academic historians': Windschuttle, 'Doctored Evidence and Invented Incidents', in Bain Attwood and S. G. Foster (eds), *Frontier Conflict: The Australian Experience*, Canberra: National Museum of Australia, 2003, p. 106; he identifies the genocide thesis on p. 100.

'uncovers the truth': Janet Albrechtsen, 'False History Acts as Barrier to Reconciliation', *Australian*, 30 April 2003.

'one of the most important and devastating': Geoffrey Blainey, 'Native Fiction', *The New Criterion*, <http://www.newcriterion.com/archive/21/apr03/blainey.htm>.

a deliberate politicisation of history: Keith Windschuttle, *The Fabrication of Aboriginal History. Volume One: Van Diemen's Land*, Paddington, NSW: Macleay Press, 2002, p. 400.

they victimise dissidents: *The Fabrication*, pp. 6, 199–200.

other historians had long since challenged: Bain Attwood, 'Historiography on the Australian Frontier', in Attwood and Foster, *Frontier Conflict*, pp. 169–84.

the counsel for the defence: Windschuttle, *The Fabrication*, pp. 3, 32, 130, 360.

SOURCES 254

Both Ryan and Reynolds: Lyndall Ryan, *The Tasmanian Aboriginals*, St Lucia: University of Queensland Press, 1981; Henry Reynolds, *Fate of a Free People*, Ringwood, Vic.: Penguin, 1995.

Windschuttle's counter-history: *The Fabrication*, pp. 65–73, 95–111; his reference to the *Hobart Town Gazette* is on p. 66.

Windschuttle made a count: The calculation of deaths is explained on pp. 361–4 of *The Fabrication* and presented in a table on pp. 387–97.

'nothing that resembled genocide': *The Fabrication*, p. 399.

he revised downwards the size of the Aboriginal population: *The Fabrication*, pp. 364–86; the tasteless reference to their 'good fortune' is on p. 386.

'You can't really be serious': Jane Cadzow, 'Who's Right, Then?', *Age*, Good Weekend, 17 May 2003, who also quotes the threat to sue Manne.

Robert Manne made an early and cogent criticism: *Age*, 12 December 2002.

'it is a measure of how desperate my critics are': Keith Windschuttle, 'Why I'm a Bad Historian', *Age*, 16 December 2002.

Suggestions from some historians: Raymond Evans in the *Courier-Mail*, 20 December 2002; Lyndall Ryan in the *Australian*, 17 December 2002.

She has replied: Lyndall Ryan, 'Ryan v. Windschuttle: Who is the Fabricator?', which is to appear in Robert Manne (ed.) *Whitewash: On Keith Windschuttle's* Fabrication of Aboriginal History, Melbourne: Black Inc., 2003.

At the closing session of the forum: Tim Rowse reported in *Frontier Conflict*, pp. 22–3.

9 WHAT DO THEY TEACH OUR CHILDREN?

educational untruths: Howard Hutchins, letter, 'Yes, We Can Thank God for Captain Cook', *Age*, 31 December 2001.

'**Black Armband' view of history:** Geoffrey Blainey, 'Drawing Up a Balance Sheet of Our History', *Quadrant*, vol. 37, nos 7–8, July–August 1993, pp. 10–15.

A national document on history curriculum: Kevin Donnelly, 'The Black Armband View of Australian History', *Agora*, vol. 32, no. 2, 1997, p. 15.

First appearing: Alan Barcan, 'A History of History Teaching', in Norman Little and Judy Mackinolty (eds), *A New Look at History Teaching*, Marrickville, NSW: History Teachers' Association of New South Wales, 1977, pp. 37–47; S. G. Firth, 'Social Values in the New South Wales Primary School 1880–1914: An Analysis of School Texts', *Melbourne Studies in Education*, Melbourne University Press, 1970, pp. 123–59; Graeme Davison, 'Learning History: Reflections on Some Australian School Textbooks', *Agora*, vol. 22, no. 3, 1987, pp. 27–32.

'**the aim of the course**': *Syllabus in History*, Sydney: New South Wales Department of Education, 1957, pp. 5, 17.

students imagine themselves as a squatter: A. Witcombe, 'Junior History Assignments', *Agora*, vol. 3, no. 3, 1969, p. 32.

theories of 'knowledge acquired in active process': Leonie Kramer, 'A Recipe for Lower School Standards', *Sydney Morning Herald*, 25 August 1975.

ran the cover story: Peter Samuel, 'Australia's Educational Scandal: We're Turning Out Millions of Dunces', *Bulletin*, 15 May 1976, pp. 30–3. The two articles by Kramer and Samuel are discussed in Alan Barcan, *Two Centuries of Education in New South Wales*, Kensington: New South Wales University Press, 1988, pp. 278–82.

Ideals of increasing equality: Alan Barcan, *A History of Australian Education*, Melbourne: Oxford University Press, 1980, p. 362.

contributed a critical article on the state of the subject: Patrick O'Farrell, 'A Basic History Education: Its Aims and Uses', *Teaching History*, July 1983, p. 10.

endangered 'our children': Geoffrey Partington, 'History Education in Bicentennial Australia', *Forum*, December 1987, p. 32.

criticised the negative momentum: Ken Baker, 'The Bicentenary: Celebration or Apology?', *IPA Review*, vol. 38, no. 4, Summer 1985, pp. 175–7, 179–82.

systematic exposure of their dark side: Ken Baker, 'The New History', *IPA Review*, vol. 42, no. 3, December–February 1988–89, p. 50.

ignoring Australia's proud pioneering settlement: 'The Rocky Horror History of Australia', *IPA Review*, vol. 38, no. 4, Summer 1985, pp. 283–5.

In a similar attack: Partington, 'History Teaching in Bicentennial Australia', p. 29.

By 1988 governments were developing: Steve Burrell et al., 'Govt Bid To Head Off Black Protests', *Sydney Morning Herald*, 8 January 1988; David Kennedy, '1988 Ban a Matter of History, Say Teachers', *Sydney Morning Herald*, 8 January 1988.

Defending the threat: Quoted in Kennedy, '1988 Ban a Matter of History, Say Teachers'.

Aboriginal people had a right to lawful and peaceful dissent: Burrell et al., 'Govt Bid To Head Off Black Protests'.

According to the Sydney journalist: P. P. McGuinness, 'Big Brother Writes the Syllabus', *Weekend Australian*, 17–18 August 1991; 'History of Invasion Ignores More Balanced School of Thought', *Australian*, 15 June 1994.

An information sheet in the sourcebook: *Social Studies Units 1 and 2, Year 5 Replacement*, Brisbane: Queensland Department of Education, 1995 (original emphasis).

the book was a disgrace: Tony Koch, 'Furore over "Invasion" Text: Govt Refuses To Intervene', *Courier-Mail*, 8 February 1994.

the shadow minister for education agreed: Melissa Ketchell, 'Explorers Axed in "Correct" Syllabus', *Courier-Mail*, 7 February 1994.

There was a need: Tony Koch, 'Goss Cans "Invasion" Textbook', *Courier-Mail*, 9 February 1994.

'I think that just about all Australians': Julie Lewis, 'Goss Repels "Invaders"', *Sydney Morning Herald*, 9 February 1994.

Editorials complaining of government attempts: Editorial, 'Our History: It Needs To Be Fully Understood', *Courier-Mail*, 10 February 1994.

double standards: Geoff Temby, letter, *Courier-Mail*, 11 February 1994.

reluctance to use terms: Barry Shield, letter, *Courier-Mail*, 15 February 1994.

Goss maintained: Quoted in Jennifer Craik, 'Was This an Invasion? Framing History in the Media', in Ray Land (ed.), *Invasion and After: A Case Study in Curriculum Politics*, Brisbane: Queensland Studies Centre, Griffith University, 1994.

the previous sourcebook: *Primary Social Studies Sourcebook Year 5*, Brisbane: Queensland Department of Education, 1988.

condemned for allowing the word 'invasion': 'Nats Condemn Minister's "Distortion" of History', *Sydney Morning Herald*, 20 June 1994.

The delegate who initiated the motion: Michael Wilkins, 'Nationals Condemn Chadwick "Invasion"', *Sunday Telegraph*, 19 June 1994.

The draft was consequently: Julie Lewis, 'Teachers Threaten Syllabus Ban', *Sydney Morning Herald*, 29 June 1994.

Its members were guilty: Quoted in Henry Reynolds, *Why Weren't We Told? A Personal Search for the Truth about Our History*, Ringwood, Vic.: Viking, 1998, p. 160.

'The description "invasion"': Editorial, 'An Invasion Indeed', *Sydney Morning Herald*, 26 September 1995.

Howard denounced the history curriculum: Judith Brett, 'Opinion', *Age*, 8 November 1996.

the unbroken legacy of the Anzac legend: John Howard, Anzac Day speech, Gallipoli, 2000. Published as 'Pilgrimage To Define the Future of a Nation', *Sydney Morning Herald*, 26 April 2000.

In the unit of Koori history: *History Study Design*, Melbourne: Victorian Curriculum and Assessment Authority, 1991, p. 76.

By 1996: *History Study Design*, Melbourne: Victorian Board of Studies, 1996, p. 97.

Japanese Ministry of Education was embroiled: Ian Buruma, *The Wages of Guilt: Memories of War in Germany and Japan*, London: Vintage, 1995, p. 194.

According to Nobukatsu Fujioka: Burton Bollag, 'A Confrontation with the Past: The Japanese Textbook Dispute', *American Educator*, vol. 25, no. 4, Winter 2001, p. 22.

In 2002 the German ambassador: Becky Barrow, 'Lessons "Biased against Germany"', *Daily Telegraph*, 9 December 2002.

History teaching in Scotland: Graham Grant, 'Braveheart Approach to Teaching of History "Helps Fuel Anti-English Bigotry"', *Daily Mail*, 12 December 2002.

revived memories of the debate over the English curriculum: Mary Braid, 'Determined To Make History a Matter of Fact', *Independent*, 5 April 1990; Ray Massay, 'This History is Bunk', *Daily Mail*, 15 October 1992. For a detailed examination of the curriculum, see Robert Phillips, *History Teaching, Nationhood and the State: A Study in Educational Politics*, London: Cassell, 1998.

Initiated with a view to national testing: Linda Symcox, *Whose History?: The Struggle for National Standards in American Classrooms*, New York: Teachers College Press, 2002, pp. 9–10, 102.

spoke out angrily against the new Standards: Lynne Cheney, 'The End of History', *Wall Street Journal*, 20 October 1994.

The educationalist: Diane Ravitch, 'Standards in U.S. History: An Assessment', *Education Week*, 7 December 1994, p. 48.

dismissed the Standards: Charles Krauthammer, 'History Hijacked', *Washington Post*, 4 November 1994.

The resolutions were passed: Symcox, *Whose History?*, pp. 1, 137.

In response, Gary Nash: 'Plan to Teach U.S. History is Said to Slight White Males', *New York Times*, 24 October 1994.

In his later analysis: Gary B. Nash, Charlotte Crabtree and Ross E. Dunn, *History on Trial: Culture Wars and the Teaching of the Past*, New York: Alfred A. Knopf, 1997.

'Captain Cook and Sir Robert Menzies do not feature': Martin Thomas, 'School Syllabus Swings to the Left', *Courier-Mail*, 10 June 2000.

the syllabus was gravely misrepresentative: Ted Wilson, letter, *Courier-Mail*, 13 June 2000.

a new national curriculum framework: Colin Marsh, 'Conceptual Strands of Studies of Society and Environment', in Colin Marsh (ed.), *Teaching Studies of Society and Environment*, 2nd edn, Sydney: Prentice Hall, pp. 167–91.

The incorporation of history: An analysis of teaching history within a SOSE framework may be found in Tony Taylor's *National Inquiry into School History*, Canberra: Department of Education, Training and Youth Affairs, 2000.

criticised SOSE for its tendency: John Lidstone, 'Sapping Education', *Courier-Mail*, 16 June 2000.

The Melbourne journalist: Andrew Bolt, 'Class Revolution', *Courier-Mail*, 10 June 2000.

Writing to the *Courier-Mail*: John Meredith, letter, *Courier-Mail*, 13 June 2000.

the syllabus 'ought to be dumped': Editorial, 'Ideology in the Classroom', *Courier-Mail*, 10 June 2000.

'Our children need knowledge': Editorial, 'Trouble with Syllabus is Fundamental', *Courier-Mail*, 2 September.

State school principals: Tom Hardy et al., letter, *Courier-Mail*, 15 September 2000.

'new syllabus is serious': Barry Salmon, Queensland School Curriculum Council, unpublished letter to *Courier-Mail*, 13 June

2000, <http://www.qscc.qld.edu.au/kla/sose/faq.html#updates> (accessed 15 January 2002).

its coverage of the debate: Malcolm Cole, 'SOSE Debate Enrages the Ants', *Courier-Mail*, 23 September 2000.

Labor Premier Bob Carr: 'NSW Students To Be Versed in Nation Issues', ABC, 13 October 2002, <http://abc.net.au/news/newsitems/s700070.htm> (accessed 14 October 2002).

Carr campaigned with the promise: Julie Lewis, 'Carr Calls for a Return to Educational Basics', *Sydney Morning Herald*, 6 June 1994.

Between 1997 and 2001: The funding for the Discovering Democracy program was reported by Tony Taylor, 'Disputed Territory: Some Political Contexts for the Development of Australian Historical Consciousness', a paper presented at the Canadian Historical Consciousness in an International Context: Theoretical Frameworks conference, University of British Columbia, 2001.

Launching the report: David Kemp commented on the National Inquiry in a press release on 15 October 2000.

President George W. Bush announced massive increases: Bush's speech was reproduced on the History News Network, <http://hnn.us/articles/980.html> (accessed 19 September 2002). The funding for Bush's history initiatives was reported by the National Coalition for History, NCH Washington Update, vol. 9, no. 5, 3 February 2003, <http://h-net.msu.edu/cgi-bin/logbrowse.pl?trx=vx&list=H-NCH&month=0302&week=a&msg=MSiSZpOjx5r59duVuaQ1MA&user=&pw=> (accessed 5 February 2003).

10 WORKING THROUGH THE MUSEUM'S LABELS

'I am still working . . . through these labels': David Barnett quoted in *Sydney Morning Herald*, 5 June 2001.

Blainey recommended Graeme Davison: Senate Environment, Communications, Information Technology and the Arts Legislation Committee, 'Consideration of Additional Estimates', 11 February 2003, p. 221.

'a very bland museum': Graeme Davison's assessment was reported in the *Sydney Morning Herald*, 5 June 2001.

Dr Brian Kennedy: Lauren Martin, 'Left? Right? The Centre of Attraction', *Sydney Morning Herald*, 18 April 2001.

Miranda Devine: 'A Nation Trivialised', *Daily Telegraph*, 12 March 2001, and 'Trivial Pursuit of Our History', Adelaide *Advertiser*, 14 March 2001.

Piers Ackerman: 'Museum Is an Original Limitation', *Sunday Telegraph*, 9 April 2001.

Pru Goward: 'Making an Exhibition of Ourselves', *Australian*, 13 March 2001. The other headlines are taken from the *Age*, 10 March 2001 and the *Bulletin*, 13 March 2001.

Keith Windschuttle took up the campaign: 'How Not to Run a Museum: People's History at the Postmodern Museum', *Quadrant*, vol. 45, no. 9, September 2001, p. 19.

By December Windschuttle: 'Doctored Evidence and Invented Incidents in Aboriginal Historiography', in Bain Attwood and S. G. Foster, *Frontier Conflict: The Australian Experience*, Canberra: National Museum of Australia, 2003, pp. 99–112.

Windschuttle repeated this claim: *The Fabrication of Aboriginal History. Volume One: Van Diemen's Land*, Paddington, NSW: Macleay Press, 2002, pp. 2, 9; 'Submission to the Review', 3 March 2003, <http://www.sydneyline.com/National%20Museum%20submission. htm> (accessed 20 May 2003).

Rod Kemp . . . chose John Carroll to chair it: Senate Committee, 11 February 2003, pp. 227, 235.

It is a political maxim: The review of the National Museum's exhibitions and public programs appears on its website, <http://www.gov.au>.

'to understand Australian history and nationhood better': Dawn Casey, 'The New Museum', keynote address to the conference of Museums Australia Queensland, 15 September 2001, <http://www.maq.org.au/progams/conf/01/proceedings/dawn.html> (accessed 20 May 2003).

When Senator Alston announced: Richard Alston, press release, 15 December 1996, parliamentary website, <http://aph.gov.au>, quoted in James Michael Gore, 'Representations of History and Nations in Museums in Australia and Aotearoa New Zealand', PhD thesis, University of Melbourne, 2002, p. 198.

Two members of that committee: Blainey and Mulvaney's contribution to the Pigott report, *Museums in Australia 1975: Report of the Committee of Inquiry into Museums and National Collections*, Canberra: Australian Government Publishing Service, 1975, p. 73, is quoted by Graeme Davison, 'Conflict in the Museum', in Attwood and Foster (eds), *Frontier Conflict*, p. 202, and by Gore, 'Representations of History', p. 104.

'telling the wonderful story of Australia': Dr William Jonas, statement to the Joint Committee on Public Works on 8 December 1997, quoted in Gore, 'Representations of History', p. 200.

Mulvaney worried: *Age*, 9 November 1998, quoted in Gore, 'Representations of History', p. 201.

They prepared guidelines: Graeme Davison quotes from the guidelines of the National Museum in 'Museums and the Burden of National Identity', keynote address to the Museums Australia conference, Adelaide, March 2002.

He has pointed out: Davison explicates national identity in Graeme Davison, John Hirst and Stuart Macintyre (eds), *The Oxford Companion to Australian History*, Melbourne: Oxford University Press, rev. edn, 2001, pp. 456–8.

'endless and agonised navel-gazing': Sir Robert Menzies Lecture, 18 November 1996.

'the prime minister was adamant': I quote here from Barnett's letter to Staley, n.d. and my copy comes, along with Davison's letter in response, 18 October 2000, from John Faulkner.

C. E. W. Bean . . . wrote an article: 'Australian Records Preserved as Sacred Things', *Commonwealth Gazette*, 15 January 1918, pp. 45–7, cited in Michael McKernan, *Here Is Their Spirit: A History of* *the Australian War Memorial 1917–1990*, St Lucia: University of Queensland Press, p. 42.

'I don't think Dr Bean would approve': Quoted by McKernan, *Here Is Their Spirit*, p. 320.

'It's a memorial': *Canberra Times*, 16 December 1984, quoted by McKernan, *Here Is Their Spirit*, pp. 329–30.

'a small dishonest cadre': Quoted by Jack Waterford, 'War at the Memorial', *Eureka Street*, vol. 5, no. 9, November 1995, p. 18.

'trendy attitudes': Council minutes, 28 November 1985, quoted by McKernan, *Here Is Their Spirit*, p. 334.

a chapter on frontier conflict: Richard Broome's chapter appeared in Michael McKernan and Margaret Browne (eds), *Australia: Two Centuries of War and Peace*, Canberra/Sydney: Australian War Memorial/Allen & Unwin, 1988.

Blainey recommended: AWM 93 234/3/7, part 1, cited in McKernan, *Here Is Their Spirit*, pp. 293–4.

the Entombment of the Unknown Australian Soldier: K. S. Inglis, *Sacred Places: War Memorials in the Australian Landscape*, Melbourne: Melbourne University Press, 1998, pp. 451–8.

biographer remarks on the symbolism: Michael McKernan, *Beryl Beaurepaire*, St Lucia: University of Queensland Press, 1999, pp. 292–4.

a speech by Paul Keating: Mark Ryan (ed.), *Advancing Australia: The Speeches of Paul Keating, Prime Minister*, Cremorne Point, NSW: Big Picture Publications, 1995, pp. 287–8.

'the total culture of New Zealand': A Concept for the Museum, 1989, quoted in Gore, 'Representations of History', pp. 223–4.

'traditionally held views of New Zealand are being scrutinised': A Plan for Development, 1985, quoted in Gore, 'Representations of History', p. 220.

'filled with Maori junk': Gore, 'Representations of History', p. 233, quotes excerpts from the visitors' book for the exhibition, Voices, which were broadcast on Radio New Zealand on 1 March 1993.

He came up with a similar approach: Jock Phillips, 'Our History, Our Selves: The Historian and National Identity', *New Zealand Journal of History*, vol. 30, no. 2, October 1996, p. 115.

'vision statement': Quoted by Gore, 'Representations of History', pp. 248–9.

John McDonald: 'From There to Eternity', *Sydney Morning Herald*, 10 March 2001, quoted by Gore, 'Representations of History', p. 264.

Christian Heritage Party: *Christianity Today*, 15 June 1998, quoted by Gore, 'Representations of History', p. 262.

Prime Minister Helen Clark: Gore, 'Representations of History', pp. 265–6.

Paul Keating was not persuaded: Speech at the opening of the National Portrait Gallery, 30 March 1994, quoted by Gore, 'Representations of History', p. 189.

'a book upon a wall': Phillips, 'Our History, Our Selves', p. 113; Davison, 'Conflict in the Museum', provides a more extended discussion.

The team working on the Horizons gallery: I draw here on information from Nicole McLennan.

As Tony Staley put it: *Sydney Morning Herald*, 5 June 2001.

When Keith Windschuttle took up the attack: the quotations in this paragraph and the next come from Windschuttle, 'How Not to Run a Museum'.

Windschuttle accused: His charges in 'How Not to Run a Museum' are rebutted by Davison in 'Conflict in the Museum'.

Davison's paper . . . was in fact delivered in July 1999: It appeared as 'National Museums in a Global Age: Observations Abroad and Reflections at Home', in Darryl McIntyre and Kirsten

Wehner (eds), *National Museums: Negotiating Histories Conference Proceedings*, Canberra: National Museum of Australia, 2001, pp. 12–28.

Windschuttle alleged that these names: Davison notes the existence of the placenames that Windschuttle says were invented in 'Conflict in the Museum', p. 209.

Cathie Clement . . . has pointed to more than thirty examples: In her submission to the Museum Review.

The story had been examined: David Roberts, 'Bells Falls Massacre and Bathurst's History of Violence: Local Tradition and Australian Historiography', *Australian Historical Studies*, vol. 26, no. 105, October 1995, pp. 615–33.

Windschuttle cited Roberts' investigation: He enlarged on his criticism on the ABC current affairs program 'PM', 13 August 2001, and Roberts quotes from it in his own reconsideration of 'The Bells Falls Massacre and Oral Tradition' in Attwood and Foster, *Frontier Conflict*, pp. 150–7.

CONCLUSION

'the attempt to rewrite Australian history': John Howard, Sir Thomas Playford Memorial Lecture, 5 July 1996.

Keith Windschuttle accuses: *The Fabrication of Aboriginal History. Volume One: Van Diemen's Land*, Paddington, NSW: Macleay Press, 2002, pp. 6, 402–4.

'our University must be a great seminary of politicians': J. R. Seeley, *The Growth of British Policy: An Historical Essay*, Cambridge: Cambridge University Press, 1995, vol. 1, p. xii.

'a school of statesmanship': Elkington quoted in Stuart Macintyre, *A History for a Nation: Ernest Scott and the Making of Australia History*, Melbourne: Melbourne University Press, 1994, p. 94.

'Australians are free to be proud': Howard's draft preamble to the Constitution appears in Donald Horne, *Looking for Leadership: Australia in the Howard Years*, Ringwood, Vic.: Viking, 2001, p. 271.

INDEX